THE HERITAGE OF LANCASTER

THE HERITAGE OF LANCASTER

By John Ward Willson Loose

Published under
the sponsorship of the Lancaster Association
of Commerce and Industry
Research provided by the Lancaster County
Historical Society

Windsor Publications, Inc., Woodland Hills, California

Library of Congress Catalog Card Number: 78-056667
Windsor Publications, Woodland Hills, Ca. 91365
©1978 by Windsor Publications. All rights reserved
Published 1978
Printed in the United States of America

Library of Congress Cataloging in Publication Data

Loose, John Ward Willson.
    The Heritage of Lancaster.

"Published under the sponsorship of the Lancaster
Association of Commerce and Industry; research
provided by the Lancaster County Historical Society."
    Bibliography: p. 219
    Includes index.
    1. Lancaster, Pa. — History
I. Lancaster County (Pa.) Historical Society.
II. Title. F159.L2L68
974.8'15 78-56667
ISBN 0-89781-001-5

To those who have
unselfishly given freely of
themselves in the
unfolding of the saga
of Lancaster

"

The history of the world is but the biography of great men.

"

Carlyle

During one of his trips to Lancaster in 1802, the American architect-engineer, Benjamin Latrobe, paused to paint this watercolor of Centre Square, Lancaster. The scene is from the southeast, looking towards the north and northeast sides of the Square. At this time the County Office Building (Old City Hall) at the extreme left was the office building for the state government then using Lancaster as the state capital. The courthouse in the middle held the legislative chambers, with the House of Representatives on the first floor and the Senate on the second floor. Latrobe never finished coloring in some of the areas of the scene.

Contents

Preface

The Heritage of Lancaster is an impressionistic survey — a panorama — of Lancaster's history, culture, and life. Every effort has been made to ensure historical accuracy, but this work was not written for historians. It is intended primarily for the general reader who wants to know and understand those events and responses that have made Lancaster what it is. Space limitations necessitated omitting many details. Choosing details to include or exclude was the most difficult part of the generally pleasant task of writing about Lancaster and its people. Those readers whose particular interests were slighted or ignored are urged to consult the thousands of excellent monographs and articles published since 1896 by the Lancaster County Historical Society.

If the reader senses a "love affair" between the author and the community of Lancaster, that perception is well founded. The author's German, Scottish, English, and Huguenot ancestors put down roots here before the creation of Lancaster County. Holding that people are the most valuable asset of any community, the author has focused his attention on the human aspects of the community. Here, for the first time, are references to those groups that have contributed greatly, albeit anonymously, to Lancaster's heritage, some of which have given the community much of its vitality, color, and cultural diversity. A constant tranquillity will convert stability to stagnation. Lancaster, happily, has those persons that make us justify the status quo, evoking new assessments of reality and principle.

Next to people expressing their identities in the arts, literature, religion, and life itself, we are interested in their economic activities. Lancaster has gone through four generations or stages of manufacturing, the products of each stage being replaced by new responses to challenges of the marketplace. Whether by accident or design — it probably was fortuitous circumstance — Lancaster's economy has been quite diversified. It is balanced between agriculture and manufacturing, hard goods and soft goods, capital goods and consumer goods, and stable commodities and ephemeral products. A healthy ratio has existed between skilled workers and unskilled labor. Lancaster never has been a one-industry town.

It is the fond hope of the author that readers — newcomers as well as longtime residents — come to understand and appreciate, if not love, this wonderful old community of the Red Rose.

JOHN WARD WILLSON LOOSE

Honoring the men of Lancaster County who had served in the War Between the States and other conflicts, the Soldiers and Sailors Monument was dedicated on 4 July 1874, marking the site where courthouses had stood, where the Continental Congress had met, and the Pennsylvania Legislature had assembled.

Acknowledgments

This book owes its existence to a widely shared interest in the history of Lancaster on the part of its people, among them the members of the Lancaster Association of Commerce and Industry. Credit for making this book possible goes most deservedly to Gerald L. Molloy, past president of the Association, who was the prime mover on this project; to Dean H. Keller, under whose presidency the project saw fruition; to Charles K. Perella, the Association's Vice President for Manufacturing, who provided continuing assistance throughout; and to the entire staff for the various and sundry tasks associated with this venture.

It has been said that a "picture is worth a thousand words," but no number of words could have substituted for the superb picture chronicle of Lancaster contained in these pages. Except as otherwise indicated, the large majority of these photographs were provided by the Lancaster County Historical Society, with the very able assistance of John W. Aungst, Jr., staff administrator, and Ann Hoeck, head librarian-archivist. Appropriate credits appear with those photographs provided by other sources. The color photography is primarily the work of Robert Fuschetto, a professional photographer residing in New York.

Many citizens and organizations, public and private, cheerfully assisted photographer Robert Fuschetto; among them, Samuel E. Dyke, Vincent W. Nolt, Arthur L. Reist and family, Ezra F. Bowman Sons, Inc., Commonwealth National Bank, Fulton Bank, Lancaster Milling Co., Inc., Lapp's Carriage Shop, RCA Corporation, Fulton Opera House, Rock Ford Plantation, and Wheatland. To these and to the anonymous others, a special thanks.

Additional appreciation is extended to Frederic S. Klein, for recommending the author for this project, and to Jean F. Molloy for her promotion and marketing endeavors.

Jane Eastman, well known in our community for her work with various organizations and volunteer boards, is the industrious and talented free-lance writer who researched and wrote the business biographies for the chapter entitled "Partners in Progress," which contributes significantly to the interest of this book.

The author is greatly indebted to JoAnn Levy of Windsor Publications, Inc., for her editing, coordinating, and inspiration. Any success this book may earn must be traced in large part to her efforts.

Errors of fact are, of course, the responsibility of the author solely.

J.W.W.L.

Two Cultures Meet

Central to the dispute between William Penn and Lord Baltimore over the proper location of the boundary between Pennsylvania and Maryland was the situation of the Susquehannock Fort built by the Iroquois branch along the Susquehanna River. Penn assumed the Indian fort was much farther south, possibly opposite the mouth of Octoraro Creek. Lord Baltimore thought it was on the fortieth degree of latitude, beneath which Maryland lay, according to his charter. Early twentieth-century research revealed Baltimore's valid claim; the fort was on the fortieth degree — opposite Washington Boro.

Lancaster — the city and county seat — historically has been the hub of social, economic, political, and intellectual activity of Lancaster County. Before we explore the heritage of Lancaster we ought to understand the surrounding countryside and the folk that have populated it, those that have given Lancaster its character and nourishment the past 250 years.

Lancaster County is a remarkable study in contrasts, a circumstance that may explain its extraordinary strengths as well as its tendency to baffle the casual visitor, if not the newly arrived resident. Excluding the Amish-Mennonites and the other groups of sectarians we call the Plain People, one may be tempted to view Lancaster County as quite typical of those prosperous semirural paradises that dot middle America. Nothing could be further from the truth! The Lancaster mind defies classification, and woe unto the person that creates a stereotypical Lancastrian!

Lack of economic opportunities and rigid land-tenure systems forced most of our settlers to break their ties with Europe. Although by the early 1700s religious persecution was more a memory and a threat than a reality, that threat occasionally sparked the decision to come to Pennsylvania. Religious wars had laid waste vast areas of the Rhineland, causing severe economic problems for several generations; from these later generations came the early settlers. They realized only too well the persecution, warfare, and destruction of the human spirit caused by state-sponsored religion. William Penn's land of promise seemed a beacon of hope to the oppressed and the disheartened as well as to ambitious immigrants.

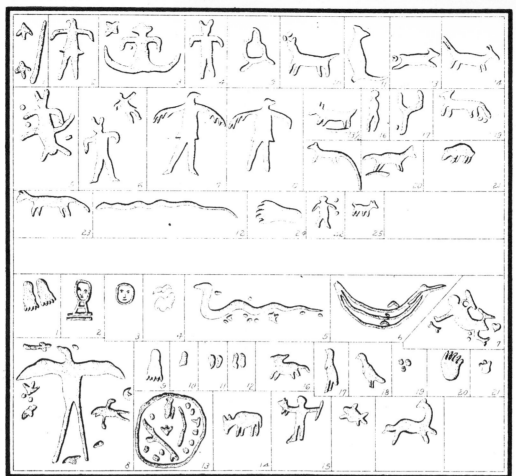

Before the construction of the hydroelectric power plants on the Susquehanna River, many islands and the shore contained large rocks on which the Indians had carved numerous characters in their sign language. The state archaeologist made casts of those rocks too large to move; others were taken to the state museum and to North Museum in Lancaster. The Susquehannocks and Conestogas that lived in Lancaster County when white men arrived here were not the first Indians to inhabit this area. American Indians, who came originally from Asia, were in Pennsylvania approximately 15,000 years ago, long before the period of Egyptian civilization.

Before Lancaster County was erected on 10 May 1729 (the English always "erected" counties!), Pennsylvania consisted of three original counties — Bucks, Philadelphia, and Chester — all created in 1682 by William Penn, the Quaker proprietor. Then, Chester County was defined vaguely as that area west of Philadelphia County as far west as the South Mountain and as far north as the Blue Mountain.

As settlers moved into the wild backwoods of Chester County, problems of law enforcement developed. Clearly, local government was needed. In 1718 Chester County created Conestoga Township, which included all the area west and north of the Octoraro Creek. Scots from Ulster took up land — often without bothering to acquire rights from the proprietor — in the Chikiswalungo Valley near the Susquehanna River, while Germans rapidly filled up the broad, flat limestone valley of the Conestoga River with their farms. Chester County again created a new township, West Conestoga, in 1720; it included all the land north of the Pequea Creek. That move brought down the wrath of the Scots upon the heads of the English government, for Conestoga was an Indian name and Scots regarded Indians as natural enemies to be rooted out as quickly as possible. The Quaker administration, always unhappy with the belligerent Scots, yielded in 1722, and West Conestoga was changed to Donegal Township. Meanwhile the influx of settlers, many of them Welsh, to the headwaters of the Pequea Creek caused the formation of Pequea Township in 1721. No specific boundaries were recorded for this township, but it was included in the present Salisbury and East Earl townships. Never officially established nor even placed before the court, but nevertheless cited in early deeds, was a township named West Strasburg that probably included parts of today's East and West Lampeter, and Lancaster, townships, and even part of Lancaster city.

Lands west and north of the present Lancaster County were unorganized and possessed no local government until the Lancaster County Quarter Sessions Court began approving the creation of townships between 1729 and 1785 in what later was to become York, Cumberland, Dauphin, Northumberland, Lebanon, and Berks counties.

Indian traders traveled through the Susquehanna Valley from the earliest days of the colony. Here and there they maintained trading posts, often connected to each other and the coastal market town by trails that eventually became roads. Peter Bezaillion's trading post on the Susquehanna River in Donegal Township was connected to his home base at Compassville by a trail that bore his name: Old Peter's Road. That road later formed the northern boundaries of East Hempfield, Manheim, and Leacock townships.

Lancaster County's first permanent settlers, tradition claims, were the Swiss Mennonites that took up residence between Lampeter and Willow Street. The Herrs, Mylins, and Kendigs were noteworthy members of that small band of pioneers. More recent research provides two rivals to the claim of being the first settlers. A Scot named Gault was established in Salisbury Township by 1710, and an English Quaker family was keeping the hearth fire burning in Little

Introduction

Britain Township possibly prior to 1710. There can be no doubt that the Herr-Mylin-Kendig community made a great and permanent mark upon the county's heritage. Germanic Switzerland and the German Rhineland were quite similar culturally. Not always is it possible to say with certainty that one family came from Switzerland and another from Germany.

French Huguenots (Protestants) began arriving here in 1712, and they settled generally in the area near present-day Paradise and Strasburg. Their names, occasionally Anglicized, betray their Gallic origins. Madame Marie Ferree led the little community, and thereby became Lancaster County's first "outstanding woman" in a heritage that now numbers many hundreds of acknowledged women in the arts, sciences, government, medicine, and commerce. Early records mention the family names of LeFevre, Diller, Mathiot, DuBois, and Bushong (Anglicized from Beauchamps). In religion the Huguenots of Lancaster mainly affiliated with the Reformed, Lutheran, and Presbyterian churches.

Following on the heels of the Huguenots were the Scot Presbyterians from Ulster. They did not relish their transplanting from Scotland to Ulster at the hands of the English, nor did they find their Irish neighbors agreeable. As the first wave of Scots moved westward from Philadelphia where they tarried no longer than necessary, settlements were made in what was to become Donegal Township. A Presbyterian church was built at Donegal Springs; it served not only as the focal point of the community of Scots but it gave birth to one of the nation's most historic presbyteries. A second wave of Scots was diverted to the Drumore area near the Maryland border by the Quaker government, it is thought, because the Quakers could not repel the Marylanders without using force, an activity unthinkable to the more devout Friends. The Maryland government with its Roman Catholic associations insisted the Maryland-Pennsylvania boundary line lay about three miles south of Lancaster town, and sent raiding parties in to assert possession. Penn believed the line lay much farther south, perhaps at Annapolis, but certainly not north of the mouth of the Octoraro Creek. The Quaker government knew that Scots were not sympathetic to Catholics, and that Scots enjoyed a good fight. Therefore what better place for the Scots than in southern Lancaster County (then Chester County). Presbyterian churches sprang up at Chestnut Level, Muddy Run, Middle Octoraro, and Little Britain. Local tradition has maintained the Scots were indifferent farmers and lacked the patience of the Germans in building fertile farmland. Recent research suggests the Scots compared rather favorably with the Germans when they put down their roots and overcame their wanderlust. It is true, of course, that many Scots continued moving westward, and their places were taken by German farmers.

English Quakers and members of the Church of England (Anglicans) began arriving about 1716, and they settled in a belt running east to west across the girth of the county, from Salisbury to Hempfield townships.

Development of the county seat drew Englishmen to that "urban" center but never in numbers that would rival the Germans. Welsh settlers, mostly members of the Church of England, occupied the eastern areas of the county, providing such place names as Caernarvon and Brecknock townships, and Bangor.

During the 1720s the central limestone plain of the county became home to hundreds of German farmers and mechanics representing every mode of religious expression, from the highly liturgical Lutherans and cerebral Calvinists (German Reformed) to the extremely individualistic sects, including the Anabaptists, which fall into two major groups: Mennonites and German Baptist Brethren (Dunkers). Among the Mennonites were the Amish that migrated slowly down the Conestoga Valley in the latter half of the eighteenth century, and many splinter groups led by charismatic ideologists. Not all Germans found the impersonality of the Lutheran and Reformed churches satisfying to their spiritual needs. Later in the eighteenth century these disaffected persons would flock to the "German Methodist" congregations: United Brethren in Christ and Evangelical Association.

The German Baptist Brethren experienced defections, the most colorful being that of Johann Conrad Beissel, founder of the Ephrata Cloister. Beissel observed Saturday, the seventh day of the week, as the Sabbath, and his movement resulted in the German Seventh-day Baptist Society that eventually took over his defunct community. A small and quite conservative religious association known as the River Brethren was formed in western Lancaster County as a theological compromise between the German Baptists and the German Methodists. Still active today, in appearance and custom they resemble somewhat the Old Order Mennonites. The men wear broad-brimmed hats not unlike the Amishmen. Like the Horning Mennonites, they cover the chromium parts of their motorcars with black paint.

Among the American colonies no province was more pluralistic or cosmopolitan than Pennsylvania, and nowhere in Penn's Woods did this diversity flourish with more richness and vigor than in what was to become Lancaster County. Late-nineteenth-century historians attributed the genius of Lancaster Countians to the ethnic characteristics supposedly possessed by its natives. A more acceptable explanation for the thought and behavior patterns — the culture — of Lancastrians is suggested by their responses historically to challenges, primarily those presented by their environment. The relationship that developed between man and nature, as each confronted the other, produced complex and often unique situations. To what extent man and his environment influenced each other at every turn has given us that heritage we celebrate in these pages. Out of this constant process of action and reaction, resistance and acquiescence, challenge and response, has evolved a principled pragmatism. Whether the challenges were religious, economic, or environmental in origin, the work ethic was ingrained deeply in the typical Lancastrian.

During colonial days Lancaster's ethnic and religious diversity fostered a tolerance and harmony forged out of necessity, making a united effort against the

Johann Conrad Beissel, a charismatic defector from the German Baptist Brethren sect known as "Dunkers," in 1732 began a community along the Cocalico Creek for those who wished to avoid a life of ease, pleasure, and worldliness.

Mills for making flour, paper, linseed oil, and lumber were started, and a large printing press was established. The economic potentialities of the community encouraged the brothers Eckerling to displace the spiritual life promoted by Beissel. In 1745 the entrepreneurs were expelled but Beissel's charisma had just about run its course. Following his death in 1768, the Cloister went into a decline which was hastened by the use (and subsequent destruction) of several Cloister buildings as hospitals after the Battle of the Brandywine.

Bethania, the solitary brothers' house of the Ephrata Cloister, was built in 1746 and was razed in 1911, a year after this photo was taken. It has not been reconstructed. As in the case of all Cloister buildings except one, the construction is entirely wooden, including chimneys. This four-story building was divided into many small cells. Doorways were kept very low to encourage humility.

When the Moravian congregation in Lancaster built their meeting house of stone in 1750, its immense size bothered the Lutheran and German Reformed churches. This stone building stood along North Market Street until the present century. A tiny portion of it survived as part of the later Moravian Church that occupied the site until the property was sold to the Lancaster Association of Commerce and Industry in the 1960s.

relentless frontier. All energies — none could be wasted on bickering or foolish contentiousness — had to be turned to survival in the wilderness. Such diversity produced a wealth of worship patterns and liturgies; it generated within churches a continuum of expression ranging from the liberal to the conservative; from the plain and austere to the rich pageantry of the old established churches. Lancaster County also was the scene of many schisms — perhaps more than found in any other part of the nation — as ideas and institutions clashed towards the end of its first century of growth. Lancastrians seemed to prefer forming new congregations rather than fighting long and acrimonious battles within their churches.

Lancaster County often is considered by natives and newcomers alike to be an exceptionally conservative community. But the county always has had a strong and influential liberal tradition that balances the inherent conservatism. It should be understood that by *liberal* we mean the individualistic spirit manifested by the Republic's founding fathers that expressed great faith in the ability of free men and women to manage their own lives and enterprises with a minimum of regulation by the government, however benign. From its Quakers, Moravians, Swedenborgians, German university-trained clergy, and German sectarians has come a subtle, albeit efficacious, spirit that cuts through orthodoxy and blunts the hard, cold edges of political and religious conservatism. Extreme or obviously impractical solutions to problems meet with little acceptance among Lancastrians. "Change is a vehicle to be kept under control and to be steered properly; it must not be a runaway juggernaut" sums up the conventional wisdom of the Lancaster County mind.

Visitors to Lancaster usually betray their origins when they begin pronouncing words. The Pennsylvania-Dutch dialect (more accurately Pennsylvania German) amuses the tourists probably as much as the New Yorker's speech entertains the local natives. A lesson in linguistics may be in order. Most Lancaster natives employ the broad and flat *a* vowel sound in preference to the long *a* and rising diphthongal *āĕ* of the trans-Appalachian visitor. When a tourist wishes to know the distance from *Lan-CAST-er* to *HAY-riss-burg*, Teutonically tuned ears know a westerner is in their midst. Ironically, the Philadelphia or Baltimore society matron that inquires for the price of *to-MAH-toes* in the Central Market may find her cost elevated a trifle. Usually the first notice natives have of a visitor's presence is the pronunciation of a shrill, long *A* in Amish. Lancastrians know the *A* is broad: *AH-mish*, not *A-mish! Lancaster* itself is a telltale word. Our Lancaster is pronounced exactly as the English say it, and they took it from Lancashire (*LAN-ka-sher*). Legend has it that all places named Lancaster in the United States except those in Massachusetts and Pennsylvania were named by former residents of our county. Our county was named by its first commissioner, John Wright, a native of Lancashire, England. He would have pronounced it *LAN-kas-ter* as the natives do today, using a flat *a* in the second syllable.

Scottish influence can be detected in Lancaster speech, particularly in the clearly enunciated *r*, although our northeastern county "Dutchmen" mute the *r* sound similar to the New York-spoken *r*. Another vestige of the Scottish presence is the expression "redding up," meaning to tidy up a disorderly area. To this day some Quaker families in southern Lancaster County employ *thee* and *thou* in addressing members of their families; it is a token of closeness and respect for human dignity. Many Amish persons are trilingual, using German in their lengthy worship services, Pennsylvania-German dialect in conversation among themselves and other countrymen, and English (usually superior to that spoken by the general population) when talking with worldly folk.

This, briefly, is the human background from which the heritage of Lancaster has grown.

§ § § § §

When Lancaster County was established 10 May 1729, the provincial government reminded the new commissioners some important tasks had to be accomplished. A county seat had to be selected, and a courthouse and *gaol* (jail) erected. It happened that Lancaster County's most influential citizens in 1729 were clustered about a hamlet known as Wright's Ferry on the Susquehanna River. John Wright, Robert Barber, and Samuel Blunston were the movers and shakers; they also were Quakers, which the Philadelphians found most agreeable. Meanwhile,

Lancaster County's first Methodist church was Boehm's, built in 1790 near Willow Street. The structure is well preserved today. This photo was taken in 1900.

Barber, the first sheriff, built a log jail at Wright's Ferry, hoping that would make the river community the logical place for the county seat. But several miles southeast of Wright's Ferry, along the Old Conestoga Road near Rock Hill, John Postlethwaite kept an inn, and he was able to keep up with the news of the day and exert influence on his guests. He also entertained notions of having the county seat at his site, and that seemed a logical choice when the first county court was held at his inn.

Residents in the eastern part of the county desired to have the seat of government closer to the center of population, and that apparently appealed to the provincial government. Commissioners located a tract of some five hundred acres about one mile north of the Conestoga River, and recommended that site be chosen. The governor, however, wondered who owned the tract, whereupon the Provincial Prothonotary Andrew Hamilton, Esquire, was asked to check the records. The tract had been warranted by the proprietor to a Richard Wooller of London. He never took up his rights, leading local officials to assume the tract remained in the hands of the Penns, which technically it did. Wooller had died, and his heirs sold his rights to Samuel Arnold of London. Hamilton directed James Steele, then in England buying up old rights for Hamilton, to acquire the tract from Arnold, which he did, paying the princely sum of £30 10s. Steele, the Hamilton agent, took nominal title, which later was granted to Hamilton and Hamilton's son, James.

The socially prominent Hamilton, often regarded as the most brilliant lawyer in the colonies, intended the Lancaster site to be a good investment for his son and family. The elder Hamilton successfully defended John Zenger in a famous case that established freedom of the press, and he designed Independence Hall. Lancastrians like to think his third major achievement was the founding of their town.

When Hamilton began laying out his town the principal landmark, according to legend, was an inn kept by George Gibson. It was supposed to be located a hundred yards east of Penn Square on the north side of present East King Street, near a spring and a hickory tree. Legend also claims the early settlement was known as Hickory Town. Hamilton did something thought foolish: he laid out his town a mile away from the Conestoga River, with no good waterway within its limits and isolated from the southern route to Philadelphia by a large swamp. The site was hilly and not conducive to development. Nevertheless, Lancaster Townstead, as it was called originally, grew and prospered as its inhabitants worked to overcome the hostile environment.

When Andrew Hamilton, father of Lancaster founder James Hamilton, successfully defended John P. Zenger on libeling the royal governor of New York, thereby establishing freedom of the press, the city of New York presented Hamilton with this silver snuffbox.

Postlethwaite's tavern along Long Lane near Rock Hill was Lancaster County's first "courthouse" in 1729. The structure still stands although covered with clapboard.

Chapter I

Founding of the Townstead

1730-1760

James Hamilton, son of the celebrated Andrew Hamilton, was Lancaster's founder and proprietor. He was a businessman rather than a politician, and his Whiggish inclinations helped Lancaster become an enterprising community.

One spring day in 1736 James Hamilton stood along High Street, the principal thoroughfare of his new town, inhaling the pungent breeze wafted northward from Dark Hazel Swamp and observing the progress of Lancaster town. Houses were rising on the seventeen lots purchased the previous year. In fact, ten lots were claimed as early as 1730 — before Hamilton had a legal right to lay out his town and sell lots. Hamilton may well have mused that day that having a prominent and politically powerful father steered the project through some legal shoals that would have ruined lesser persons.

Additional streets would be needed. One's loyalty to the English monarchy could be demonstrated amply, a not inconsiderable factor in retaining royal favor. The main east-west street, now High Street, would become King George Street, while the chief north-south road would honor his consort, Queen Caroline. Parallel to Queen Caroline Street would be Duke of Cumberland Street one block to the east, and Prince of Wales Street one block to the west. Orange Street would recognize the royal house of King William III. Identifications with English royalty were dropped from common usage long before the Revolution, those streets being called simply King, Queen, Duke, and Prince. Dear to the English heart was the custom for naming streets for trees, nuts, fruits, berries, and vines. James Hamilton was dutybound to surround the royal streets with Chestnut, Lime, Lemon, Mulberry, and Vine streets. Water Street was a pathway along Roaring Brook, a powerful stream bearing an idyllic name that would be transformed later

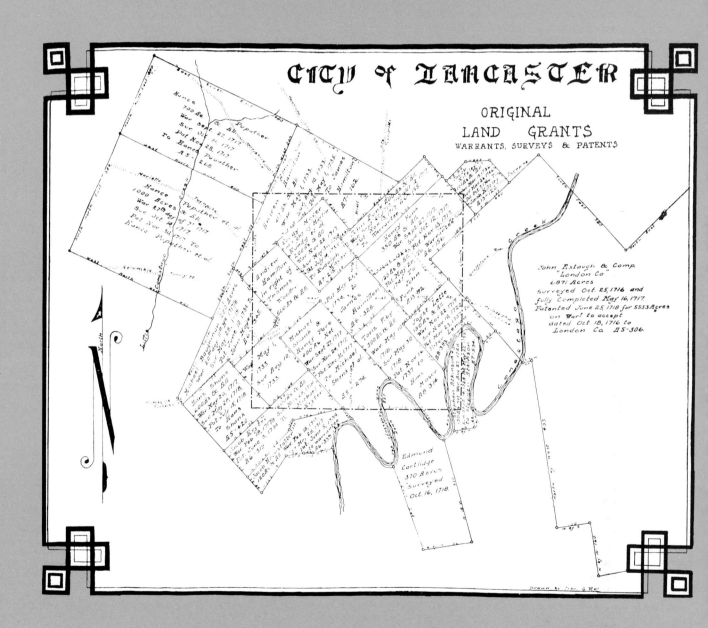

into Hoffman's Run before being christened with the final ignominy, Gas House Run.

Hamilton provided his town with one of its first distinctions by locating the county courthouse in the middle of Centre Square, the enlarged intersection of the two principal streets. The next three county seats (York, Carlisle, and Reading) had their courthouses in or on the squares, in reality, rectangles. One historical geographer has presumed the shape of Lancaster's square to have been influenced by an Ulster Scot surveyor, James Mitchell, of Donegal Township. Lancaster's focal point resembles the Londonderry square. James Hamilton with the aid of John Jones, a Philadelphia-trained surveyor — not Mitchell — planned Lancaster, including the orientation of Centre Square.

With the exception of the forty-foot-wide Water Street, all the early streets were sixty-five feet wide. Most lots were 64-feet, 4-1/2-inches wide, with depths of 245 feet to 14-foot alleys. Usually eight lots comprised one block, but regularity was not maintained. Holders of town lots were able to acquire outlots of five acres each for pasturing animals. Larger tracts of fifteen to twenty acres were available to innkeepers for pasture.

None of the lot holders could purchase rights in fee simple; they were required to pay an annual ground rent to the Hamiltons. Such rents at first were seven shillings for house lots unless the lots faced Centre Square; these "more desirable" lots carried rentals of £1 4s. Frugal Lancastrians, however, avoided the costly lots on the Square until all other lots were taken. Lots on the west side of Queen Street were taken up in 1745-46; on the east side they were not purchased until 1749. Lots on the west side of South Queen Street, lettered instead of numbered, were bought in 1762. Except for the lot of Roger Hunt, now Watt and Shand's main entrance, lots along the south side of East King Street were bought in 1745-46; Roger, who helped Hamilton lay out the outlots, acquired his lot in 1735, which made him the first inhabitant on Centre Square. Holders of outlots paid rentals of seven shillings, although the innkeepers were charged as much as six pounds sterling yearly for their pasturelands.

Mr. Hamilton's generosity was not revered in his town. Lot holders often refused to pay their rents, insisting that they paid for their rights at time of purchase. Considering that two-thirds to three-quarters of the young town's residents were German, the legal technicalities of fee simple apparently were incomprehensible, or at least that is what Hamilton's agent was supposed to believe! The stoic serenity of the Pennsylvania German gives his silence an eloquence that surpasses the Gallic body language! The English and Scots found his "ja, wohl" absolutely maddening; even the usually imperturbable Benjamin Franklin found dealing with the "Dutchmen" despairing. Little wonder Jasper Yeates advised Hamilton to go easy on the German delinquents. As time passed, ways were found to extinguish the ground rents, although some ground rents still were being collected for the Hamilton heirs after World War II.

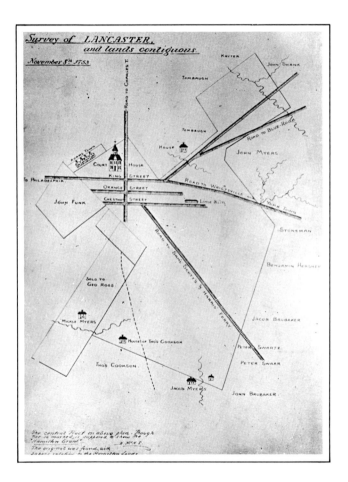

Upon purchasing a lot, the holder was required to erect within one year a "substantial Dwelling-house of the Dimensions of Sixteen feet square at least, with a good chimney of Brick or Stone, to be laid in or built with Lime or Sand." Hamilton wanted to prevent house fires, of course, but he also specified substantial construction in order to keep out the lower classes unskilled in trades, for he realized the success of his town depended on the development of a population consisting largely of skilled middle-class artisans, merchants, and professional men. In that objective he was extremely successful.

By 1740 more than 140 lots were developed, with each year exceeding the previous one in growth. Observers commented on the size of the town, and the number of persons and houses, but their estimates vary greatly. It would appear that Lancaster had about five hundred inhabitants in 1740. At the same time there were about one hundred houses, an amount that tripled during the following six years. By 1755 British travelers remarked that Lancaster exceeded in size most inland towns of England.

Travelers from Philadelphia and Upland (now Chester) to Lancaster came up the Great Conestoga Road, built about 1714, to a point nearly a mile east of the Hans Herr house, at which place a crude road led north to Lancaster. This feeder road later became segments of the Beaver Valley Pike, Gypsy Hill Road, and Eshleman Mill Road. Crossing the Conestoga River near Rock Ford, the traveler was ready to embark on the most dangerous part of his journey. Dark Hazel Swamp, with its wolves and other wild animals, lay between the river and the town. Before long the route was moved northeast of the swamp, to the vicinity of present-day South Duke Street. Traffic to the Susquehanna River continued westward along the Great Conestoga Road without coming into Lancaster.

About the time Lancaster County was erected, the proprietors of Wright's Ferry (Columbia) petitioned the newly constituted court to lay out a road from Wright's Ferry eastward to Christian Steinman's Mill (Maple Grove) and then on to White Horse in Salisbury Township. There is no record that a road was built at that time, but later this route would become the Columbia Pike and the Old Philadelphia Pike, known earlier as King's Highway.

By 1742 Lancaster had grown to become one of the largest inland towns in the British empire. Nearly 750 persons lived in the houses thought to number about 270. Despite the chronic difficulty of collecting rents, the Hamiltons were pleased that their speculative venture was turning out so well. They were so gratified, in fact, that they requested a borough charter for Lancaster in 1742. Reasons given for the request were that great improvements and new buildings were being constructed; that inhabitants were increasing in number; and that there was an urgent necessity for the promotion of trade, industry, rule, and good order. The charter, granted 1 May 1742 by Governor George Thomas in the name of King George II, contained among other things the condition that "the streets of the said Borough shall forever continue as they are now laid out and regulated." That part of the document was

honored with rare scrupulosity, because the borough, and later the city, retained its two-mile-square boundaries until the years after World War II.

As a borough, Lancaster had its own government. Two men were to be slated for burgess, the one receiving the greater number of votes becoming the chief burgess and the other simply burgess — the second in command. The burgesses were provided with six assistants, all of which constituted the legislative body. In addition, the two burgesses had powers similar to those of justices of the peace. The assistants were expected to advise and help their principals as well as keep peace and order in the borough. Thomas Cookson, a native of Durham, England, was the first chief burgess. He also laid out York Town, and speculated in land.

The borough corporation, as the government was styled, got right down to business, thanking James Hamilton for his leadership, encouragement, and liberal spirit. Following that the borough fathers adopted a series of resolutions and ordinances designed to "crack down" on the lawless element. Under the provincial government and primitive county judicial system, wrongdoers were encouraged by a lack of enforcement officials. With the population growing in Lancaster, some means had to be found to protect the innocent as well as apprehend and punish the lawbreakers.

Thanks to the Hamiltonian influence in Philadelphia and London, Lancaster's borough charter was quite liberal. It granted the borough a high degree of autonomy. The borough officials were given great latitude in solving problems that would develop. Self-government in Lancaster was an actuality. Moreover, Lancastrians came to assume gradually their autonomy was a natural state of affairs, a position that would make the townspeople, particularly their leaders, resent the authority of the Provincial Council and the British government in the 1760s. With all the freedom given in the charter, there was one drawback. The borough could not assess property and levy taxes for borough needs.

Among the problems faced by the fledgling borough government were those of public safety. Despite the "substantial" construction order by Hamilton in his deeds to lot holders, the density of buildings constructed largely of wood was a hazard. Wood-shingle roofs frequently were ignited by flying embers from the many fireplaces. One burning house soon ignited nearby structures. Adjacent stables with supplies of hay and straw were serious menaces to safety. Virtually all illumination was by an open flame, which aggravated the dangerous situation.

Drafting Lancaster's first "construction code," the burgesses required the residents to keep buckets and ladders available for firefighting, specified how fireplaces were to be constructed, regulated the cleaning of chimneys, and ordered the erection of stone fire walls in blacksmith shops and forges where such buildings were adjacent to wooden structures. Allowing fire to blaze forth from a chimney top was punishable by a stiff fine.

The first burgesses also busied themselves in gathering together some firefighting and salvage

Half-timbered structures were fairly common in Germanic Lancaster County. This structure was located about one-half mile east of Landis Valley Farm Museum on the John Grosh farm. It fell down about 1900.

Few of the earliest log houses in Lancaster survived more than a century, but this relic managed to hold on until the end of the nineteenth century. It is representative of those houses found in large numbers in colonial Lancaster.

equipment, which they used in a most informal arrangement. Whenever a fire started, every able-bodied man was expected to respond with his own bucket and to follow the directions of the burgesses. The cry of "Fire!" always brought out the most propertied gentry — those who had the most to lose in a conflagration — and the idle curious who were of little assistance. Not long after the borough was chartered the burgesses and the leading citizens decided that any worthwhile efforts to extinguish fires would have to be their responsibility. To compound the problem, the borough was not able to pay for firefighting equipment because its only revenues came from rentals of market stalls and stands at the fairs, and from fines and forfeitures, amounting to approximately one hundred pounds a year. Pleading to James Hamilton, the borough fathers asked, ". . . whether wee can Raise any money on the Inhabitants within the Borough by Assessment?" The answer was a regretful no.

With that the burgesses posed the problem of finance to the leading townsmen, and thus was born the Union Fire Company No. 1 of Lancaster. Starting with a select group limited to thirty gentlemen, the "firemen" took it upon themselves to provide necessary equipment, except for the engine. Eventually sufficient funds were obtained from the county commissioners and borough treasury to purchase fire engines — small hand-drawn tubs on wheels in which hand pumps were mounted. Roaring Brook along Water Street was dammed to furnish water to the engines and bucket brigades. It may be difficult for us today to imagine several dozen of the town's most distinguished leaders lugging a fire engine through the muddy streets, rushing into burning houses with large linen salvage bags, directing the hose stream on the fire, and keeping the curious behind the fire lines! But that is exactly what Lancaster's most prominent lawyers, George Ross and Jasper Yeates, would do when the alarm was given.

Inasmuch as several of the assigned men were neither propertied nor members of the Union Fire Company, it may be assumed some of the portly gentry were not quite able to climb ladders, brandish fire axes, and pull heavy equipment.

Fines were levied against those members that were absent from meetings. In an act of magnanimity, George Ross had his fine refunded on his absence to sign the Declaration of Independence!

Joseph Simon was the patriarch of the Lancaster Jewish community. He was a trader and merchant, and was respected as one of the town's most valuable citizens. John Joseph Henry became a distinguished justice, as did Jasper Yeates. Christopher Hager was the founder of the famous department store bearing his name. Matthias Slough was the town's leading innkeeper, holding forth at the Sign of the White Swan on the southeastern corner of Centre Square and South Queen Street.

More formal organization was essential for effective management of firefighting. On 14 August 1760 the Union Fire Company No. 1 drew up a set of bylaws, and became a formal institution with officers and members associated with but independent

of the borough government.

Adequacy of water for household consumption bothered the burgesses. Wells were ordered dug at specific locations, hand pumps were installed, and efforts were made to prevent vandalism to the pumps. A crier was employed to patrol the borough, making announcements, giving the fire alarm, and reassuring the citizenry.

Sharp practices by stand holders in the marketplace resulted in ordinances that would fine butchers for pumping air into shrunken meat. Apparently butchers had heavy thumbs in the 1740s, for the burgesses sought in vain for funds to buy the Clerk of the Market a set of weights and measures.

All public announcements and ordinances had to be printed in English and German, making an additional drain on the public treasury. It is a tribute to the borough officials that the government could operate from 1742 until 1812 without property taxes.

Law and order were maintained by the high constable and his assistants. Justice was swift and sure. Stocks and a pillory were kept in Centre Square near the courthouse, where lawbreakers could be displayed in agonizing positions, often with bare backs streaked with dried blood and purple welts. Anne Toews, a hapless young lady, added a zero to a one-shilling note, raising it to ten shillings. Her cleverness cost her an ear and a public whipping with twenty-one lashes "well laid" on her bare back. Tradition claims the pillory and stocks were located at the northwestern corner of Centre Square.

George Ross (1730-1779) was Lancaster's most illustrious lawyer and wealthiest citizen in the pre-Revolutionary era. He was a signer of the Declaration of Independence and active member of the Union Fire Company No. 1.

Francis Bailey, a Lancaster printer of the Revolutionary era, was the first to proclaim George Washington as "Father of His Country" in this 1779 almanac published in Lancaster. This print shows the cover of the almanac. Like most publications of the time, it was printed in German.

Benjamin Franklin visited Lancaster on many occasions in his official capacities; he also is reported to have been instrumental in organizing the local lodge of Freemasons which exists today as Lodge 43. Franklin's first encounter with the Lancaster County "Dutchmen" occurred while he was bargaining for wagons to be used in the French and Indian wars. Ben — a son of the Humanist Enlightenment — learned to be wary during his dealings in Lancaster County.

Lancaster County erected its first prison in the 1730s at the northwest corner of North Prince and West King streets. Attached to the jail was a workhouse. This structure, with occasional additions, survived until the present prison was built in 1852. A portion of the rear stone wall along Water Street was incorporated into the Fulton Hall.

Adam Simon Kuhn, M.D., built this large house in 1763 on East King Street adjacent to his development, Adamstown. In 1788 it was sold to Michael Lightner who named it the Indian Queen Tavern. It existed as a hotel until 1883 when it was razed to make way for the Eastern Market House, still standing. It was one of Lancaster's largest structures in the eighteenth century.

A debtors prison operated in the county workhouse. Inhabitants convicted of misdemeanors and felonies were confined to the *gaol* where the more uncooperative felons were chained to the wall. Persons found guilty of "artful" murder were hanged in the prison yard.

Despite the tales of Indian dangers, the redmen skulking around Lancaster rarely caused trouble. Possibly the most serious incident happened in March 1738 when a pair of youthful Indians in hot pursuit of firewater stormed Samuel Bethel's tavern. Bethel bounced the Indians. A plank came hurtling through a window into the tavern, whereupon two customers went outside to remonstrate with the braves. The Indians slashed one patron, and in the fracas that followed one Indian was captured. Townspeople decided after that episode to discourage the carrying of unshielded knives by Indians.

When the burgesses and their assistants could not solve a problem without difficulty, they dropped the matter in the laps of the citizenry. Town assemblies were held quite frequently, with the high constable being directed to inform the inhabitants two days in advance. The borough charter required the burgesses to have the consent of the "greatest part of the Inhabitants" before adopting an ordinance. Evidence suggests that as time passed the public meetings attracted fewer persons.

While the town assemblies saw less public participation, the citizens would turn out in force at elections of the town officials. A sociological explanation is that Lancastrians preferred to select their borough leaders carefully and then permit the officials to function with a minimum of public supervision and participation. Of course, without the thorny question of taxes the public had little with which to be exercised! Another possible explanation for public indifference to the town meetings may be the absence of much popular participation in government by the German-reared inhabitants.

Voting in early Lancaster was done at the courthouse — in fact, that was the polling place for the entire county. The various factions would print tickets of their respective candidates. These tickets would be distributed to prospective voters, who were virtually all the male adults in the community. Susannah Wright, an extraordinary woman from Wright's Ferry, once took a second-story room in a Lancaster inn and distributed tickets of her faction (the Quakers) to whoever would climb an outside ladder to her window. Miss Wright, obviously one of the strongest and most colorful personalities of colonial Pennsylvania, carried on an extensive correspondence with the most distinguished scientists, philosophers, and politicians of the mid-eighteenth century. Her sharply worded campaign diatribes against the Scot Presbyterians caused those folk to complain bitterly to the authorities. Not to be outdone, the wife of Andrew Galbraith, who was a Scot Presbyterian, campaigned for her husband, riding horseback around the county and through the borough. Women were not permitted to vote then. Her efforts were to influence the male voters.

Lancaster's charter permitted any white male who lived in the town for at least one year, and who owned property or rented a house at a cost of five pounds or more, to vote. These qualifications guaranteed a wide electorate.

One problem that was solved somehow without dipping too deeply into the town treasury was the draining of the swamp that lay in the vicinity of present-day Walnut and Lime streets, and conducting the streams from numerous springs downtown to Roaring Brook through stone sewers. Weirs were built to impound water for firefighting and to facilitate the use of the stream for waterpower. Several mills, a tannery, and a brewery were located on Water Street in the 1750s.

A problem the borough fathers found more difficult to handle was the stench caused by numerous swine and cattle pens in the town. Ordinances were passed and fines were levied, but the unpleasant odor persisted until the land thus occupied became too valuable for such employment.

With the advent of the French and Indian wars of the 1750s, Lancaster's artisans and mechanics turned their skills into providing guns, wagons, clothing, and military hardware for the British and colonial militia. Although the struggles occurred on the western frontier of Pennsylvania, no place was so well equipped as Lancaster to arm and supply an army. Soon it became the staging area for the militia, with local residents learning what "quartering troops" involved — an education that evoked unpleasant memories during the revolutionary and constitutional periods of our history.

Benjamin Franklin was dispatched to Lancaster to purchase wagons for the British army, and he too received an education — in dealing with the Pennsylvania-German commercial mentality!

With the French and Indian wars being fought to the west, the presence of any Indians near Lancaster caused alarm. False alarms were common. One day Thomas Doyle fired his pistol, and virtually every inhabitant of Lancaster ran to the courthouse. All were armed and none had ammunition! The multitude then sheepishly returned to their homes.

From 1730 to 1742 Lancaster had grown rapidly. The Hamilton tract was nearly filled with householders. Buildings could be seen from Water Street to Lime Street, and from Vine Street to Chestnut Street. The Hamilton tract ended at the northern boundary of a parcel warranted to Theodorus Eby in 1718, but which Eby never was able to take up. After Eby's death his heirs sold their warrant to John Musser, who paid Penn's land agent and received the patent of three hundred acres. This tract, as others in the Lancaster vicinity, was oriented at an angle to lines of latitude and longitude. The Eby-Musser tract formed the northern boundary of Lancaster Township in 1729, and therefore the Hamilton tract ended against that diagonal boundary.

In 1744 John Musser sold to Dr. Adam Simon Kuhn, a prominent physician and layman of Trinity Lutheran Church, a tract of land extending from East King and Church streets south to the Conestoga River at the tip of South Duke Street. Rockland Street formed the southwestern boundary. Dr. Kuhn laid out a town of forty-six lots along two streets, Church Street and Middle Street, now called Howard Avenue. First Alley, later Freiburg Street, and then changed in 1917 to Pershing Avenue, and Second Alley, now part of South Lime Street, were the cross streets. Dr. Kuhn sold most of his lots by lottery, disposing of thirty-two in the first year. The winner received a free lot but was required to pay the legal fees and annual ground rent of seven shillings. Adamstown, derived from "Adam's Town," had more liberal requirements than Hamilton's tract; lot holders had two years to build their "substantial" houses.

John Musser, Jr. decided to follow Dr. Kuhn's example, and he then laid out Mussertown. Rockland Street divided the two towns. Musser extended Church and Middle streets to East Strawberry Street, and laid out two cross streets, Diamond Street, now South Duke Street, and Pearl Street, now South Christian Street. Gradually more streets were opened.

Somewhat later Samuel Bethel laid out a town named Betheltown to the southwest of the Hamilton tract, and this was at an angle to both Lancaster borough and Mussertown. Betheltown did not have a regular shape. It was located along South Queen, South Prince, and South Water streets, extending as far to the northwest as Strawberry Street.

Eventually these towns were brought into the borough, but the strange pattern of street grids continues to infuriate motorists and honors the rugged individualism of Lancaster's founders!

An event in 1744 propelled Lancaster into the colonial limelight. The town served as the meeting place of the treaty-making sessions of the Six Nations of Indians and the colonies of Maryland, Virginia, and Pennsylvania. Visitors from Maryland and Virginia were astonished at the growth and sophistication of the town in the wilderness.

By 1759 Lancaster had the following artisans at work:

34 Shoemakers	4 Stocking-weavers
19 Saddlers	1 Blue Dyer
7 Tanners	1 Buttonmaker
5 Skinners	5 Hatters
11 Blacksmiths	2 Potters
5 Locksmiths	2 Barbers
4 Gunsmiths	3 Tinsmiths
4 Nailsmiths	1 Coppersmith
27 Carpenter/Joiners	1 Saddletreemaker
22 Masons	8 Wheelwrights
1 Brickmaker	2 Clockmakers
1 Glazier	1 Watchmaker
4 Coopers	1 Silversmith
21 Bakers	7 Tobacconists
3 Butchers	1 Soapboiler
2 Brewers	1 Bookbinder
20 Tailors	4 Ropemakers
13 Weavers	

Religious needs of the Lancastrians were met by the gradual organization of congregations, frequently from earlier missions. The Anglican (Church of England), German Reformed (Calvinist), Lutheran, Presbyterian (Covenanter), Moravian (Unitas Fratum), and Roman Catholic congregations required educated clergymen.

The frontier was not an inviting place for the bright young graduate of Heidelberg or Edinburgh. Moreover, congregations in the boondocks could not afford to pay their ministers salaries sufficient to permit full-time attention to church affairs. When university graduates could be induced to accept calls to local churches, the clerics usually operated schools and academies in conjunction with their pastoral duties. Considering the growth of Lancaster's population, church development lagged significantly during the first few decades, particularly among the English segments of the community. Meanwhile the absence of regularly scheduled and organized religious services hindered the growth of that spirit conducive to ardent denominationalism.

Establishing a thriving congregation was no easy task for the average clergyman. About the time enough souls had been gathered together to warrant discussion on building a church, the founding minister would see his flock trotting off behind a newly arrived preacher whose only stock in trade were his enthusiastic exhortations and his charisma. Snorting deprecations in the direction of the pied pipers, the hapless clergymen would turn once more to the nuts and bolts of assembling congregations that could survive good times and bad, through theological tensions and all-too-human spiritual leadership.

Charismatic preachers rarely espoused the middle path. Some advocated a form of "universal

18

St. John's Episcopal Church of Pequea (Compassville) was established in 1729. It is on the boundary of Lancaster and Chester counties. This communion set (flagon, plate, and chalice) was made in 1766, and is of the style produced by famed Lancaster pewterer Johann Christopher Heyne. Lancaster silversmiths and pewterers were highly skilled craftsmen considered among the finest of the colonies.

Christianity," or nondenominationalism exemplified by the Reverend Lorenz Nyberg, a Swedish Lutheran sent to Trinity Lutheran Church during its earliest days. Said he, "The congregation should be a free church in which every servant of Christ should be at liberty to preach." Mr. Nyberg's Swedenborgian-tinged Moravianism not only disrupted his own church, it sparked heated discussions and caused dissension in other congregations. Other preachers were adamant in their views that only one truth prevailed, and that they were the sole possessors of the revealed truth. Moderate pastors and ministers, plagued with material shortages and vexing administrative problems, found their energies and inclinations for disputation depleted. Tolerance and decent compromise seemed sensible under the adverse conditions in the backwoods of Lancaster.

Some members of early Lancaster congregations expressed displeasure with the cold personalities of their clergy and the impersonal liturgies of the churches. The Reverend John B. Rieger of First Reformed Church (1739-1743), for example, was characterized as "cold, languid and heartless" in his ministry. Others complained the ministers neglected their communicants that were sick in body and spirit. On the other hand, clergymen in Lancaster were bitter about harassment from members of their churches. Charges of heterodoxy were common. Even the personal lives of the ministers came under close scrutiny, as the Lutheran pastor John Frederick Handshue discovered in 1750. The Reverend Mr. Handshue, every inch a stern disciplinarian and "no nonsense" pastor, decided he needed a housekeeper. Susanna Belzner, daughter of a deacon, was engaged for this purpose, and, before long, Handshue began admiring her piety, honor, and industry. His diary tells us: "I began to wrestle with the Lord concerning marriage and finally God convinced me that I was to have this woman and no other for my wife." The church councilmen, however, were miffed that their pastor had not sought their advice in choosing a wife; and their wives were furious that Handshue would select a girl of lowly position rather than a more appropriate young lady — after all, Susanna tended the cake stand in the Lancaster market! The social chill persuaded Handshue to take his bride and seek a pastorate elsewhere.

As early as 1729 Lutherans in the Lancaster area began worshiping informally. The Reverend Johann Christian Schultze ministered to the Lancastrians about 1730 before returning to Europe to coordinate that denomination's activities in eastern Pennsylvania. The first permanent pastor for the Lutherans in Lancaster was the Reverend Johann Casper Stoever who served as a missionary to about 150 communicants in 1733. Three years later he was called to become the first regular pastor of Trinity Lutheran Church. The first church was built in 1738, and was on the site of the present parish house. Requiring six years for completion, the pipe organ was the first instrument of its kind in Lancaster. That consummate Lutheran, Johann Sebastian Bach, completed his Cantata no. 116 that year, but it is not likely Lancastrians heard it performed for many years afterward! It might be noted in passing that the glorious *Passion According to St. Matthew* was written in 1729, the year Lancaster County was created, and the Christmas and Easter oratorios of Bach were heard first just about the time Trinity Lutheran Church was founded.

The renowned patriarch of American Lutheranism, the Reverend Dr. Heinrich Melchior Muhlenberg, watched over the development of Trinity Lutheran Church, and doubtless influenced its ability to survive a series of disruptions. The shortage of German pastors in Pennsylvania necessitated use of Swedish Lutheran clergymen remaining as vestiges of the Swedish rule over the province before William Penn's proprietorship. Apparently the Swedes held theological views that occasionally seemed heterodox, resulting in disputes.

The Lutheran congregation established a parochial school in Lancaster about 1748, following the lead of the Reformed Church. In 1749 the second annual Ministerium of the Lutheran Church was held in Lancaster, which emphasized the importance of that town to the progress of Lutheranism in Pennsylvania.

The second denomination to form a congregation in Lancaster was the German Reformed Church. Although members of that denomination were active earlier in Philadelphia County, and in rural Lancaster County, First Reformed Church was established in 1736. As with the Lutherans, Reformed settlers in Lancaster were served by traveling ministers prior to formal organization of a congregation. A log structure was

Hamilton gave lots to the mission for burials and chapel purposes. Burned, supposedly by an arsonist, in 1760, the chapel was replaced by a fine stone structure two years later. This parish eventually became St. Mary's, the original parish of the present diocese, and mother church of all Catholic parishes in Lancaster County.

In 1744 the members of the Anglican Communion living in Lancaster were astonished to find the Reverend Mr. Richard Locke "accidentally" arriving in the town. They made the best use of the new visitor, and convinced him to remain among them as their rector. Thus St. James's Church (Church of England) was established in 1744, ending the tedious search for a spiritual leader. By 1753 a building was completed, but without a steeple. A Georgian-style cupola for the bell was added in 1761. A lottery was used to finance construction of the church. The twenty-four pews were built and paid for by the pewholders. The Reverend Thomas Barton came to St. James's in 1761, but periodically threatened to resign unless his salary was increased so his family might not live in poverty. Barton's wife was the sister of David Rittenhouse, early Pennsylvania scientist. The Hamiltons and the Penns (William's sons were Anglicans, not Quakers) provided a liberal gift that kept Barton at St. James's until the Revolution.

The Moravians, or "United Brethren," not to be confused with the later sects, United Brethren in Christ, and Evangelical United Brethren, are noted for their settlements in Bethlehem and Lititz, Pennsylvania, and Winston-Salem, North Carolina. They established a church in Lancaster in 1746 through a series of peculiar circumstances. The Lutheran pastor, Lorenz Nyberg, was influenced strongly by the teachings of Emanual Swedenborg and Count Zinzendorf, the Moravian leader. The latter preached in the courthouse in 1742, and attracted many persons. The Zinzendorf plea was for interdenominational unity, which seemed appealing and logical to Lancaster's burghers. To the local Lutheran and Reformed clergy it was a serious challenge, and ministers urged the Moravians "to be driven out of town." Three years later Moravian bishop Augustus Spangenberg delivered another plea for ecumenical cooperation, and for this he was splattered with mud. Nyberg's affection for the Moravians caused a serious rift in Trinity Lutheran Church, resulting in physical violence, court actions, and appeals to the

built for First Reformed Church during 1736 — two years before the Lutherans completed their stone church. This log church stood on the present church site until 1753, when it was replaced with a much larger building constructed of regularly dressed stone. The old log building was dismantled, sold, and re-erected on the opposite side of Orange Street, where it served as a dwelling until fire destroyed it in 1836.

The Reformed congregation lost no time in starting a school during the first year of that body's corporate existence. This was Lancaster's first parochial school.

John Jacob Hoch served the Reformed congregation as its first minister. It is believed he was a ruling elder rather than a European-trained clergyman. Despite his lack of formal theological education, he served the young congregation well for nearly two years. The Reverend John B. Rieger ministered to the church from 1739 to 1743. Although he was reputed to be rather forbidding in manner, he built the congregation into a large and active body. He returned briefly after his resignation, but eventually concentrated all his efforts on the practice of medicine, which he studied in Germany.

The next congregation to become established was the Roman Catholic mission of St. John Nepomucene. A chapel was built of logs in 1742, and this soon became the second-largest Roman Catholic congregation in Pennsylvania outside Philadelphia. The Bishop of London and the Society of Jesus (Jesuits) in Germany provided priests for the burgeoning parish. As with the other congregations in Lancaster, James

In 1750 the Moravian congregation of Lancaster built a stone church along Market Street near West Orange Street. This structure was torn away in 1820 when the congregation built a large brick church. A portion of the original building was incorporated into the new brick structure. In the 1960s the entire property was sold to the Lancaster Association of Commerce and Industry and was cleared, the Moravians having built a large new church in the suburbs.

Lutheran Ministerium. When the Reverend J.B. Rieger of the Reformed Church invited Zinzendorf to his church the congregation pressed their minister to resign. Nyberg and the Lutheran-Reformed apostates then erected a nondenominational church in 1746, which they named St. Andrew's Church. It had a free pulpit open "to all who would seek the Truth." Two years later St. Andrew's became the Moravian Church, and in 1750 the little congregation constructed a large stone structure, overshadowing all other buildings in Lancaster of that date. Other clergymen were fearful of the Moravian influence. Muhlenberg in 1748 stated, ". . . we must either drive them [Moravians] out or they us." In cultural attainments the Moravians surpassed the other Pennsylvania Germans. Their music, particularly, was of the highest quality, employing organs, orchestral instruments, and trained choirs to augment their worship. The Moravian Church in Lancaster occupied the western side of North Market Street near West Orange Street, now the site of the Lancaster Association of Commerce and Industry.

Ten males are required for the holding of Jewish religious rites, and that was about all the Lancaster Jewish community could muster in the 1740s. The respect and affection earned by the German Jewish merchants in early Lancaster paved the way for a tradition in which prejudice would be absent to a remarkable degree. Joseph Simon, that venerable patriarch, owned two Torahs and an ark that were used in services held in his home from 1747 until the Revolution. Simon's home was on the southwestern corner of Centre Square. In 1747 the Jewish community bought a lot in the northern liberties of Lancaster for use as a burying ground. Today this cemetery, now owned by Temple Shaarai Shomayim, is the fourth oldest Jewish cemetery in the nation.

Despite the power and influence of the Quakers, or the Religious Society of Friends, in Lancaster, that group was unable to set up a meetinghouse until 1752, and then it never enjoyed much strength. The Lancaster Meeting was located along South Queen Street near Vine Street.

The last major denomination to establish a congregation in Lancaster was the Presbyterian, or Covenanter. Powerful in the southern and northwestern parts of the county, Presbyterianism did not have many adherents in Lancaster. Those few Presbyterians that

did reside in the borough were maligned by the American rector, the Reverend Mr. Locke: "[They] receive their sacrament with a gun charged and drawn sword; and profess they will fight for Christ against civil magistrates." The Scottish opinion of English pomp and glory was fully equal to the occasion. By 1760 there were enough Covenanters in Lancaster to found a congregation, which is known today as First Presbyterian Church. The present church and auxiliary structures continue to occupy historic land granted them by James Hamilton.

§ § § § §

From 1730 to 1760 the hamlet of Lancaster evolved into a borough of major economic, political, and social importance in the American colonies. Lancastrians and their community gradually assumed a greater role in history. The town itself, created by a businessman seeking a reasonable return on his investment, attracted a then disproportionate number of skilled mechanics and artisans of the middle class. Enlightened professional men, albeit relatively few in number, encouraged the growth of Whiggery, or the desire for freedom to pursue economic opportunities unhindered by excessive regulation. An unusually liberal charter for the new borough aided the attainment of that objective in the sense that the local government was able to regulate matters at home without possessing the authority to impose taxes. Hence Lancastrians were encouraged to find their own solutions to problems, and to live in relative independence.

Geography, too, aided fortuitously the development of Lancaster. The town's location was conducive to the establishment of artisans' workshops and mercantile business. The distant Conestoga River discouraged the growth of large industries requiring much waterpower in central Lancaster; its proximity, however, to the town's border enabled essential enterprises to sustain the community without difficulty. The availability of skilled artisans and nearby industries, coupled with an experienced mercantile community, thrust Lancaster into the role of manufacturing and supplying goods for winning the French and Indian wars, and for western expansion. Hamilton's town by 1760 had proved itself fully capable of contributing mightily to the American Revolution which was to follow.

Chapter II

Lancaster Goes to War

1760-1817

General George Washington visited Lancaster on five occasions. His visit on 4 July 1791 was a gala event, with a banquet and ball in the courthouse in Centre Square. This is an artist's conception of the visit. The courthouse was nearly square rather than decidedly rectangular.

Lancaster enjoyed a breathing spell between the conclusion of the French and Indian wars and the American Revolution. It was a time of accelerated population growth, maturity of institutions, and realization that Lancaster possessed a spirit born out of its most important asset — its people. Hamilton's planning and the earnest industriousness of Lancastrians had made the community worthy of comment by visitors. The Reverend Manasseh Cutler observed in 1788, "Lancaster is a large and antient [*sic*] town; the best built inland in America." From 1760 to the early nineteenth century Lancaster *was* the largest inland town, but not the oldest as the Pennsylvania Historical and Museum Commission markers proclaim. (More than thirty inland towns of Massachusetts antedate our Lancaster!)

By the advent of the Revolution many of the early log houses and stone structures had been replaced with larger brick buildings. Along King and Queen streets were to be found many brick homes, some of them "elegant" and "very handsome" in the words of an eighteenth-century tourist. Mr. Cutler discovered King Street contained many "very handsome" houses, and south of the town "a great number of small 'Dutch' houses." The modest homes probably were one-and-one-half-story houses illumined by one or two dormer windows protruding from the steeply pitched roofs. Some of these buildings were half-timbered on the gable ends. Several of the larger two-story houses were half-timbered above the first floor; a number of these survived to the beginning of the present century.

Among the larger structures were the major inns. A description of Henry Helm's Sign of the Boot and Crown hostelry on Queen Street reveals that it was three stories high with a large cellar under it. An arched vault, or cold cellar, with a never-failing stream of water flowing through it, was located under the pavement in front of the inn. Sixty horses could be stabled in an adjoining brick stable. In addition, the inn complex contained a large courtyard, shed with feeding troughs for the threescore horses, and a pump. Every inn and many of the other buildings in town had cold cellars under the pavements. Rebuilding of streets and structures frequently turns up the hidden vaults, which inevitably starts a rash of stories about tunnels "to hide from Indians," or "for smuggling of slaves to the underground railway." Such myths, dear to the heart of the romantic soul, are completely false in Lancaster's history.

Center of attention in the town was the courthouse, built 1736-38. It apparently was of a rather plain design — a simplified domestic Georgian architecture, it is surmised. A contemporary description tells us it was "a very large brick building two stories high. The ground room where the justices of this county hold their court is very spacious. There is a handsome bench, and railed in, whereon they sit, and a chair in the midst of it, which is filled by the judge." Other accounts say a large half-oval table, covered with a green cloth and situated below the bench and within the bar, was used by the court clerk and the attorneys. Provisions were made for the other court officers. The other three sides of the court chamber contained steps or risers "like the steps leading into the north portal of St. Paul's in London." Spectators stood on these steps when court was in session. We also are told the courtroom could hold an astonishingly large crowd of eight hundred persons without discomfort! Discounting the much smaller size of eighteenth-century Lancastrians, it still is difficult to determine how eight hundred persons could be crowded into a room sixty feet by sixty feet maximum. The second floor contained another room for the deliberation of the justices and, unlike the downstairs chamber, this one was heated. A jury room was located upstairs. Atop the structure was a cupola in which eventually were placed a clock and bell. Improvements and more comfortable appointments were made from time to time, usually accompanied by cries of outraged citizens who

perceived a cause-and-effect relationship between improvements and higher taxes.

It was in this courthouse that the Indian treaties of 1744 were negotiated, and it was here that the Continental Congress met on 27 September 1777. The Pennsylvania government used the building for nine months during the British occupation of Philadelphia, September 1777 to June 1778. And it was in this ancient building that thirteen persons heard the dreaded sentence of death intoned, from John Jones in 1759 for burglary, to Negro York in 1781 for rape. All were executed by hanging. One, Catherine Fisher, was the only woman ever to have been sentenced to death in Lancaster County.

While the perpetual remodeling was going on, a fire broke out on 9 June 1784, destroying the venerable structure. Blame was attributed to careless plasterers or a negligent clock repairman or an arsonist. (Most old-time fires were thought to be the fiendish work of arsonists.) Apparently the fire did not race rapidly through the building, for a large amount of records was saved.

With the courthouse in ruins, agitation began to rebuild the structure on a site other than in the middle of Centre Square. The proprietor of the town was of similar opinion, and asked, "Pray could it not be contrived to have the new one raised in some other Place and to leave the Square unencumbered with any building in its Center? It would certainly conduce very much to the Beauty of the Town. The public might have any Lot of mine that would suit the Purpose." By 1784 Hamilton had few lots in central Lancaster, and none were very desirable. Most Lancastrians had grown accustomed to seeing the courthouse in the Square, and that is where they wanted to see a new courthouse.

Within two months efforts had begun to rebuild the structure. Meanwhile court was held in Frederick Hubley's tavern. Townspeople kept wary eyes on the progress, wondering what it was going to look like and how much it was going to cost in taxes. The county commissioners acted traditionally. The new structure did not differ too greatly in appearance from the original building.

Each of the four faces and gables of the courthouse looked directly into the four streets that entered the Square, with the south facade being the main entrance. The bell and clock were housed in a tall square tower surmounted by a classical cupola, topped off by a fine

This large clock movement was made about 1785 by John Eberman, Jr., for the Lancaster County courthouse tower. The works proper stands fifty-three inches high. Eberman was paid L550 for making the clock. When the third courthouse was built in 1852-1854, this movement was installed in the new tower where it served until replaced in 1898. Eberman's son, Jacob, lost a hand while working on the clock in 1796. The Lancaster County Historical Society has custody of the clock, which is restored and keeps excellent time when demonstrated. (Photo by S.E. Kramer, III.)

In 1763 the last of the Conestoga Indians were massacred in the prison yard by Scot Presbyterians known as the Paxtang Boys from the Harris Ferry locale (Harrisburg). The Indians had been attacked earlier, and the survivors were put under protective custody in the Lancaster prison. The massacre took place on a Sunday morning when the townspeople and prisonkeeper were in their churches. Women and children were murdered along with the braves. This sketch by an unidentified Quaker was drawn with great artistic license.

weather vane. The John Eberman clock is still in excellent running order, and has been preserved by the Lancaster County Historical Society.

The courtroom was heated by two Franklin stoves set into fireplaces in the northeast and northwest corners, and two cannon stoves in the spectators' section. Apparently the commissioners did not plan to heat the new courtroom with eight hundred bodies. A circular staircase inside the east entrance permitted access to the second floor. Three large rooms there were used for the district and orphans courts, city council meetings, school board gatherings, and jury deliberations. From 1799 until 1812, when Lancaster was the capital of Pennsylvania, the state legislators met in the courthouse. It is traditional for the upper house (Senate) to regard itself as superior to the lower house (House of Representatives), and therefore a separate stairway had to be constructed outside the south wall so that senators could assemble upstairs without mingling with the representatives downstairs. Other state and county offices occupied the new county office building at the west side of the Square, known to generations of Lancastrians as Old City Hall.

During the first two decades of its corporate existence the borough government proved quite equal to the problems of the developing town despite their inability to impose taxes to pay for public improvements. Solutions were found by use of moral pressure, generation of broad public support, personal obligation, and ingenious resourcefulness. As the borough moved into its third decade, growth of the population and the increasing complexity of civic problems, much of which was caused by a spirit of political change in the wind, brought to the governmental leaders many trying hours. Gradually the borough fathers sought and obtained authority to deal effectively with the new problems. As the number of persons increased, wrongdoing and crime kept pace. A serious need for additional justices of the peace existed, but the borough was kept waiting until after the Revolution began.

The borough was thrown into an uproar on Sunday morning, 27 December 1763, when a frightful massacre occurred in its midst. Some days earlier a band of approximately fifty-seven Scot Presbyterians from the Paxtang area, near Harrisburg, decided to eliminate the Indians that caused the settlers much concern on the western frontier. Rather than attacking

in western Pennsylvania, however, the Scots, called the Paxtang Boys, raided the Conestoga Indiantown in Manor Township, killing all the elderly Indians in the village. These particular Indians were quite peaceable and lived amicably with their white neighbors, making baskets and peddling them in the township. When the massacre occurred most of the younger Indians were out of the village, going on their peddling rounds. The county authorities at once brought the survivors to the county jail at Prince and King streets and placed them in protective custody. The following Sabbath morning, while the people of Lancaster were at worship, the Paxtang Boys made a second raid, breaking into the jail and murdering every man, woman, and child that survived the earlier attack. Even the smallest infants were bludgeoned to death. A Presbyterian minister, Lazarus Stewart, was believed to be the leader of the gang. Despite the widespread expression of revulsion, the Paxtang Boys were never prosecuted. This act of wanton barbarism marked the end of Indian community life in our county.

Until 1775 the borough corporation met approximately four times annually, which suggests the high burgess and his assistants handled issues informally as all but the most severe problems occurred. Serious matters could be debated and solutions found quarterly. Council meetings apparently operated by consensus and with the advice of the borough's leading citizenry. We may assume that if Jasper Yeates, Edward Shippen, George Ross, Adam Reigart, William Henry, and William A. Atlee agreed on a solution, the borough fathers needed no additional sanction from Jonathan Q. Publick!

During the Revolution borough government was in disarray; its major personalities had duties either in manufacturing and procurement for the Pennsylvania militia and the Continental Congress or on the battlefield. The corporation met irregularly and informally. Much of its work appears to have been *ad hoc* in nature. State and Continental requirements and authority frequently overlapped borough jurisdiction. During 1777 and 1778 Lancaster borough found itself hosting the Continental Congress for one day and the state government for nine months; matters like these could weigh heavily upon burghers accustomed to stretching market-stand rentals to cover the cost of protecting the community's humanity and property. To make matters worse, the borough officials usually were

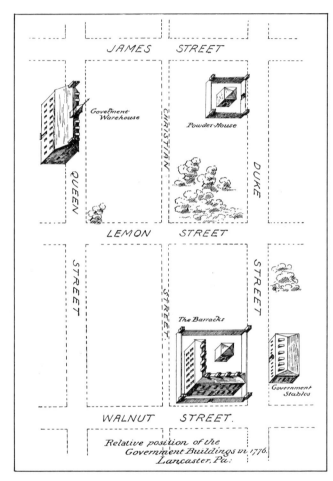

Relative position of the Government Buildings in 1776. Lancaster, Pa.

of their borough government. Some of the indifference might be attributed to the large numbers of German-speaking residents that saw little purpose in sitting through an English-language discussion. Other factors causing lack of interest may have been unfamiliarity with governmental processes — although Lancaster's burgesses functioned on a quite informal, common-sense basis — and willingness to allow trusted and respected leaders to handle all the matters themselves.

An attempt to bypass the apathetic citizens was undertaken by the corporation when it petitioned the House of Representatives to permit the burgesses to function as did the county justices of the peace in making rules and ordinances without submitting such proposals to the electorate for their approval. The issue that precipitated this petition was the need for better street regulation and a building code. It was suggested that by staying home the fiercely independent Lancastrians could prevent regulation-making! The Pennsylvania General Assembly turned down the request. However, the burgesses were given the power to act as justices of the peace within the borough, and in time this move permitted the borough government to function more effectively, albeit less democratically.

An important trend was seen in the election of burgesses in the 1760s. Heretofore these borough officers were elected from the wealthiest and most respected residents, who usually were professional politicians and lawyers. After 1760 the town's businessmen assumed a major role in running the borough, and before long the majority of burgesses were men of business. Innkeepers, merchants, and skilled artisans held the reins of control throughout this period and thereafter. Lancaster's business mentality, already well developed, turned its special talents and way of perceiving problems — its pragmatism and readiness to compromise — to solving the ills of the fast-growing "largest inland town."

Some of the matters receiving the attention of the burgesses in the 1770s were improvement of streets. Roaring Brook, that stream along Water Street, was a special vexation to the burgesses. Travelers from the west were forced to slosh through the water only a little more than one block from the center of Lancaster. The road was a king's road, and under the authority of the province/state. Finally the county paid to have a bridge built over the "rivulet." The borough had brick arches

not informed in advance how many thousands of extra mouths had to be fed and bodies housed when armies and groups of prisoners and refugees arrived in town during the Revolution. Moreover, local officials wondered how much authority they had under the charter granted by a king from whom the nation declared its independence. Were royal commissions still valid? By the 1780s local government had begun to make some order out of the chaos.

In 1782 corporation meetings again returned to the quarterly schedule. Another problem arose. It was difficult to obtain a majority for the adoption of ordinances as required by law. Finally the borough officials were obliged to go around town, knocking on doors, to urge the citizenry to attend their meetings! Lancastrians had become apathetic to the functioning

THE
CHARTER,
LAWS,
CATALOGUE of BOOKS,
LIST OF
PHILOSOPHICAL INSTRUMENTS, &c.
OF THE
Juliana Library-Company,
IN
LANCASTER.

To which are prefixed,

Some *Reflections* on the *Advantages* of KNOWLEDGE; the Origin of BOOKS and LIBRARIES, shewing how they have been encouraged and patronized by the Wise and Virtuous of every Age.

WITH

A Short Account of its INSTITUTION, FRIENDS and BENEFACTORS.

Sine Libris Justitia quiescit, torpet Medicina, Philosophia manca est, Literæ mutæ, omnia Tenebris involuta Cimmeriis —— *Barth. de Libris Legend. Diss.*

Books are the Legacies which a great Genius leaves to Mankind, which are delivered down from Generation to Generation, as Presents to Posterity.——What an inestimable Price would a *Virgil*, or a *Homer*, a *Cicero*, or an *Aristotle* bear, were their Works, like a Statue, a Building, or a Picture, to be confined only in one Place, and made the Property of a single Person? SPECTATOR.

Published by ORDER of the DIRECTORS.

PHILADELPHIA:
Printed by D. HALL, and W. SELLERS. MDCCLXVI.

Lancaster's better-educated persons of the colonial period loved books. Personal libraries were the mark of the cultivated gentleman, and leadership in establishing libraries was the sign of civilized society. Lancaster's Juliana Library of 1763 grew out of the Lancaster Library Company of 1759. The Lancaster County Library traces its origins to the 1759 library.

Bridges, roads, and churches were built by lottery in old Lancaster. These lottery tickets of 1761 were issued to pay for building a bridge over the Conestoga River. They are signed by Joseph Simon, the beloved patriarch of the Jewish community and town leader whose support of humanitarian and civic improvement projects always could be expected.

erected to divert water from the gutters of West King Street into the stream. A similar arrangement was constructed at the bridge built across South Queen Street at Vine Street.

With their usual independence, local property owners were laying out streets, lanes, and alleys upon which other citizens encroached and "made nuisances." Placement of party walls created numerous quarrels, and buildings were erected without regard to the distance from the street or the street line. In 1774 the provincial legislature granted the borough authority to regulate the buildings and streets of Lancaster, and to appoint three "discreet persons" to oversee such regulation. Existing buildings were not required to be removed but when they needed repair or replacement the owners were directed to comply with the regulations. Moreover, Lancastrians were not allowed to throw in the streets material that would be offensive or an obstacle to passage. Cellar excavations were to be done so earth or clay would not be left on the streets. Houses could not be built with bay windows, rain spouts, or gutters protruding beyond the sidewalk line. Any nasty Lancastrian that willfully or maliciously broke or extinguished a street lamp would be fined. Distillers were not allowed to drain "foul" liquors into the streets. Soapboilers and tallow-chandlers were not to dump the malodorous debris of their trades on the public pathways, unless they wished to pay fines of thirty shillings. Slaughterers were admonished to stop leaving "dead carcasses, excrement, or filth from necessary-houses" unburied. Stopping up gutters and common sewers could result in a fine not to exceed twenty pounds.

Following the Revolution the burgesses sought additional power from the Pennsylvania assembly. Increasing complexity of governing the town required the appointment of agencies or bureaucracies that were not dreamed of when the charter of 1742 was granted, and maintaining the streets could no longer be done without taxing the residents.

Fires always were a problem and, as the community grew more densely constructed, the threat of a serious conflagration worried the town fathers. When the courthouse burned in 1784 a strong wind from the southwest carried burning embers over much of the borough, setting afire the Reformed Church and other buildings, all of which were saved, happily, by the swift work of the volunteer fire companies. The Union Fire Company, always seeking better methods of safeguarding the burghers' properties, urged a reliable source of water to be available at all times for firefighting. A well was dug near the barracks at Duke and Walnut streets, then some distance from the downtown area. These structures, mostly survivors of the French and Indian wars, were flimsy "tinderboxes," and would be entirely consumed by the "fire fiend" before the usual bucket brigade could be organized. Imagine a line of citizens stretched from Water and King streets to the barracks, five blocks away! Asking the Court of Quarter Sessions to direct the county commissioners to purchase another fire engine and additional buckets, the Union Fire Company pointed to the need for protection of public buildings. Not only the courthouse but the jail and workhouse were in Lancaster, which placed a burden on the town's firefighting facilities. The county officials demurred, as was their tradition.

Casper Singer, a tanner whose yard was along Water Street, had an idea. He would lay a wooden pipe under Water Street to King Street where a *jet d'eau*, a stream of water spouting upward, would be installed wherever the borough officials desired, all at his own expense, provided the borough would permit him to dig up Water Street and would not deprive him of water necessary for the tanning vats. Approval came swiftly, along with the proviso that Singer, his heirs, and assigns, keep the system in repair forever. An ordinance then was adopted to penalize anyone who would "willfully or maliciously" interfere with or destroy the system.

The success of Singer's *jet d'eau* prompted the borough to dig cisterns in King Street and other parts of the town for holding water in large quantities when needed for firefighting. Numerous springs that lay in the vicinity of East King and North Duke streets were connected to the cisterns, using wooden pipes, or "conduits" as the borough officials were fond of calling them. One of the larger springs was under the Sign of the Leopard Tavern, a hundred feet east of Duke Street on the north side of East King Street.

A fuel shortage led the burgesses to encourage the selling of wood at the market, with the market clerk and three assistants being charged with examining each cord to determine full measure. If the farmer selling the

The Krug house at the southwest corner of South Prince and West King streets was built in the late-eighteenth century. Behind the house, along West King Street to Water Street, was Krug's tannery. This house was razed in 1872 when the Stevens House hotel was built.

wood gave short measure the market examiners would receive sixpence; if good measure, the purchaser would give the examiners the same amount. That was the Lancaster method of consumer protection!

If Lancastrians were indifferent to their borough government, many of them had definite opinions concerning British rule. Strong feelings were found among all the English and Scots, and the more worldly Germans. Quakers and sectarian Germans were not as interested in political matters, particularly when the status quo served their own interests handsomely.

Parliament's restrictions on colonial trade fostered immediate anger among Lancastrians. On 15 June 1774 a public meeting took place at which it was agreed Lancastrians would "join and concur with the patriotic Merchants, Manufacturers, Tradesmen, and Freeholders of the City and County of Philadelphia, and other Parts of this Province, in an Association of Solemn Agreement to this purpose, if the same shall by them be thought necessary." Within a fortnight local patriots met and adopted resolutions under the leadership of George Ross, wealthy local attorney who was to become a signer of the Declaration of Independence. The essence of these resolutions was

that King George III treat the colonists as English subjects possessed with all the constitutional rights of Englishmen, that he recognize that the colonists had been loyal to His Majesty, and that he ought to act in kind. Topping off their resolutions, the Lancastrians threatened that if the Crown persisted in abridging the rights of the colonists, they would gladly support and encourage the General Congress of the Colonies.

Having gone that far, the local patriots selected a Committee of Observation that included Edward Shippen, William Bausman, Dr. Adam Simon Kuhn, George Ross, Sr., Adam Reigart, Jasper Yeates, James Webb, Christian Voght, William Augustus Atlee, Casper Shaffner, Eberhardt Michael, and Charles Hall. All were respected leaders in the borough and most of them were businessmen or had commercial interests. The committee was charged with many powers and authority to supervise virtually every aspect of Lancaster life and economy. They had an opportunity to function as a revolutionary tribunal with life and death powers of a military junta. That, however, was wholly foreign to the English tradition. The Lancaster committee was quite effective without losing its benign self-control.

Wherever and whenever human beings agree to live
in a community, various viewpoints surface, with most
of the persons taking sides with one leader or another.
Lancaster was not different. Political factions had
existed from the earliest days. Thus far the issues
generating factions were focused on proper
representation for the fast-growing county to the west
of the Philadelphia Establishment, interests of the Penn
family versus interests of the provincial government,
and adequate defense against Indians on Pennsylvania's
frontier. With a revolutionary spirit in the air, new
factions sprang up.

One group, the revolutionary firebrands — mostly
Scots — wanted to break the ties with England at once,
regardless of the cost. Another faction recognized the
injustice of the British restrictions and the great threat
to the colonial economy, but they hoped the matter
could be solved without cutting the bond with England.
The third group sided with the British, and were
regarded as Tories. Each of these factions had its
subgroups. The Tories, for example, included those
who held no views based on political principle; they
were concerned solely with maintaining their economic
opportunities, and they later could be found dealing
with the enemy because British gold was more
negotiable than American paper money. Another Tory
group genuinely believed the English position was
correct. Counted among the Tories were the pacifists
such as the Quakers that refused to take military action.
The Tory rector of St. James's Church was required to
leave, and the church was closed during the war.

As the Revolution progressed, most of the moderate
group turned from their hope for reconciliation to
outright support of the colonial patriots. By education
and social temperament the non-Tory aristocratic
classes and middle classes exercised a beneficial

restraint on excesses of the radicals. It has been claimed
by some historians that the Revolution was actually a
struggle between the classes. Evidence does not
support that argument persuasively. The more
excitable Lancaster patriots were a fairly tame bunch
when contrasted to fiery Sam Adams. Possibly the most
inflammatory patriot locally was Christopher Marshall,
the apothecary and diarist. Living in Lancaster, but
rather apart from the mainstream of local thought, was
the famed pamphleteer Thomas Paine, whose explosive
prose was penned in William Henry's house — but
after the writer roused himself from too-long bouts with
slumber. Lancastrians didn't take too kindly to the
"foreign upstart" whose slovenly habits, heterodox
ways of religious thinking, and mid-morning
awakenings were hardly in the Lancaster tradition with
its emphasis on cleanliness, Godliness, and crack-of-
dawn waking. William Henry's son loathed Paine, as
did Matthias Slough, the pious Lutheran.

A goodly number of Lancastrians were involved
significantly in the war effort, but not on the battlefield.
These patriots bore the military title of colonel but they
were for the most part engaged in the very important
task of making and procuring supplies for the
Continental and state militia forces. William Henry was
a well-known gunsmith, inventor, and early Lancaster's
version of a Renaissance Man. As Colonel Henry, he
was assistant commissary general, in charge of
procurement of guns (his own shop produced
thousands), foodstuffs, clothing, hides, and shoes. So
important were his employees in the gun manufactory
that they were exempt from military duty. The Henry
Gunshop was on the eastern side of the southeastern
corner of Centre Square where the Watt and Shand
store now stands. As treasurer of Lancaster County
from 1777 to 1785 he was responsible for keeping the

William Henry (1729-1786) was
an ardent patriot of Lancaster
during the Revolution. A gunmaker
and mechanical inventor, Henry
was a universal man in his
accomplishments: patron of the
arts; friend of writers, scientists,
and politicians. During the
Revolution he was the chief
procurement offficer in this region.

The White Swan, Lancaster's finest hostelry during the Revolutionary period, was located on the southeastern corner of Centre Square during the late-eighteenth and throughout the nineteenth centuries. This 1850 print shows the inn, now Hubly's Hotel, a few years before its decline and eventual conversion into store buildings.

Drawing of a parlor door in the Jasper Yeates mansion, South Queen and West Mifflin streets, by David McN. Stauffer in 1879. Yeates, one of Lancaster's most famous lawyers and justices, was a Revolutionary patriot. His mansion, although greatly altered, still stands.

county finances in shape at a time when the value of money dropped to virtually nothing. When he died, Mrs. Henry was appointed in his place. Henry also served as justice of the peace, member of the Pennsylvania assembly, and member of the Council of Safety for Pennsylvania. In religion he was a Moravian. The Henry home hosted Thomas Paine, David Rittenhouse, and Benjamin West, the artist. It is thought young Robert Fulton was influenced greatly by William Henry who also held advanced ideas on steam navigation. The screw auger is one of Henry's inventions. Persons of artistic, social, and intellectual achievement never failed to visit the Henry home north of the marketplace when going through Lancaster.

Another revolutionary leader was Colonel Matthias Slough whose inn, the White Swan, was *the* place to stay for Lancaster's most elegant visitors. It also was the place where the town's aristocrats gathered to plan elections and solve procurement problems. Indeed, it served pretty much as Lancaster's Union League during the revolutionary years. The hostelry was on the southern side of the southeastern corner of Centre Square; it hosted "the great" while Adam Reigart's Grape Tavern took care of "the near great." While Continental Congress stayed in Lancaster (27 September 1777) John Adams and other luminaries were put up by Slough, and the documents of the young government, including the Declaration of Independence, were kept in a guarded wagon in Slough's courtyard.

Five prominent attorneys, William Augustus Atlee, Jasper Yeates, George Ross, Sr., John Hubley, and Edward Shippen, demonstrated superb leadership during this period. Atlee had served as chief burgess, and was instrumental in the founding of the local Committee of Correspondence. He was a delegate to the Pennsylvania convention that paved the way for the province to participate in the First Continental Congress. With the actual break with England, Atlee was picked to head the Committee on Public Safety. When the Continental Congress and Pennsylvania government were forced to leave Philadelphia in September 1777, they turned to Atlee for safe transporting of men and documents to Lancaster. Back home, Atlee was attracting attention with his execution of a difficult task — supervising the prisoners of war and the British officers on parole. The war over, Atlee was appointed to the Pennsylvania Supreme Court and later to the judicial district of Chester, Dauphin, Lancaster, and York counties. Of course, he was active in the Union Fire Co. No. 1!

Jasper Yeates was the original Philadelphia Lawyer, it would seem. While still a very young man his reputation as an exceedingly brilliant lawyer earned him a large income which was invested wisely. Like his fellow patriots, Yeates served on the Committee of Correspondence and Safety. As chairman of the Committee on Public Safety, he organized the entire county, which then included Dauphin, Lebanon, and part of Northumberland counties, into military and governmental units. The indefatigable attorney whipped the trigger-happy Scots and hesitant Germans into groups that could and did make magnificent contributions to the winning of the Revolution. He even found time to take on the enormous job of determining which of the crown statutes should be retained in the Pennsylvania revolutionary government and, by so doing, earned himself the title of Father of Statute Law in Pennsylvania. In 1787 he was a delegate to the convention that ratified the new federal Constitution. He served with distinction on the state supreme court from 1791 until his death in 1817.

George Ross, Sr. was Lancaster's distinguished elder statesman, wealthy attorney, proper churchman (his father had been rector of historic New Castle's Episcopal Church), and assistant chief engineer of the Union Fire Co. Ross had a finely tuned political sense that permitted him to work with the various factions. He appeared to be a person commanding great respect, he had the astute attorney's sense of compromise, and he won elections. He was a delegate to both the First and Second Continental Congress although he was forced to stay on the sidelines for a short time during 1776 when the local radicals discarded every leader except the most fanatical patriots. He came back in time to sign the Declaration of Independence. Later he contributed his wisdom to the Pennsylvania Constitutional Convention in 1776 as its vice president, but he was disappointed in the radical document that emerged. He refused to support it, and by 1790 his views were vindicated fully. His last service was on the Admiralty Court.

John Hubley, scion of one of Lancaster's most respected old German families, served on the active committees of the Revolution, and had the responsibility of constructing the powder magazine. He

Rock Ford, *country home of General Edward Hand.*

was a delegate to the state constitutional convention, and the ratification committee for the federal Constitution. Hubley also managed to serve at one time or another in virtually every county office.

Edward Shippen, by every measure employed to characterize men, was the last person early Lancastrians might expect to find in the revolutionary movement. He was a classical scholar, extremely moderate in temperament, a stickler for neatness, order, and legal perfection, and the local philosopher of civil obedience. While Shippen's nature rebelled against the very thought of revolution, his heart was led, albeit with caution, prudence, and propriety, to support the patriotic cause. By the time of the Revolution Shippen had passed his seventieth birthday. Earlier he had held important offices, including mayor, in Philadelphia. Local zealots regarded Shippen's tempered support as good; it gave the revolutionary fervor respectability, and no one was more respectable than good old Edward Shippen! He even found himself the honorary chairman of the local committee on revolutionary activity. After the British treatment of the Bostonians, the ancient symbol of "safe and sane" revolting lost his temper, and tore into organizing a relief fund with all the zest of impulsive youth! Edward's son, bearing the same name, stayed behind in Philadelphia, and waxed fat on the pleasures of

Philadelphia colonial society. The elder Shippen's distress when his granddaughter, Peggy, married Benedict Arnold can be imagined.

One Lancastrian that saw military service, and rose to become General Washington's adjutant and confidant, was General Edward Hand, the physician-soldier-politician. Participating throughout the war, General Hand had little time to spare in Lancaster. He kept up his correspondence with his beloved Kitty (Catherine), whom he had married in 1775 after resigning from the British service as surgeon of the Eighteenth Royal Irish Foot Regiment. Mrs. Hand was a daughter of Captain John Ewing and Sarah Yeates, sister of the redoubtable Jasper. Obviously the young surgeon was well-placed socially. During one of Washington's five visits to Lancaster he was entertained at tea by Mrs. Hand. It is thought the Hands then were living on West King Street, possibly near Mulberry Street. Later General Hand would purchase the "plantation" along the Conestoga River south of Lancaster. This fine home, built in the mid-1780s, has been preserved with loving care and utmost authenticity by the Rock Ford Plantation Foundation. General Hand, an ardent Federalist, was elected to the Pennsylvania House of Representatives. He also served in the Continental Congress under the Articles of Confederation in 1784-85. The state constitution was

General Edward Hand, Irish-born
physician and military leader, was
one of Lancaster's most noted
citizens. His close and trusted
friendship with General
Washington earned him the post of
adjutant-general. Hand's fine
country home, Rock Ford, has been
preserved.

Major John Andre, young British aristocrat and officer, was quartered at Caleb Cope's house on North Lime and East Grant streets for several months following his capture during the Revolution. Andre formed a very close relationship with Cope's son, John, and the boy tried to run away to join his friend after Andre's exchange. Andre later was executed.

Caleb Cope, prominent Lancastrian and burgess, lived in this brick house at the northeast corner of Lime and Grant streets during the Revolution. Here Major John Andre was paroled, during which time the English officer-prisoner taught Cope's son drawing and other skills. The major later was executed. The house was demolished in 1903.

redrawn in 1790 to reflect more conservative views, and in this undertaking Hand was Lancaster's delegate. He had served his town as chief burgess, his state and his nation in war and peace and, finally, as a collector of revenue for the national government during its Federalist years. As a loyal aide to Washington, General Hand became one of the founding members of the Order of the Cincinnati, this nation's oldest hereditary military society.

While the distinguished men and women of Lancaster achieved much in winning the struggle for independence, the role of the less-noted townfolk cannot be diminished. William Henry's gunmakers, Paul Zantzinger's tailors and shoemakers, and Adam Reigart's bartenders all rose to the occasion — sometimes with justifiable grumbling — when they were called upon to feed and clothe and equip the troops of the state militia and the Continental army. Relatively few turned their backs on this nation's birth struggle. Only seven Loyalists had their properties confiscated, and only one person was accused officially of buying boycotted goods. It is only fair to say, however, the townspeople viewed the Revolution somewhat more sympathetically than did many rural persons. The pacifists were around the countryside.

Inasmuch as the revolutionary war did not involve

Thomas Wharton, President of Pennsylvania during the Revolution, was a prominent Philadelphia merchant and patriot. He is buried at Trinity Lutheran Church, South Duke Street.

General "Mad" Anthony Wayne was born in Chester County of Welsh ancestry. He shared Benjamin Franklin's frustrations in dealing with the Lancaster County "Dutchmen." On one occasion when uniforms were scarce and soldiers were freezing, Wayne grumbled to the Commissioner of Clothing in Lancaster to get clothing, "even if they had to take the pants off the Dutchmen." Many of the local Germans understood the value of gold more than the abstractions of political independence.

Lancaster militarily, the town's major role lay in providing goods for the fighting men. There were a few incidents, nevertheless, in which Lancaster figured centrally in American history. One was the arrival of the Continental Congress in Lancaster after fleeing from the British in Philadelphia. They met on 27 September 1777 in the courthouse in the Square, and there heard a few routine reports before leaving for York across the Susquehanna River. We are told the reason for adjourning to York was fear that the British would take Lancaster. Of much greater validity is the impossibility of finding lodging and other accommodations in Lancaster for the congressmen and other government officials. Lancaster was playing host to hundreds of refugees, the entire Pennsylvania government, and thousands of prisoners of war. The state government stayed and the Congress went to York for nine months during which time they put the finishing touches on the Articles of Confederation, preparatory to submitting them to the thirteen states for ratification. The Conway Cabal, an alleged plot to overthrow General Washington, also was supposed to have been hatched in York. Often overlooked but surely very significant historically was the position of General Washington toward confiscation of personal property for use by his army. When it was suggested that a group of Virginia riflemen passing through Lancaster could be outfitted here by confiscating goods from local citizens, Washington insisted that all goods taken must be acquired with tact and the owners compensated. Due process was part of the English heritage, and it would remain intact in the legal tradition of the new Republic! "Mad" Anthony Wayne, however, once ordered his procurement agents in Lancaster to obtain clothing for his troops "even if they had to take the pants off the Dutchmen."

British and Hessian prisoners of war were kept in huge stockades, but their officers were "paroled" to live in rented quarters among the townspeople — if they could find a landlord that would tolerate the sullen stares and whispered criticism of their neighbors. Caleb Cope, a burgess, and a plasterer by trade, provided lodging for Major John Andre, a talented and scholarly young English gentleman. Major Andre taught the children of Mr. Cope, and it may be presumed the youngsters learned civility as well as the officer's skill as an artist. Later, Lancastrians who had come to admire the young officer were distressed to learn that he had been hanged in a spy conspiracy. Major Thomas Hughes, an English ensign, also was a "parolee," and has left in his diary an interesting picture of Lancaster during the war.

The Conestoga wagon of local invention and construction was the heavy-freight hauler of the eighteenth and nineteenth centuries. Its broad iron tires rumbled over Lancaster streets carrying goods to Philadelphia and to the West. The boatlike shape of the body was designed to keep freight from shifting on hills.

Workingmen's houses on Middle Street (now Howard Avenue) exhibit curious half-timbered construction. These houses date from the pre-Revolutionary period, and some were used to house British prisoners of war. A few of these structures still exist.

The Lancaster, or Pennsylvania, rifle was a development of gunsmiths in the Conestoga valley of Lancaster County beginning in the 1720s and reaching its highest state of the art in the late 1700s. No one knows today who made the first Pennsylvania rifle — certainly it was not Martin Meylin who has been credited with it. It may have been his son-in-law, John Baker. This rifle, erroneously attributed to Meylin, is a very early weapon. Its long barrel and curly maple markings make it a handsome piece.

The several thousands of prisoners of war — English as well as the Hessian and Brunswick mercenaries — were confined to the stockades and barracks. Conditions apparently were fairly bad. Crowding was commonplace, and disease was prevalent. The townsfolk always were worrying when Lancaster would be wiped out. As if the presence of so many enemies and rampant disease were not enough, the Lancastrians had another complaint: their daughters were sneaking off to fraternize with the prisoners, especially the German-speaking soldiers. General Moses Hazen, commandant of the prison-guarding unit, had his headquarters at the old stone Sign of the Cat on North Prince Street south of West James Street.

Of the many war goods manufactured and processed in Lancaster for the Revolution, none were more celebrated than the Pennsylvania rifle, a magnificently handsome and deadly precise firearm developed in the Conestoga Valley. Now called (erroneously) the Kentucky rifle, the weapon in the hands of patriots was nicknamed the widow-maker. Because the rifle required so much time to prepare for the next shot, it was not used as extensively as many persons assume. The musket, also made by Lancaster craftsmen, remained the standard weapon; it was used in close formation by ranks of soldiers.

Other goods supplied in great quantity by local manufacturers were wagons, clothing, shoes and boots, blankets, hardware and leather equipment, harness and saddles, beef, pork, and flour. The purchasing agents of the Continental Congress discovered inflation made needed goods virtually impossible to buy with the nearly worthless paper money. Lancastrians, as a rule, were not greedy, but they were not excessively generous in bargaining with the government buyers. Lancaster riflemakers apparently engaged in a slowdown when their bills were overdue. Procurement officials observed that Philadelphia-made guns were cheaper. Lancaster manufacturers, knowing their products were superior, suggested that if the government wanted good rifles, they should increase their payments. Moreover, argued the local gunsmiths, iron had gone up in price, as had wages. With that, the Lancaster gun shops were authorized to receive more money, and guns soon were forthcoming. Lancaster flour and beef also became very scarce — unless the buyer had plenty of ready cash, especially hard cash. Some of the important materials of war made in Lancaster County were produced at the nearby charcoal iron blast furnaces. None of these were in the borough, however.

Horses were hard to find, and British agents were known to pay some countians, whose sense of gold was more acutely developed than their sense of patriotism, to steal horses from known patriots. Two of these characters were discovered and hanged without trial in the Lancaster jail yard.

Christopher Marshall had only contempt for those whose activities contributed nothing to the war effort. Grumbling to his diary, Marshall commented bitterly on the demeanor of some local folk that came in to Lancaster from the countryside: "You may Speak and Converse with Some whose Sweet Countenances will tell you that you are highly agreeable to them while you talk to them in their way, but change the Discourse by asking them to Spare you some Hay, Oats, Wheat, Rye, Wood, butter, Syder [cider] for your Selfe &c.&c. to be paid for in Congress Money . . . O then their serene Countenances is [sic] all overcast. A Lowering heavy Cloud Spreads all over their horizon; they have nothing to Say, nay Scarcely to bid you farewell. . . ." The old druggist was equally severe with fancy balls and frivolous parties in Lancaster when the officers should have been with their troops. The presence of paroled British officers strutting around town in their fine uniforms was thought to be an effort at subverting the local patriotic gentry who always were searching for someone or something to be the subject of a rousing toast! Victories and rumors of victories always produced rounds of parties, much celebrating, "illuminations" in the windows, and barbed remonstrances from Christopher Marshall.

Either the courthouse or Slough's inn were the scenes of much merrymaking on such occasions. The gentry and their ladies, bewigged and in silks and satins, probably were observed with some amusement by the borough's watchman as he made his rounds on King and Queen streets. He may have helped more than a few to their homes after an evening of rejoicing. At Slough's White Swan and Reigart's Grape, the preferred beverage was Madeira wine. A swig of country rye was relished, but not in mixed company

unless the possibility of a fever or some other ailment was present. Down by the Sign of the Drovers the house beverage was beer brewed on the premises from vague recipes, using procedures mysterious even to the brewer, and producing a beverage with incalculable qualities.

With the theater of war shifting from the middle Atlantic states, Lancaster began to experience peace and quiet, broken only by outraged cries of merchants, businessmen, and consumers as inflation tore into the local economy. Beef, which sold for £2.8 per barrel in 1775, cost £600 for the same quantity in 1780. Common flour climbed from £12.5 per hundredweight in 1775 to £109.4 in 1780. The mainstay of the rural kitchen was pork, an item that increased from £2.88 per barrel in 1775 to £750 in 1780! After the latter date prices began dropping to a level about sixty percent above the market price at the beginning of the Revolution. Other prices that may interest present-day homemakers are:

(in 1779)

Butter, $5 per pound	Rye, $37.33 per bushel
Firewood, $44 per cord	Milk, 66¢ per quart

(in 1780)

Eggs, $6 per dozen	Butter, $12 per pound
Oats, $18 per bushel	White beans, $20 per peck
Eightpenny nails,	Loaf of bread, $4
$20 per pound	Beef, hind quarter,
Madeira wine,	$4.50 per pound
$50 per pint	

When the war came to an end, Lancastrians had much to be thankful for. The independent spirit that was so much a part of the Lancaster soul had become a national potentiality.

Turning from the sword to the plough, Lancastrians settled down to enjoy the fruits of independence. There would be the new Constitution of 1787, replacing the largely unworkable Articles of Confederation; and there was the new state constitution of 1790, a document, good and gray, in which Lancaster's Federalists took immense pride. As the young nation's political factions struggled for supremacy, Lancaster became a stronghold for the Federalists — indeed, that party continued to win elections here long after its death nationally.

Newspapers were the means of spreading the gospel of political philosophy. In 1794 Henry Willcocks and

BY DESIRE OF

GOVERNOR M'KEAN,

Who means to honor the Theatre with his presence.

THIS EVENING, January 2, 1800,

At the House of Mr. LENEGAN, in East King-street, Lancaster,

At the Sign of the White Horse.

———

The LADIES & GENTLEMEN of Lancaster are respectfully informed, that this evening will be presented the greatest variety of amusements that has ever been exhibited in this town, consisting of

Pantomime, Singing, Hornpipe *Dancing*, Tumbling, SPEAKING, &c. &c.

And in particular an Indian WAR and SCALP Dance,
by Mr. Durang and Mr. F. Ricketts.

Doors to be opened at six and the performance to begin at 7 o'clock.
Tickets to be had at Mr. Lenegan's and at Hamilton's Printing-Office.

Ladies and Gentlemen who wish to engage seats may have calling upon Mr. Rowson at the Theatre.

ROWSON *& Co.*

———

Printed by William Hamilton, King-street, Lancaster.

NB one Box was appropriated and occupied by the Governor.

Made about 1800 by an unknown artist, this view of Lancaster from the southwest hills, now the 8th Ward, shows the approximate locations of the town's major buildings: (1) Store House, (2) Barracks, (3) German Reformed Church, (4) Courthouse, (5) St. James's Episcopal Church, (6) Presbyterian Church, (7) Trinity Lutheran Church.

William Hamilton started the Lancaster *Journal*, which was published at the Euclid's Head on West King Street. Hamilton soon became the sole proprietor. In its infancy the *Journal* naively stated its guiding principle to be: "Not too rash, yet not too fearful; open to all parties, but not influenced by any." During the 1796 presidential campaign, correspondents used the *Journal* to launch attacks upon Robert Coleman and Charles Smith, Esq., two of the borough's leading Federalist candidates. Messrs. Coleman and Smith were furious, and urged local businessmen to not use the *Journal* for advertising. Hamilton was distraught, but he rallied quickly, announcing triumphantly that the dastardly attempt to "ruin a young man just entering upon the theatre of the world, and to trample under feet the sacred liberties of the press" had resulted in only

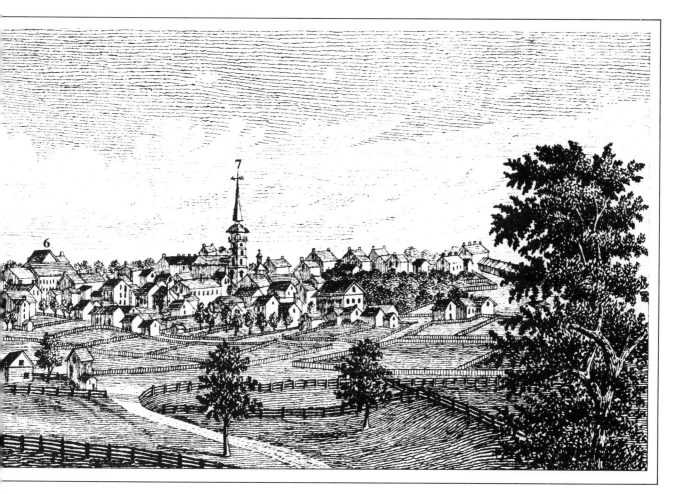

twenty-seven cancellations by subscribers but the acquisition of thirty-five new patrons. Then, doing what any intelligent and highly practical young man would do, Hamilton switched his editorial policies to the Federalist cause and became that party's most outspoken supporter, lambasting the "Jacobean anarchists" and the European rabble that spilled over from the French Revolution! In 1820 the *Journal* was acquired by John Reynolds, after which it supported the Democracy.

Robert and William Dickson published the Lancaster *Intelligencer* on North Queen Street, beginning in 1799. It was a vigorously anti-Federalist paper, and its editor's high-flown rhetoric occasionally got the paper into trouble. Some reporting on alleged corruption in Governor McKean's administration resulted in a celebrated libel suit. Judge Robert Coleman presided over the trial which was heard by ten Federalist and two Republican jurors. With obvious relish the Federalist judge sentenced William Dickson to three months in jail and a five-hundred-dollar fine. Undaunted, he continued to edit the *Intelligencer* while sitting in prison, to which the great and near great among the anti-Federalist faction came in a constant stream. William Dickson probably was the only inmate in Lancaster's prison history to have been entertained at a banquet while in jail! In 1839 the *Intelligencer* was merged into the *Journal,* and the newspaper appears every morning in Lancaster nearly 185 years later.

The borough, already the largest inland community in the United States, became the Pennsylvania capital in 1799. For the next thirteen years Lancaster was the

Lancaſter Journal

NOT TOO RASH.—YET NOT FEARFUL:—OPEN TO ALL PARTIES,—BUT NOT INFLUENCED BY ANY.

LANCASTER: Printed every Wedneſday & Saturday, by WILLIAM HAMILTON, at the Printing-Office, FRANKLIN'S HEAD, KING-STREET, Weſt of the Court-Houſe, at the low Price of Two Dollars per Annum. Advertiſements, Eſſays, and Articles of Intelligence thankfully received, and every kind of Printing executed with Accuracy and Diſpatch.

[No. 22. SATURDAY, NOVEMBER 9, 1799. [VOL. VI.

TAKE NOTICE.

ALL perſons indebted to the eſtate of Anna Zantzinger, of the City of Philadelphia, wi chaut deceaſed, are deſired to ſettle no account due to ſaid eſtate, nor to pay any money to any perſon but the ſubſcriber, or his written order.

H... RY ZANTZINGER.

Philadelphia, October 29. 10 t. w. & ſ.

Ten Dollars Reward.

WHEREAS on the night of Thurſday the 3rd. inſtant ſome malicious, evil diſpoſed perſon entered the yard of the ſubſcriber, and cut off the tail of his Cow. Whoever will give information ſo that the Villain may be brought to Juſtice ſhall receive the above reward.

JOHN BRADBURN.

Lancaſter. Oct 5th 1799.

Ching's celebrated Lozenges,

PROPER to be taken at every Seaſon of the yee by Men, Women and Children for Deſtroying Worms, removing Pains in the Head, Stomach and Bowels, purging the Body &c.

Likewiſe Sovereign Ointment for the Itch, an infallible cure at one dreſſing, without a Particle of Mercury or other pernicious ingredient in its Compoſition and may be uſed with ſafety by Women with Child, and on infants newly born, prepared by B. SHAW in London and ſold by appointment at CHARLES HEINITSH's, King-ſtreet Lancaſter.

Notice is hereby given to the

Creditors of Jacob Brenneman, of Straſburg, that he has applied to the court of Common Pleas, of Lancaſter County, for the benefic of the Laws of Pennſylvania, made for the releief of Inſolvent debtors, and the ſaid court have appointed the ſecond Monday in November next, at the Court houſe in the Borough of Lancaſter, for the hearing of him and his creditors, at which time and place they may attend if they think proper.

TO BE SOLD,

ON Tueſday the fifth day of November, Anno Domini 1799, at the late dwelling houſe of Jacob S...man deceaſed, late of Manor townſhip, Lancaſter county, the following articles, viz. houſehold and kitchen furniture, chairs, tables, beds, bedſteads, ſtoves, cheſts cupboards; alſo horſes, cows, ſheep and hogs, three waggons, ploughs, harrows, hops, a quantity of wheat and rye in the ground, hay ſecond crop, with various other articles, too tedious to mention.

The vendue will begin preciſely at nine o'clock, on ſaid day, where the terms of ſale, reaſonable credit, and due attendance will be given by the Subſcribers.

ABRAHAM STEMAN.
JACOB BRENNEMAN. } Exec's.
JACOB WITMER.

October 26.

New Line of STAGES.

THE ſubſcriber begs leave to inform the public, that he has erected a Stage to run from Harriſburgh to Lancaſter, by the way of Middletown and Elizabethtown, twice a week—viz. the Stage to ſet out every Monday and Friday mornings, preciſely at five o'clock, from the houſe of Henry Shepler, ſign of the king of Pruſſia, in Harriſburgh, and arrive on each of the ſaid days at the houſe of Adam Weber in Lancaſter, and return to Harriſburg the ſame days following.

Alſo a Stage to ſet out from the houſe of Henry Shepler in Harriſburg, every Wedneſday morning at five o'clock, and arrive in Sppinſburg ſaid day, and return to Harriſburg the day following.

A ſtage will return to Carliſle every Sunday —viz the ſtage to ſet out from the houſe of Henry Shepler on Sunday morning at five o'clock, and arrive the ſame evening in Harriſburg.

Fare for paſſengers and baggage as uſual.

The ſubſcriber flatters himſelf that by his aſſiduous attention to the buſineſs, to pleaſe all that may favour him with their cuſtom.

HENRY SHEPLER.

TO MILLERS,

The Patent Boulting Cloths

MANUFACTURED BY

ROBERT DAWSON

Eaſt King Street, LANCASTER:

WHERE *Millers & Retailers* of BOULTING CLOTHS will be ſupplied at the moſt reduced prices for CASH only.—There is no neceſſity for recommending them to the Public—As all Millers who have tried them or thoſe that have ſeen them at work, acknowledges them to be far ſuperior to the imported cloths. I rely on my former Cuſtomers and all thoſe that have ſeen them at work. And I invite thoſe that wiſh to have good Cloths and that have the proſperity of their Country at heart, by encourageing ſuch a valuable undertaking in the United States.

N. B. All the cloths of this Manufactory are Warranted.

November 2, 1799.

TWEL's and MORRIS's fine ALE, and HARE's beſt bottled PORTER for ſale at MY Bottling Cellar.

ROBERT DAWSON.

LOOKING-GLASSES,

Hardware, Dry Goods, &c.

JAMES STOKES,

At the corner of Market and Front-Streets.

HAS FOR SALE,

A large and general aſſortment of the following articles, wholeſale or retail, on reaſonable terms;

Looking-glaſſes and tea trays.	Slate and pencils,
Andirons, ſhovels & tongs,	Knives and forks;
Candleſticks & ſnuffers,	Razors & corkſcrews,
Iron pots and bake-ovens,	Ivory & horn combs,
Flat irons & ſtands,	Pocket books & ink-holders,
London pewter,	Pocket knives & pencils,
Copper & tea kettles,	Penknives & ſciſſars,
Frying pans & bellows,	Watch chains, ſtrings, ſeals and keys,
Tea pots, ſpoons, & ſoup ladles,	Plated ſpurs and ſpectacles,
Fiſhhooks and needles,	Shoe & knee buckles,
Straw and hay knives,	Guns and piſtols,
	And a variety of ſaddlery.

A L S O,

Cloth, & caſſimeers,	muſlins,
Chintzes & calicoes,	Callimancoes and durants,
Silk, cotton & thread ſtockings,	Silk and cotton handkerchiefs,
Ladies & gentlemen's gloves,	Money purſes & ribbons,
Sacking bottoms and blankets,	Hat bands, looping and twine,
Linens, checks, and thickſetts,	A vaſt variety of other articles too tedious to mention.
Red leather ſkins,	
Dimities, nankeens &	

Philadelphia, Nov. 2, 1799. 6t.

TO PRINTERS.

For ſale at this Office,
About 200 lbs. of French Great Primer, of which this is a ſpecimen. It is well aſſorted, is all new or nearly ſo. *The price is a quarter of a dollar a pound, caſh.*

Twenty Dollars Reward.

RAN AWAY from Spring Forge, in York county, a Negro man named Iſaac, otherwiſe Cudjo, about 21 years old, the property of Robert Coleman Eſq. He is about 5 feet 8 inches high, has a blemiſh in his eyes, more white in them than common, by trade a forgeman; had on and took with him, a drab coloured broadcloth coat, almoſt new, a ſailors jacket and pantaloons, printed fancy-cord, a ſwandown ſtriped jacket, a rorum hat, one fine and one coarſe ſhirt, one muſlin handkerchief, ſ. rigged, two ditto ſtriped border, a blue perſian under jacket, and two pair cotton ſtockings. Whoever takes up ſaid Negro, and lodges him in any jail, in this, or any of the neighboring ſtates, ſhall have the above reward or reaſonable expences if brought home.

JOHN BRIEN.

Spring Forge, Oct. 26.

N. B. As ſaid Negro formerly lived in Cheſter county, it is probable he may return there.

A STRAY

CAME to the Suſcriber, in Manor Townſhip, about five weeks ago. A ſmall red Heiffer; the owner is deſired to come prove property, and take her away.

JAMES ARMSTRONG.

WANTED IMMEDIATELY,

A JOURNEYMAN FULLER,

AT the Fulling Mill of the Subſcriber, near the Village of Straſburg, Lancaſter county. Good encouragement will be given to any one that underſtands the buſineſs properly.

JACOB NEFF, jun.

October 30, 1799.

ADVERTISEMENT.

WILL be ſold by way of Public Vendue, on Wedneſday the 6th day of November, at the houſe of the ſubſcriber living in Church ſtreet, Adamſtown, in the Borough of Lancaſter, three ten plated ſtoves with the appurtenances, a good milk cow, a houſe clock, tables, chairs, bedſteads, kitchen furniture and many other articles too tedious to mention. The Vendue will begin at one o'clock in the afternoon, when attendance will be given by the Owner.

MICHAEL HEISLY.

October 30.

To be ſold by public vendue,

ON Friday the 8th day of November next, at the late dwelling-houſe of PETER ECKMAN, late of Lampeter townſhip, deceaſed—Houſehold furniture, ſuch as feather beads, cheſts, deſks, and Kitchen furniture, ſuch as pewter, iron pots, and cedar ware, green linen cloth, and many other articles too tedious to mention. The Vendue to begin at 10 o'clock of ſaid day, where due attendance and Credit will be given by

JOHN ECKMAN,
HENRY LEFEVER, } Ex'rs

October 30, 1999.

All perſons indebted to the Eſtate of ſaid Peter Eckman, deceaſed, either by bond, note or book debt, are deſired to make payment, and all that have any demands againſt ſaid Eſtate are deſired to come forward with their accounts for ſettlement to the Executors

NOTICE

IS hereby given, to the creditors of THOMAS KNOX; that the ſubſcribers, auditors appointed by the court of Common Pleas of Laneaſter county, will meet at the honſe of William Ferree, Innkeeper in the Borough of Lancaſter, on Monday the 25th day of Nov. next, to execute the duties of their appointment; when all claims againſt the ſaid Thomas Knox, muſt be exhibited, in order to make a final adjuſtment.

ADAM REIGART, jun.
JOHN FREY.
JOHN GRAFF

October, 26.

WILL BE SOLD,

ON the Premiſes, on Friday the 22d inſt. a valuable Tract of LAND, containing about 53 acres, adjoining land of Thomas Miller and Chriſtian Garver, ſituate in Allen townſhip, Cumberland county, on the North ſide Yellow Breeches creek, where it empties into the Suſquehannah, on the main Road leading from Chambers's ferry, to Carliſle; about ten acres of ſaid tract are cleared and under good fence, five acres of which is meadow of the firſt quality, the remaining 43 acres is of the firſt quality woodland, 20 acres of which would make excellent meadow, the other 23 well adapted for Wheat, or any other kind of Grain. The improvements are a large two ſtory log dwelling houſe, well finiſhed, with a ſpring of excellent water at the door, a good Barn and Saw mill, erected about a year ſince, with about ten feet fall. The place is well ſituated for tavern keeping, or any kind of public buſineſs. Iron works or water works, of any deſcription, might be erected on ſaid premiſes, without a ſcarcity of water, in the drieſt ſeaſons. Poſſeſſion and a clear title will be given immediately after ſale, or as ſoon after as may beſt ſuit the purchaſer. For terms apply to James Douglas, living on the premiſes, or to John Douglas, in Dauphin county, or Jacob Stoner in Manor townſhip, Lancaſter county.

JOHN DOUGLAS,
JAMES DOUGLAS,
JACOB STONER.

November 6.

N. B. At the ſame time and place will be ſold, Houſehold Furniture, Cows, Hogs, and a quantity of Boards and Scantling.

TO BE LET,

And Poſſeſſion given, on the 1ſt of May next,

THAT large, commodious and well ſituated Houſe, and two Lots of Ground, ſituate at the corner of Lime and Orange ſtreets, in Lancaſter, the property of Joſeph Shippen, Eſq of Cheſter county, and now in the tenure of Col. Alexander Anderſon.—For TERMS, apply to Judge YEATES.

JOHN SHIPPEN.

Nov. 6. 1799.

TO BE LET,

A THREE-Story Brick HOUSE, in Queen ſtreet, Lancaſter, wherein James Hopkins, Eſq. now lives.—Poſſeſſion will be given after the 9th of November inſtant.

Enquire of JASPER YEATES.

Nov. 6.

TEN DOLLARS REWARD.

RANAWAY on the night of Tueſday the 28th inſt. A NEGRO WOMAN, named PRISCILLA, about 28 years of age, middling tall, of a hanſome countenance, ſpeaks plain Engliſh and has no toes on her right foot, in conſequence of which ſhe limps a little in walking. She was formerly the property of John Edie, of Yorktown. Has a Huſband named CLEM. Took with her a large quantity of cloathing, which I cannot deſcribe, except a white felt Hat with green underneath. The above reward will be paid to any perſon who will ſecure the ſaid Negro ſo that I may get her again, with reaſonab charges if brought home.

SAMUEL FAHNESTOCK.

living in the Borough of Lancaſter,

July 13.

INFANTRY.

Captain Barton's Company of Infantry will parade on ... day the 9th inſt. at ... o'clock preciſely. ... tendan[illegible]

[illegible]

political center of the Commonwealth of Pennsylvania. The general assembly met in the courthouse while other offices were housed in the county office building at the west side of the Square. The local inns served as lodgings, caucus rooms, and hearing rooms for the government.

When the seat of state government was moved from Philadelphia to Lancaster, the persons responsible for the transportation were able to use the new Lancaster and Philadelphia turnpike, the first long macadam road in the United States. This road, begun in 1792, cost a total of $465,000. Stagecoach lines were organized to operate over its length, with Lancastrians cashing in on the numerous benefits to the economy.

During the early nineteenth century Lancaster was connected to the outside world with excellent turnpikes.

No sooner had the state government moved its offices to Harrisburg than Lancaster discovered its economy was flagging. A flourishing handicraft-industry town in earlier years, the challenge no longer was present. Even the War of 1812, which came no closer to the borough than Havre de Grace, Maryland, did little to spur the economy. Unemployment was becoming a serious problem. Societies and committees were formed to deal with the matter of assisting the victims of the faltering economy and to encourage the creation of new industries.

Abraham Witmer built this fine nine-arch stone bridge over the Conestoga River at the Philadelphia Pike at the beginning of the nineteenth century, and the structure continued to carry all traffic until its removal in 1930. It was too narrow for the motorcar traffic on the Lincoln Highway East.

Lancaster's "Old Factory" along South Duke Street near the Conestoga River was the community's first textile factory, but it was not too successful. After being used for other manufacturing purposes, it burned in the 1870s. The exposed wooden truss bridge in the background was later replaced with a covered bridge.

When Gottlieb Sehner built his handsome house on Prince Street about 1784, little did he realize it would become the home of Andrew Ellicott, the surveyor and engineer that laid out Washington, D.C., replacing Major Pierre L'Enfant who had annoyed Washington and Jefferson. To this house Captain Merriwether Lewis came for instructions in navigating the wilderness in the proposed Lewis and Clark Expedition. Ellicott later became superintendent of West Point. The house is now being restored.

Lancaster's working class lived in modest homes such as these along Lamparter Row in the southeastern corner of the city. These were built originally for workers at the textile mill at nearby Humesville early in the nineteenth century.

One such enterprise was the Lancaster Manufacturing Company, founded in 1815 as an outgrowth of the Lancaster Cotton Works that Jacob Miller and others owned along the Conestoga River south of the borough. The textile mill was not especially successful, but it was Lancaster's first corporation. Waterwheels powered the spinning machines that twisted about fifteen tons of cotton annually. Beset by problems caused by fire, and the flooding of the market by cheap British cotton textiles, the works ceased, and by the panic of 1819 Lancaster's fond hopes for a new industry had evaporated.

Unemployment, no wars to supply, an aging population, and opportunity seemingly gravitating westward bothered the townspeople. Like a troubled woman buying a new hat to ease her cares, Lancaster decided to become a city.

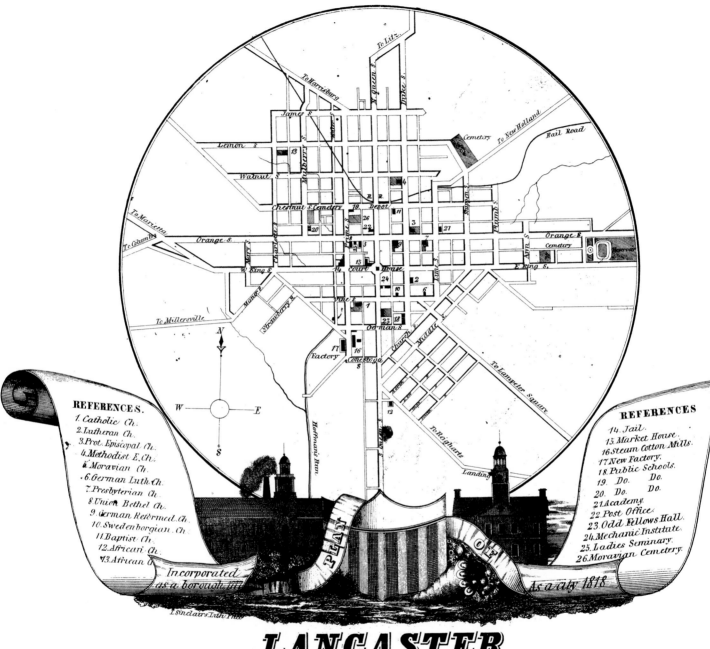

REFERENCES.
1. Catholic Ch.
2. Lutheran Ch.
3. Prot. Episcopal Ch.
4. Methodist E. Ch.
5. Moravian Ch.
6. German Luth. Ch.
7. Presbyterian Ch.
8. Union Bethel Ch.
9. German Reformed Ch.
10. Swedenborgian Ch.
11. Baptist Ch.
12. African Ch.
13. African Ch.

REFERENCES
14. Jail.
15. Market House.
16. Steam Cotton Mills.
17. New Factory.
18. Public Schools.
19. Do. Do.
20. Do. Do.
21. Academy.
22. Post Office.
23. Odd Fellows Hall.
24. Mechanic Institute.
25. Ladies Seminary.
26. Moravian Cemetery.

Incorporated as a borough. 1777.

As a city 1818.

PLAN OF

LANCASTER.

Chapter III

The Emergence of a City

1818-1860

Civic consciousness had developed by 1848 when this map of Lancaster was engraved. The city extended east along King and Orange streets to the reservoir at Franklin Street, west to Charlotte Street, north to James Street, and south to Conestoga Street, with Mussertown appended to the southeast.

Beset by a declining economy and seemingly moving quickly from vibrant young maturity to premature senility, Lancaster took stock of itself and wondered what it could do. Those glorious leaders of the revolutionary era no longer were available for advice and, in all likelihood, they too would have been bewildered by the challenges.

Part of the problem was the natural consequence of the economic policies pursued in the previous century. Under the mercantilist system the government exercised considerable regulation over the economy in order to couple private interests with national goals. The British advocacy of mercantilism was a factor in the Revolution, but the colonial and state legislatures found the system an accepted way of life and simply converted it to the objectives of the states. Pennsylvania, particularly, involved itself in an extraordinary amount of economic regulation, labor controls, market rules, inspection measures, and price fixing. It was the Philadelphian-turned-Lancastrian Christopher Marshall that was responsible for establishing price controls in the capital city, and who did much to influence similar practices in the hinterland.

Regional competition began to assert itself early in the nineteenth century. The Susquehanna Valley found Baltimore a ready market for agricultural goods via natural and modified waterways, thus ending some freight traffic through Lancaster to Philadelphia. Indeed, one of the major reasons for the construction of the Lancaster and Philadelphia turnpike was to regain

RATES

Of Toll to be Collected on the Philadelphia and Lancaster Turnpike Road, at Gate No.

DESCRIPTION OF THE CARRIAGE. &c.	No. of Horses	Amount of Toll per mile.		Amount when toll at 6.2 miles
		Cents.	Mills.	
Every Sulkey, Chair, or Chaise, with one Horse and two wheels,	1	1		62 cents
Every Sulkey, Chair, or Chaise, with one Horse and four wheels,	1	1	5	43 cts
Every Chariot, Coach, Phæton, or Chaise, with two Horses and four wheels, (stages and vehicles used for the transportation of passengers and the mail, excepted,)	2	2		124 cts
Either of the foregoing Carriages, with four Horses,	4	3		186
Every other Carriage of Pleasure, under whatever name it may go, the like sum according to the number of wheels and Horses drawing the same,				
Every Pleasure Sleigh, or Pleasure vehicle on Sleigh runners, with one Horse	1	1/2		62 cts
ditto ditto ditto with two or more horses,	2	2		124 cts
Every Stage Coach, or other vehicle used for the transportation of passengers, with one Horse	1	2		124 cts
ditto ditto ditto ditto with two Horses	2	4		248
ditto ditto ditto ditto with four Horses,	4	6		372
Every vehicle employed in the transportation of the mail with one Horse,	1	2		124
ditto ditto ditto with two or more Horses,	2	4		248
If the mail be carried on Horseback, alone,	1	1		62
Every Cart or Wagon, going to market, with produce, or provisions, with one Horse,	1	1		62
ditto ditto ditto ditto with two Horses,	2	2		124
If with more than two Horses, according to the number of Horses, and when returning from market, empty, one half of said charges,				
Every Horse and his Rider, or led Horse,			5	31 cts
Every score of Sheep or Hogs,		1		62
Every score of cattle,		2		124
Every Cart or Wagon, other than market Carts or Wagons, with wheels not exceeding 4 inches and one Horse,	1	2	2 1/2	139 1/2
ditto ditto ditto ditto ditto and two Horses	2	4	5	2.79
ditto ditto ditto ditto ditto and three Horses	3	6	7 1/2	4.18 1/2
ditto ditto ditto ditto ditto and four Horses	4	9		5.58
ditto ditto ditto ditto ditto and five Horses	5	11	2 1/2	6.97 1/2
ditto ditto ditto ditto ditto and six Horses	6	13	5	8.37
Every Cart or Wagon, other than market Carts or Wagons, with wheels more than 4 inches and not exceeding 7 inches, and one Horse,	1	1		62
ditto ditto ditto ditto ditto and two Horses	2	2		124
ditto ditto ditto ditto ditto and three Horses	3	3		186
ditto ditto ditto ditto ditto and four Horses	4	4		248
ditto ditto ditto ditto ditto and five Horses	5	5		310
ditto ditto ditto ditto ditto and six Horses	6	6		372
Every Cart or Wagon, other than market Carts or Wagons, with wheels more than 7 inches and not exceeding 10 inches, or being 7 inches shall roll 10 inches, and two Horses	2	1	5	93
ditto ditto ditto ditto ditto and three Horses	3	2	2 1/2	139 1/2
ditto ditto ditto ditto ditto and four Horses	4	3		186
ditto ditto ditto ditto ditto and five Horses	5	3	7 1/2	232 1/2
ditto ditto ditto ditto ditto and six Horses	6	4	5	279
Every Cart or Wagon, other than market Carts or Wagons, with wheels more than 10 inches or being 10 inches shall roll more than 15 inches, and two Horses	2	1		62
ditto ditto ditto ditto ditto and three Horses	3	1	5	93
ditto ditto ditto ditto ditto and four Horses	4	2		124
ditto ditto ditto ditto ditto and five Horses	5	2	5	155
ditto ditto ditto ditto ditto and six Horses	6	3		186
Every Cart, or Wagon, other than market Carts or Wagons, with wheels more than 12 inches, and two Horses,	2		6	37 2/10
ditto ditto ditto ditto ditto and three Horses	3		9	55 4/5
ditto ditto ditto ditto ditto and four Horses	4	1	2	65 1/10
ditto ditto ditto ditto ditto and five Horses	5	1	5	93 1/10
ditto ditto ditto ditto ditto and six Horses	6	1	8	1.11 6/10

All such Carriages as shall be drawn by Oxen in the whole, or partly by Horses and partly by Oxen, two Oxen shall be estimated as equal to one Horse, in charging the aforesaid tolls, and every Mule as equal to one Horse,

Empty Carts or Wagons, or such as have loading in them, not weighing more than 200 lbs. including the feed for Horses, to pay one half of the above tolls,

some of the traffic going between Lancaster County and Wilmington.

Lancastrians were taught to be resourceful in manufacturing by responding abundantly to the challenges of the French and Indian wars, the Revolution, and the War of 1812. The latter struggle particularly fostered a strong desire for the young nation to be economically self-sufficient and to be able to manufacture most, if not all, goods used here. Now Lancaster suffered from a surplus of war-work-generated craft apprentices and much unused craft-shop capacity.

The second decade of the nineteenth century was a troubled time for land speculators and town developers. A quick glance at the histories of Lancaster County villages and boroughs reveals that many of them began at this time. There were many others planned that never "got off the paper on which the plans were drawn." It was a time of bankruptcies and sheriff sales involving every class of citizen. Testifying before a Pennsylvania committee in January 1820, Lancaster's solon stated economic distress "is experienced over the whole country, and is unexampled in great part thereof. It exhibits itself in various forms, viz. by a very large number of insolvent debtors; by the embarrassment of all classes except attorneys, sheriff, constables, justices of the peace and county officers generally . . . who are benefitted; by scarcity of money, and consequent sacrifice of property; and by numerous law suits." He described the increase in the market value of land, which soared from $75 to $100 per acre in 1809, to $250 to $300 in 1813. The Farmers Bank of Lancaster, the senator assumed, marked the beginning of the speculative era in this area. In answer to the question as to what property would bring on the market in 1819-20, he replied that it would sell for a mere $75 to $100 per acre. Lancastrians, he believed, blamed the distress on the high price of real and personal property in 1812-14 when many large debts were contracted and were not paid off by the 1816-19 period when peace between the United States and Britain resulted in a flood of foreign goods on the local market, putting Americans out of work. The oversupply of goods resulted in a reduction of prices, which worked hardship on merchants and manufacturers while not enabling the unemployed persons to take advantage of the cheaper prices. Banks called in loans, refused to honor notes issued by other banks that were not known

to be strong, and were reluctant to discount notes. Lancaster's Federalist state senator, Jacob Grosh, related how a large, elegant, three-story brick house that cost $16,000 to build in 1814 was sold in 1819 at a sheriff sale for a mere $1600. Lancaster's workers were fervent supporters of the protective tariff, which signaled the candidates of the Democratic Republican and Jacksonian Democratic factions to campaign for high tariffs, much to the great chagrin of the old Federalists and Whigs that regarded themselves as the exclusive proprietors of that doctrine.

It was in this setting that Lancaster decided to obtain legislation to become a city. As early as 1798 the borough corporation urged the Pennsylvania General Assembly to charter Lancaster as a city, giving as its reason the inability to govern in a benevolent manner because too many citizens were indifferent and refused to become engaged in controversy. Noisy minorities of citizens representing special interests were not at all reluctant to be seen and heard, which put the burgesses in an awkward position because they knew the noise was not at all representative. The state was not moved by that argument.

The state government had moved from Lancaster to Harrisburg in 1812. Between 1808 and 1812 a number of communities vied to secure the state capital seat: Northumberland (Sunbury), Harrisburg, Middletown, Philadelphia, Columbia, and Lancaster. Both Lancaster and Columbia had tried to have the United States Congress select one of these towns for the site of the permanent national capital. Although General Hand had put forth strenuous efforts to convince the Congress to pick Lancaster, Wright's Ferry, quickly renamed Columbia to add more weight to its claim, came within one vote of becoming the nation's federal city. Now Lancaster and Columbia each desired to become the state capital, with Assemblyman Slaymaker leading the effort to move the state lawmakers and offices back to Lancaster in 1818. Costs and slowness of construction in Harrisburg, lack of good transportation facilities, and remoteness all were cited to persuade the state government to come back to Lancaster. As part of the promotional campaign Lancaster again sought city status, which was granted 20 March 1818 by act of the general assembly. Before the city could celebrate its second birthday, a group of Lancastrians, angered by what they thought were excessive taxes and payroll padding, petitioned the

Simon Snyder, governor of Pennsylvania 1808-1817, was born in Lancaster on 5 November 1759 on North Queen Street, above Chestnut Street. This portrait is a copy by James R. Lambdin of an original by Thomas Sully.

Lancaster's first two courthouses were Georgian-style structures located in the middle of Centre Square. The third courthouse, built 1852-1854, was designed by Samuel Sloan, prominent Philadelphia architect, in the Roman-revival style. Its copperclad dome is surmounted by an unblindfolded statue of justice holding a sword in her right hand and scales in her left. This old structure is being preserved and used in conjunction with a new seven-story annex adjoining it. (Photo by the author)

general assembly to repeal the city charter. The effort was unsuccessful. Lancaster, the largest inland community in the United States, was now the third city in Pennsylvania, Philadelphia (1701) and Pittsburgh (1816) being senior. By contrast, Reading gained a city charter in 1847, Erie in 1851, Harrisburg in 1860, Scranton and Chester in 1866, Allentown in 1867, Lebanon in 1885, and York in 1887.

The city charter created two legislative bodies, a select council consisting of nine members whose qualifications were identical to those required for the state senate, and a common council of fifteen members who possessed qualifications for the state house of representatives. After a year in office each house was to arrange staggered terms so one-third would be elected annually. For the first election the outgoing burgesses were to conduct the voting. Governor Simon Snyder, a native Lancastrian, appointed John Passmore to be the first mayor. Mr. Passmore was the heaviest mayor ever to serve Lancaster; he weighed more than four

hundred pounds!

Following Passmore's two-year term, these mayors were elected by the councils from the nine-member board of aldermen. Each alderman was elected by the voters after the city was chartered, the number being determined by the governor appointing two and the other seven coming from the ranks of former justices of the peace in the borough. Eventually each alderman was to serve a ward, hence the creation of nine wards many years later. The mayors were:

Samuel Carter, Jeffersonian Republican, 1821-1823
Nathaniel Lightner, Jacksonian Democrat, 1824-1830
John Mathiot, Federalist-supported Masonic Democrat, 1831-1843

Mathiot, an extremely popular political leader, died in office. He was the last of the mayors elected by the councils. After that they were elected by the voters. Completing this era were:

In the era before photographic portraits, only the wealthier citizens could afford to have their likenesses recorded for posterity. Jacob Eichholtz (1776-1842), trained as a coppersmith, discovered his talent for art. Largely self-taught, he received counsel and much encouragement from Sully and Stuart. In maturity he was called upon by the nation's political, financial, and professional leaders for their portraits. His ability to capture a client's inner character and strengths was remarkable. This self-portrait apparently was done using a mirror.

Old City Hall along West King Street at Centre Square began as a county office building and then the state office building before serving as the city hall. To the left of the hall are the old market stalls with the Masonic Lodge overhead, and to the right rear the newer market sheds of 1854. This 1860-era photo shows the Square minus the courthouse razed in 1853.

Michael Carpenter, Loco Foco Democrat, 1843-1851
Christian Keiffer, Native American and Whig, 1852-1854
Jacob Albright, Native American and Whig, 1855
John Zimmerman, Democrat, 1856-1857
Thomas Burrowes, Anti-slavery Whig, 1858
George Sanderson, Democrat, 1859-1869

The city did not have public buildings for its exclusive use until the county vacated its 1795-97 office building on the west side of the Square when the new courthouse was completed in 1854. Council sessions and the Mayor's Court were held in the courthouse. The mayor wore two hats; he was the city's chief operating and administrative officer, and he served as a "super" magistrate, holding court that had the same function in the city as the minor judiciary (justices of the peace) and the County Court of Quarter Sessions had outside the city. The clerk of the Mayor's Court was an elected official called a recorder. Conflicts of interest apparently did not bother the citizenry as the mayor enforced the law, headed the police department, and sat on the bench as judge!

The new city councils set about adopting ordinances to keep the city healthy, wealthy, and safe. Nothing escaped their notice. An 1820 ordinance required all "persons of colour," residents and visitors, to register with the mayor within twenty-four hours of arrival in the city, providing information as to name, address, names of all members of the families, and occupations. The penalty for violation was one dollar fine for every twenty-four hours. Moreover, it was the duty of every innkeeper and landlord to report the presence of black persons, under penalty of one dollar. Constables were to charge "any strange person of colour found in the city, or lurking therein" as disorderly or vagrant persons. Since bureaucrats always charge fees, each black registrant was required to pay twelve and a half cents for the privilege.

Another early city ordinance required all able-bodied

*James Buchanan was
Pennsylvania's only native son
U.S. President. "Gentleman Jim"
or "Old Buck" also was the only
bachelor President. Aristocratic,
highly intelligent, ambitious, and
exceedingly cautious, Buchanan
revered the law and the
Constitution more than popular
adulation. He died in Lancaster
in 1868.*

persons to form bucket-brigade lines and place themselves under the authority of the several fire companies upon the alarm of fire. Driving, riding, or trotting a horse or other animal through the city streets at a speed in excess of seven miles per hour was illegal. Upon conviction, the offender could be fined not less than three nor more than ten dollars. In 1823 the city prohibited "swine, hogs, pigs, shoats, sheep or geese" from running at large, "whether yoked, ringed or otherwise." Either the city solicitor was not a farm lad or he wanted to be certain he included every member of family *suidae!*

Ever mindful of the costs of government and the belief that "idleness is the workshop of the Devil," the city enacted an ordinance in 1825 that observed, "Whereas, it has been represented to councils, that, from the want of means for confining convicts and vagrants to hard labor in the jail of Lancaster County, the sentence . . . has not been complied with, and a confinement in the jail has ceased to be a punishment to the idle and the vicious: Therefore . . . it shall be the duty of the street commissioner to procure a quantity of hard stone . . . and compel [the inmates] to break the stones to a suitable size . . . for the repairing of streets."

As guardians of the public morality, the councils in 1820 ordered that action be taken against "the very shameful, disorderly and profane conduct of the rising generation of this city on Sabbath days, as well as on other days." The outcome was an ordinance that penalized any male or female aged ten and upwards that profanely cursed or swore "by the name of God, Jesus Christ, or the Holy Ghost . . . or by any other name or thing" the sum of fifty cents or else spend twelve hours in jail for each offense. By the same act, persons playing at any game on the Sabbath or smoking in the streets and alleys were subject to a similar punishment.

The political complexion of Lancaster in the early nineteenth century was curious. The Federalists continued to win elections, but by the 1820s their ranks had been depleted and voters were looking to a successor for leadership. Meanwhile the Republican party of Thomas Jefferson had split into two factions, one favoring full enfranchisement of all males regardless of wealth and property holdings (Democrats), and the other preferring measures that would encourage industry and internal improvement while reserving to the states more authority than the old Federalists approved. The latter group were called National Republicans, and most of its partisans eventually became Whigs. Democrats, however, had internal struggles with the local Democracy divided into opposing camps headed by James Buchanan and Colonel Reah Frazer.

Lancaster witnessed a sample of the Democracy in disarray in 1829. Buchanan, a former Federalist, had tried to unite the various factions of the Democratic party and the survivors of Federalism in the coming battle with the anti-Masonic movement. His intentions apparently disturbed George Wolf, the Democratic candidate for governor. Wolf's backers in Lancaster decided to hold a victory banquet at the courthouse as soon as the court adjourned its session. Buchanan's supporters saw the opportunity to use the dinner celebration for their own purposes and to demoralize the Wolf Democrats. Consequently the Wolf people, headed by Sheriff Adam Diller, tried to oust the Buchanan crowd. Chosen chairman of the event by a "general howl," Diller was hoisted into the chair, only to be pulled from it by the Buchanan partisans. The scene was described in the press as "one seldom witnessed in a civilized country. Howling, hissing, tumult and confusion became general." George B. Porter, James Buchanan, and Benjamin Champneys climbed atop the judges' desks to make speeches which were drowned in the bedlam. A free-for-all erupted, and the victory dinner turned into "the worst brawl within the memory of the oldest living inhabitant." For two hours the courtroom in Centre Square was a political battleground, with glasses and pitchers, inkstands, and other missiles flying through the air. The local Democratic press was not surprised by the ruckus because "that should be expected when Buchanan tried to bring the Federalists and red-blooded Democrats together."

Eventually the Democrats did unite in a more

Lydia Smith, Congressman Thaddeus Stevens's housekeeper, was a black woman. She presided over the Stevens residence on South Queen Street during the congressman's activities in Washington. Stevens's Southern enemies, whose numbers were legion, assumed Mrs. Smith was more than a housekeeper for the irascible bachelor congressman.

harmonious pooling of interests. A black cloud loomed on the political horizon: the anti-Masonic party, supported so fanatically by Thaddeus Stevens. Among some Lancastrians of English, Scottish, and worldly German ancestry, Freemasonry was highly regarded as a fraternity that fostered the highest ideals of civilized manhood and ethical conduct akin to the monotheistic religious traditions. Indeed, Lancaster's Lodge 43, warranted 21 April 1785, had antecedents as early as 1766, and Masons had resided in Lancaster from its beginning. The founder, James Hamilton, was senior grand warden of the Philadelphia lodge in 1734, at which time he was laying out Lancaster. Lodge 43 entered into an agreement with the borough of Lancaster to build a lodge hall on top of pillars over the town market, probably the first instance of "air rights" in the United States. The structure was completed in 1800, and Lodge 43 used it continuously until 1971 when it became part of the Heritage Center of Lancaster County in which a typical lodge room has been reconstructed, using original furnishings. Lodge 43 is now in its 194th year. Its roster reads like a *Who's Who* of Lancaster.

Because Freemasonry is a fraternity with symbols and allegorical interpretations disclosed only to its members, opposition arose to its existence in a democratic Republic. Those of more modest circumstances often saw in the fraternity a gathering of the better-educated, more liberal, and influential men — a conspiracy, it seemed, against the common man, a conspiracy of aristocrats who might combine to control all the elective and appointive offices. Into these ominous threats to egalitarianism rode Thaddeus Stevens, ripe for a new crusade. Stevens, of the deformed foot and the shadow over his suspension from Dartmouth, had become a fervent anti-Mason. The average Lancaster Countian traditionally was politically conservative and supported whichever party or faction that represented the conservative philosophy, delivered a low tax rate, and kept the discontented under control, whether by Calvinistic exhortations or the street commissioner's stone pile. Although the city would swing between the parties, the county outside would remain steadfast in its opposition to the Democracy. Rather than combine with or support Democrats for public office, the rural population during the 1830s cast its ballot for the anti-Masons. Historians have

Thaddeus Stevens (1793-1868) served as U.S. Representative from Lancaster County from 1859 until his death in 1868. He served in the Pennsylvania House of Representatives 1833-1835, 1837, and 1841. In 1842 he moved to Lancaster and established a law office here. Known as the "Father of the Free School Act" in Pennsylvania and as the "Father of the Reconstruction Act" in Congress, Stevens was never married. He was the prime mover in the effort to remove President Johnson.

tended to overplay the anti-Masonic sentiment in Lancaster County when virtually blind opposition to anything Democratic actually was the overriding influence. James Buchanan was worshipful master of Lodge 43 in 1823.

As soon as the Whig party emerged, Lancastrians that were associated with the anti-Masons joined it to oppose the Democrats. The Whigs in Lancaster had a short life politically, the party being divided into antislavery and neutrality-on-slavery factions, the former being headed by Thaddeus Stevens and called the Woolly Heads. Edward Darlington was the leader of the moderate Whigs, known as the Silver Grays. That disruption created a vacuum into which the Native American party jumped. If the anti-Masons were irrational, the Native Americans were psychopathic! They exhausted all their energies in fighting among themselves, spying on each other, and holding kangeroo courts to expel "untrustworthy" members of the party.

PROGRAMME AND ORDER

OF THE

CIVIC PROCESSION,

For the reception of His Excellency, the

President of the United States,

On Friday evening, August 10, 1849

TRUMPETER MOUNTED

AIDS.	CHIEF MARSHAL.	AIDS.
Maj. D. B. Vondersmith, Mr. George F. Mosser.	Maj. Gen. Geo. Ford.	Maj. Chas. M. Howell. Dr. H. A. Smith.

BAND.

Second Assistant Marshal, HENRY F. ~~████~~

Escort of Citizens on Horseback, dressed as follows :—Black coat with ~~██~~ ribbon on the'left breast; white pantaloons and black hat.

ESCORT.

4TH ASST. MARSHAL, Walter G. Evans, Esq.	President's Carriage.	3D ASST. MARSHAL, William W. Phillips.

Governor's Carriage.

Member of Cabinet's Carriage.

Committee of Arrangement in Carriages.

Officers and Soldiers of the Mexican War, in do.

His Honor, the Mayor, and the Presidents and members of the Select and Common Councils, of the city of Lancaster, in carriages.

AID. Daniel B. Miller.	FIRST ASST. MARSHAL, FRANCIS KEENAN, ESQ.	AID. Henry Hayman

High Sheriff of Lancaster county and Deputies.

Judges and Officers of the Courts.

Citizens on Horseback.

Citizens on Foot.

Conestoga Teams.

Citizens in Carriages.

The Chief Marshal, Assistant Marshal, Aids, and Committee of Escort, consisting of citizens dressed as designated in the programme, will assemble at "the Manor Hotel," (Boley's) West King st, on FRIDAY, at 5 o'clock P. M. precisely,

Carriages, Citizens on horseback, on foot, and all others will take their places in the line on the Harrisburg turnpike, at the intersection of the Railroad.

Order and Arrangement for Saturday,

For the purpose of escorting His Excellency, President TAYLOR, to the Harrisburg Railroad on Saturday morning, the 11th instant, the Procession will be re-formed agreeably to the order for Friday, at 8½ o'clock, A. M in Orange street, the right on Duke street, facing South and displaying West. At 10½ o'clock, it will then proceed by the following route down Orange street to North Queen, up Queen to the President's Quarters. After the President is in line, the procession will move out East King street to Middle, down Middle to South Queen, up South Queen to West King, out West King to Charlotte, up Charlotte to Orange, down Orange to Prince, and out Prince to the Harrisburg Turnpike. The procession will then halt, when the President, Governor and members of the Cabinet will move to the right of the line, which will then pass in review before them.

☞ All Banners, Emblems, Insignias and Mottoes of a political character, are prohibited from being introduced into the line.

By order of

GEORGE FORD,

Chief Marshal.

C. M. HOWELL,
 D. B. VONDERSMITH, } AIDS.

When President Zachary Taylor visited Lancaster 10 August 1849 the city went all out in welcoming the hero of the Mexican War. With torches lighted and trumpets blaring, everyone who was anyone joined the governor and mayor in the gala procession to escort General Taylor from the railroad track on Harrisburg Avenue to the North American House. Then, as now, Conestoga wagon teams were in the parade. Just in case a political opponent might be indiscreet, there was a prohibition against banners, emblems, insignia, and slogans.

Five months after his inauguration, President Zachary Taylor visited Lancaster amidst much ceremony on 10 August 1849. After a huge reception and parade, the President was put up at the White Swan Hotel in Centre Square where he could see the 336 sperm candles illuminating the windows of the courthouse in his honor. A banquet was held, toasts were drunk, and the President affirmed his affection for Lancaster's fighting sons and a protective tariff dear to local ironmasters' hearts.

By 1856 Lancaster city was in a shambles politically. The Democrats patched up their intraparty quarrels long enough to elect James Buchanan to the White House, although the local workingmen were unhappy with rumors that Buchanan purchased furniture and other goods made in Europe. Lancaster's professional populists still sneered that Buchanan was a stuffed shirt and a snooty aristocrat. On the other side of the political arena Lancaster's peppy reform editor J.M.W. Geist called together in Fulton Hall the leaders of the various Whig, Native American, and other political conservative factions. Geist had in mind the formation of the Republican party in Lancaster. The summit conference lasted all day Saturday, 19 May 1856, with Thaddeus Stevens glumly pondering what success he might have in the new party. Although this meeting did result in a Republican organization, city candidates were hesitant about running under the banner of the new party until the GOP could score some victories, which happened in 1857. A vexing problem in Lancaster was the lingering shadow of the Native American party that regularly spoiled the chances of Whigs or Republicans by dividing the conservative vote. By 1860 the political parties were settled, and contests generally were between Democrats and Republicans. Both parties had their factions but these diminished in importance as national party organizations became stronger.

Lancaster newspapers during the nineteenth century attacked each other vehemently while waging campaigns for their respective candidates. They used language and made accusations that would not be permitted today. Partisan politics were intense, humorless, and serious. More adult male Lancastrians participated in the voting process then than now, often turning out between eighty and eighty-five percent of the eligible voters. Very early, voting in Lancaster was done at the courthouse. One window would be opened and an official stationed there to receive ballots. Each candidate or faction would have a headquarters, usually at an inn, where ballots would be handed to friendly voters. After marking his ballot, if even that was necessary, the voter turned his ballot in at the courthouse window. In later years polling places were set up in saloons, successors to the old inns. This "improvement" permitted voters to be fortified courtesy of grateful candidates, and possibly contributed greatly to the high degree of participation.

Few places in our nation have been home to as many powerful politicians as Lancaster County during the mid-1880s. Here lived James Buchanan who served in the legislature, Congress, as secretary of state, minister to Great Britain, and President of the United States, 1856-1860. In 1842 Thaddeus Stevens moved his residence and law practice to Lancaster, and soon after represented Lancaster in Congress until his death in 1868. Stevens was one of the most powerful men in Congress, and headed the impeachment proceedings against President Andrew Johnson. Senator Simon Cameron of nearby Donegal Springs virtually ran the Republican party from the antebellum era to his retirement in 1877 when the mantle passed to his son, Donald. Early in the war he served as Lincoln's secretary of war, and his son served President Grant in the same position. Moreover, Lancaster's representatives to the general assembly were outstanding leaders eagerly sought out by other Pennsylvania politicians for their advice. The mid-1800s saw Lancaster providing political leadership to the nation just as the town furnished the material for waging war and securing American independence in the seventeenth century.

The industrial revolution that converted the United States into a major manufacturing power occurred between 1840 and 1865. Starting in the New England states and the Delaware Valley, the factory system presaged vast changes to the American economy. Lancastrian enterprisers looked longingly at these developments, but they were not very successful in transplanting a manufacturing economy to Lancaster until they had learned more sophisticated techniques for capital formation. The primitive and chaotic condition of banking at that time contributed greatly to the problem of bringing capital together for establishment and initial operation of industries employing fairly large numbers of persons.

Although flour milling was Lancaster County's major industry in value of production throughout most of the nineteenth century, it was carried out in hundreds of gristmills, few of which were large, employed many persons, or constituted a major investment of capital. Several mills close to the city furnished the wheat flour and processed other grains for the Lancaster market.

Another large industry in the county was the

J.M.W. Geist (1824-1905) was a
longtime editor, temperance
crusader, writer, politician, and
churchman. He founded the
Lancaster New Era in 1877 on the
principles of Reform
Republicanism.

The Conestoga Cork Works was
established in 1860 by Harris
Boardman at Locust and Lime
streets. The building burned in
1882. Lancaster became a center
for cork-cutting, leading to the
entrance of Armstrong Bros. & Co.
from Pittsburgh into cork
operations in Lancaster.

Eagle Furnace, later called Chickies Furnace No. 2, was one of many anthracite iron blast furnaces operating in Lancaster city and county from 1842 until the early 1900s. This furnace was built in 1854 by Stephen Eagle at Marietta. In 1889 it was rebuilt by Haldeman & Co., proprietors of an adjacent furnace (Chickies No. 1) and ore-mine operations in West Hempfield Township. (Courtesy John Ward Willson Loose Archives)

As one of Lancaster's wealthiest ironmasters, Clement Bates Grubb (1815-1899) owned the largest piece of residential property in the city. His mansion, built in 1845, is bounded by Lime, Chestnut, Shippen, and Marion streets, and is now the centerpiece of Musser Park. Grubb was a faithful Republican, Mason, and heavy contributor to the Episcopal Church. His summer mansion was at Mount Hope.

charcoal iron business conducted in a number of blast furnaces, forges, and rolling mills, none of them in the city except Conestoga Furnace located at the foot of Prince Street. Built in 1846 as a charcoal pig-iron furnace by George Ford, an enterprising Lancaster attorney, and Robert and James Colvin, practical ironmasters, the trio hoped to bring cordwood from York County up the Conestoga Navigation Canal to the furnace where it would be converted to charcoal. The Colvins already had established a record of failure at the Shawnee Furnace in Columbia, and soon Ford's money ran out. Henry Reed, a Lancaster banker, and Thomas Baumgardner, an astute business promoter and coal merchant, took the furnace in assignment and sold it to John Frederick Shroder, another private banker and promoter of industrial enterprises, and John Black, entrepreneur of the Lancaster Locomotive Works, whose foundry required much pig iron. Thirty days later they sold the furnace to Christopher Geiger, George Mayer Steinman, and John C. Hager, trading as Geiger and Company. Geiger was a practical ironmaster, Steinman was in the hardware business, and Hager was a local merchant; both Steinman and Hager were addicted to promoting business enterprise in Lancaster. Geiger and Company converted the furnace to use anthracite coal as fuel, and extended the stack to thirty-eight feet. As Lancaster County anthracite blast furnaces went, it was not a large establishment in either size or capacity. The panic of 1857 ended its operations for sixteen years. Inadequate transportation was the major cause of its shutdown, the nearby canal having become bankrupt and no nearby railroad facilities available.

The Steinman hardware store on West King Street was begun in 1744, and supplied ironmongery to the western settlers. In this 1895 photo one may see the ladders and other merchandise displayed on the sidewalk. The Steinman & Co. is now a realty owner, the hardware business being closed out in the early 1960s.

The Steinman hardware store was started in 1744, making it the oldest ironmongery in the nation at the time it closed its retail and wholesale business in the 1960s. The firm still exists as a corporate entity.

The "John Breckinridge" was built in the Lancaster Locomotive Works by John Brandt, Sr., for the Columbia and Philadelphia Railroad in 1857. Locomotive builders had their finest products lithographed in color. The appearance of early locomotives was nearly as important as their mechanical efficiency and fuel economy.

Long after the famed Pennsylvania rifle was developed in Lancaster County in mid-eighteenth century, Henry Eichholtz Leman (pronounced like the citrus fruit) was proprietor of Lancaster's largest gunworks. Throughout much of the nineteenth century Leman guns and rifles were shipped far and wide. Many of the western hunters carried Leman weapons. Leman, of French Huguenot stock, was a prominent business and civic leader.

The fact that duels were illegal in 1843 did not stop Henry E. Leman, Lancaster's fine rifle and gun manufacturer, from advertising pistols for defending gentlemanly honor from the defamations of a lowly cad.

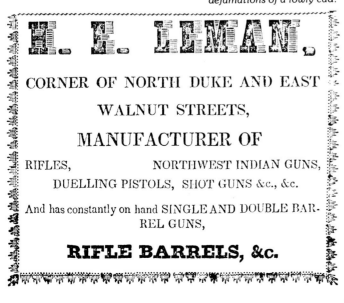

Lancaster's reputation for manufacturing the finest rifles was continued in the nineteenth century by a number of master gunsmiths working in their small shops. Henry Leman, however, produced weapons in his gunworks at the corner of Walnut and Cherry streets about 1840 after serving an apprenticeship with Melchoir Fordney and working as a journeyman in Philadelphia. The Leman works produced many hundreds of thousands of guns, many of them under government contract. Leman was a member of both city councils at various times, and was a Mason. In its later years the Leman Rifle Works was located on West James Street near Water Street.

A legacy from the revolutionary war, leatherworking in the city continued in various forms. Boot and shoemakers were numerous. As early as 1836 unionized employees of the shoemakers went on strike for higher wages, an act that upset Lancaster County

Christopher Hager was a dry-goods merchant in Lancaster, the family business being started in 1821. Hager prospered, and turned his vast energies to promotion of the local economy. He built Fulton Hall. Hager and John F. Steinman were a team dedicated to bringing industry to Lancaster, improving the banking system, and upgrading the community in educational and cultural pursuits.

This 1838 print of North Queen Street and Chestnut Street shows the courthouse in Centre Square and the railroad tracks north of Chestnut Street. In 1859 the Pennsylvania Railroad built a depot at the far left. Trains continued to stop downtown until 1929. The Hotel Brunswick occupies the site of the North American Hotel.

farmers immensely because they would have to pay more for footwear while not being able to earn a greater income from farming. The farmers met to consider boycotting the cordwainer union. Other leatherworkers in Lancaster produced large amounts of harness and saddlery. Water Street continued to be the center of Lancaster's tanning industry.

With superb mechanical skills and uncommon practical intelligence at their command, Lancaster mechanics turned to manufacturing machinery, engines, and boilers for the new age of steam. One such business was the firm of Pennell and Lehner, founders and machinists, at the northeast corner of Duke and Chestnut streets, along the railroad cut. In 1839 the firm was given an order to manufacture first-class locomotives for the Columbia and Philadelphia Rail-Road, the rail link of the State Works between Pittsburgh and Philadelphia. Early in 1853 land in the

vicinity of East Chestnut, East Fulton, Plum, and Ann streets was acquired for an extensive locomotive works. John Brandt, Sr. was the superintendent of the Lancaster Locomotive Works, and among the stockholders were the ubiquitous promoters Christopher Hager and John N. Lane. During the first year of operation eleven locomotives were made. Of an engine built in 1855, the local press rhapsodized, ". . . the 'Uncle Toby' is a first-class freight engine, combining all the latest improvements with a degree of finish and ornament heretofore, we believe, unequalled in this country." The "Uncle Toby" had sixteen-inch cylinders, twenty-two-inch stroke, and four combined driving wheels five feet in diameter. The "Wheatland," built in 1853, was used to transport the Prince of Wales, future King Edward of England, around the nation in 1860. He rode in the cab to better see the scenic splendor of Horseshoe Curve.

At the peak of production a locomotive was built each week. The panic of 1857 caused the works to close until reopened in 1863 by Edward and James Norris. Approximately four hundred employees were kept busy in the six-acre works until it ceased operations in 1868. A year later an effort was made to reactivate the works, but after a year-long attempt the works was shut down, never to make any more locomotives. In 1874 the Lancaster Manufacturing Company, of which the principal stockholder was Andrew J. Steinman, converted the works into an iron-rolling mill for the manufacture of railroad supplies, frogs and switches, and other items of hardware. Later this became the Penn Iron Works, which ceased operations in the early 1920s.

Other foundries and machine works in Lancaster were kept busy producing cast-iron machine parts, structural columns, boilers, steam engines, pressure vessels, and agricultural machines.

Before 1840 Lancaster's beer was brewed in the traditional English manner, that is to say with hope, faith, and an earnest prayer instead of a recipe. The outcome, even when relatively successful, was a short-lived concoction of murky quality, not unlike an amateur's first effort at making home brew. With the introduction of "lagering," or storing, and bottom-fermenting yeast, Lancaster brewers gradually installed equipment and deep cellars to produce lager beer. John Wittlinger supposedly was the first lager brewer in 1842; his small plant on West King Street eventually grew into the large Rieker Brewery that was a Lancaster institution for so many years before and during Prohibition. Henry Franke was a lager brewer in 1848 in the rear of 236 North Prince Street. The John Abraham Sprenger brewery produced the frothy beverage in the late 1840s and, when the brewer was stricken, his wife ran the plant until 1867 — probably one of the first women brewers in the world!

With the economy not keeping pace with the growing population of Lancaster, the city's coterie of perennial promoters — Christopher Hager, John N. Lane, Judge Alexander Hayes, John Frederick Steinman, James Evans, and now a new face, David Longenecker — put their heads together and decided to invite General Charles Tillinghast James to Lancaster to speak on building steam-powered cotton mills. Encouraging the construction of steam cotton

mills was James's passion, and he was well known for his missionary work on behalf of that enterprise.

Quite taken in by General James's enthusiasm, the promoters got busy, formed a corporation called the Conestoga Steam Cotton Mill, and sold stock to the citizenry. General James's man, Edward Warren, was dispatched to Lancaster to supervise the construction and operation of the mill, an intrusion resented by Longenecker. Warren was supposed to buy a block of stock with funds advanced to him by a commission merchant in Philadelphia who was to have exclusive selling rights for Conestoga textiles. Longenecker would have none of that deal, preferring to find his own factors. As a result Warren was forced out, and from then on the building of the mill was pretty much a Longenecker enterprise. Contracts were let 12 August 1845 for the erection of the mill, then to be the largest structure built in the city. Lancaster's brickyards worked around the clock to make the hundreds of thousands of bricks required, while masons and carpenters laid up the walls. Any other enterprises in which the managers were interested — David Longenecker was interested in virtually everything — were required to be patronized by the contractors. Judge Hayes's lime kiln was to furnish the lime for mortar, for example.

When the Carson and Kautz Brickyard fell behind in delivery of bricks, Longenecker exacted from the firm an agreement they would not deliver bricks to any other customer until the mill was fully supplied with eight hundred thousand bricks. On top of that, Christopher Hager and J.F. Steinman were sent searching for an additional four hundred thousand bricks at the lowest price, resulting in a complete stoppage of all building in Lancaster while the brickyards worked exclusively for the mill construction. When stories began to circulate that additional mills were in the planning stage, the brickmakers started to plan expansions of their own. Longenecker thought the carpenters were charging too much, so the carpenters' union protested and the matter had to be arbitrated.

Finally, in January 1847, the mill was ready to produce cotton textiles. Female operatives were sought for wages of $1.25 per week. Longenecker, Hager, and Steinman now were to be found traveling around the country buying bales of cotton, trying to beat the experienced brokers at their own game. When

Few men in Lancaster have contributed as greatly to the economic success and stability of the city as did John Frederick Steinman. Heir to the family hardware business that was begun in 1744, Steinman soon earned a reputation for integrity, industriousness, and civic leadership. He promoted all sorts of local industries, many of them successful. A son, Andrew Jackson Steinman, became the publisher of the Intelligencer Journal. Steinman was active in the Moravian Church.

Lancaster's first large industry conducted at one site was the Conestoga Steam Cotton Mills, begun in 1847. The mills provided employment to hundreds of female operatives but few dividends to stockholders.

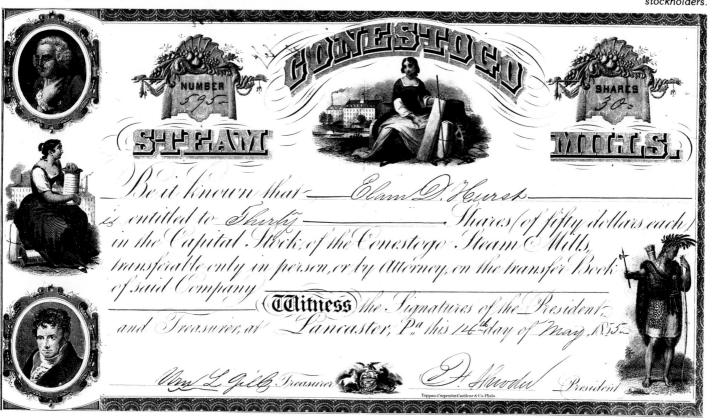

The city issued money called "shinplasters" during the panic of 1837. "Shinplaster" money were issues of script that were really municipal obligations, or transferable notes. They were about the same size as an old-fashioned "shinplaster," hence the name.

Longenecker wasn't buying cotton, he was trying to sell the goods produced. Eventually the David S. Brown Co. of Philadelphia became the principal agent of the mill. Longenecker, who by now had become president of the Lancaster Bank, which extended huge loans to him with only cotton-mill stock as security, made a practice of paying the mill's accounts payable in Lancaster Bank notes which were as worthless as the mill's stock certificates.

A few years later Conestoga Cotton Mill No. 2 on the west side of Prince Street was erected and, shortly after that, Mill No. 3 was built south of Mill No. 1 at the corner of South Prince and Conestoga streets. By 1857 the entire complex of mills, the Lancaster Bank, the Lancaster Savings Institution, and David Longenecker were in deep financial trouble. It was discovered Longenecker, now derisively called "King David," had borrowed shamelessly from his bank and was living as the city's wealthiest citizen on nothing more substantial than worthless paper notes. He fled to Philadelphia; his mansion, *Hardwick,* was sold; his imported Italian statuary, paintings, and furniture were sold at auction; and he never again appeared in Lancaster until death some thirty years later when his body was sneaked back at night for an unmarked burial in the Lancaster cemetery. Thus ended the saga of Lancaster's most energetic enterpriser and biggest swindler!

The Civil War brought activity back to the closed mills, and they operated with reasonable prosperity under the ownership of John Farnum & Company of Philadelphia. They ceased operations with the advent of the worldwide depression in 1932. There were other cotton mills in Lancaster during the mid-1800s, but none as large as the complex on South Prince Street.

Labor relations in the first half of the nineteenth century in Lancaster were confined to the unions of the carpenters, shoemakers, and railroad workers, all of which struck for higher wages at some time or another. Union activity in the city was a phenomenon seen more vividly in the last half of the last century.

Lancaster's banks came into existence at the urging of the town government in 1803, when that body invited the Bank of Pennsylvania to establish a branch bank. The branch bank was opened 18 May 1803, with twelve of the borough's most prominent businessmen as directors. On 17 January 1810 the Farmers Bank of Lancaster was organized, and today it has evolved by merger into the National Central Bank. During the chaotic days of early banking the Farmers Bank was characterized by conservative action, where caution and prudence tempered any inclination to speculate or take unnecessary risks. In 1814 the bank was chartered by the state, giving it the distinction of being the first home-owned bank in Lancaster. These early banks issued their own notes for use as currency, and they invested in other banks and enterprises, hoping to reap a profit from successful endeavors. The state also purchased heavy quantities of stock in these banks, giving the state partial ownership as a major shareholder.

The Lancaster Trading Company was the town's second locally owned bank; it was organized in 1814, and in 1818 it changed its name to the Lancaster Bank. It collapsed with the David Longenecker plundering of its deposits in 1857. Before Longenecker's adventures the Lancaster Bank was fairly well governed and prospered almost as well as the Farmers Bank.

The panic of 1837 prompted the city to issue money called *shinplasters.* Lancaster's close control over the currency avoided many of the problems encountered

Lithograph showing Lancaster's first textile mill about 1820. The mill was located on the west bank of the Conestoga River just south of the Duke Street bridge.

Lancaster businessmen could hire office clerks educated at the Lancaster Mercantile College, which was a business school on North Duke Street, now the site of the courthouse annex. This 1857 view indicates the school occupied dwellings that became known to old-timers as "Barbary Coast," or simply, "Lawyers' Row." Penmanship was the core of the curriculum at "Dear Old LMC."

elsewhere where the temptation to abuse the issuance of "homemade" notes was given free rein. Even the city redeemed its loan with fractional currency in 1838. These came in denominations of 10¢, 12-1/2¢, 25¢, and 50¢. The prevalent use of 12-1/2¢ in those days came from circulation of Spanish pieces of eight, eight of which amounted to one dollar.

In 1841 the Lancaster County Bank was founded and, like the Farmers Bank, it benefited from cautious, prudent direction. Never in its history has the bank's integrity or stability been placed in any danger.

The banking needs of the city also were met by a half-dozen private bankers such as Gyger & Co.; Reed, McGrann & Co.; and A.S. Henderson.

A flurry of building early in the 1850s changed the face of Lancaster. The old prison was replaced by a new institution built on East King Street, and on the site of the old prisonyard civic promoter Christopher Hager built Fulton Hall in 1852. Samuel Sloan, an eminent Philadelphia architect, designed the new Roman Revival courthouse at the northwest corner of Duke and King streets; this domed structure was completed in 1854. Many churches were in a mood to expand and even Trinity Lutheran Church went "modern," reorienting its sanctuary and moving its central entrance to the tower end where vestibules were constructed.

On College Hill, Franklin and Marshall College, having been formed by the merger of Lancaster's Franklin College and Mercersburg's Marshall College in 1853, began to take shape. Old Main and two identical flanking buildings, one for the Diagnothian and the other for the Goethean literary societies, were completed by 1857. The college, one of the oldest liberal arts colleges in the nation, has had a long and distinguished history in higher education.

At nearby Millersville the Lancaster County Academy was being planned, but before long it became a teacher-training school. Established in 1854 as the Millersville Academy, the school became the Commonwealth's first teacher-preparation college. In 1928 the institution was renamed Millersville State Teachers College and was granted the right to confer bachelor's degrees. In 1960, with the introduction of the liberal arts degree, the college became Millersville State College, and continues the excellent traditions it had earned in training teachers.

This row of houses at one time was John Leman's Brewery, and served for a time as the home of Franklin College. After the Civil War period the structures were used as a city jail. The site was along East Mifflin Street, east of Christian Street, and west of South Duke Street.

The Lancaster County prison was built in 1852-53, supposedly to resemble the castle at Lancashire, England. John Haviland was the architect. Still in use, although greatly altered and enlarged, the old prison has housed many thousands of short-term (two years maximum) prisoners and several dozen men sentenced to death.

Commerce could not be carried on in Lancaster unless adequate transportation facilities were available. In addition to the turnpikes there was the Conestoga Navigation Canal from Lancaster to Safe Harbor on the Susquehanna River, built in 1826 and used until its final bankruptcy in 1857. Much of Lancaster's bulk freight was shipped in and out by this canal. Advertisements of the day claimed a Lancastrian could travel from the city to Paris, France, by boat!

The rail link of the State Works ran from Philadelphia to Columbia on the Susquehanna River where the railroad connected with the Pennsylvania Canal to the west. When the original surveys showed the railroad to pass north of Lancaster, the city fathers went into a huddle, deciding to offer the railroad generous terms and real estate free from damage claims if the tracks could be brought through the center of the city. This was done, and the railroad entered Lancaster alongside the present McCaskey High School and passed through a deep cut to East Chestnut Street at North Queen Street, where the station was erected. The tracks continued across Queen Street and then westward in a straight path to Dillerville. Surveyors used the tower of Trinity Lutheran Church as the focal point of their sightings. Later this state railroad was purchased by the Pennsylvania Railroad. The station that stood there until 1929 was built in 1859.

Early in the nineteenth century those German-speaking residents that found the services of the Lutheran and Calvinist churches lacking in warmth and personal feeling associated themselves with one of

several groups that stemmed from Methodism. Had they been English-speaking they doubtless would have joined the Methodist church, which established its first congregation here in 1807, although Henry Boehm preached the first Methodist sermon, standing on a butcher block in the old market house, in 1803! The African Methodist Church, founded here in 1817 with a large congregation of black residents, continues to serve the community well. The Baptist Church in Lancaster traces its beginnings to 1841. A nondenominational Church of God existed in Lancaster from 1816 to 1833, after which informal services were held until the congregation associated itself with the Church of God in North America in 1840. It built a church on the southeast corner of Prince and Orange streets in 1842, and today occupies a large stone structure at the corner of Chestnut and Charlotte streets.

The Evangelical Association gathered a congregation in the city in 1846, and built a church on Water Street. An English-language controversy split the congregation, with the English element constructing a church at the northwest corner of Mulberry and Marion streets. St. John's Episcopal Church dates from 1853, and always has met on the present site at the northwest corner of Mulberry and Chestnut streets. The German Reformed Church also experienced an English-language dispute, which was solved when the English element withdrew in 1850 to form Second Reformed Church at the southwest corner of Duke and Orange streets. In time this congregation changed its name to St. Paul's Reformed Church. A similar issue caused

German Lutherans to separate from Trinity Lutheran Church about 1825 and to establish Zion Lutheran Church. On the western edge of the city, in 1853, younger members of Trinity Lutheran Church established a new congregation known as St. John's; a handsome Greek Revival-style church was built the same year.

St. Mary's Catholic Church served the Catholic community for many years during which time hundreds of newly arrived immigrants from Germany took up residence in the southern half of the city. German was not the language of St. Mary's in the nineteenth century, and that caused some disaffection with the newcomers. In 1850 a German parish was organized and named St. Joseph's. A building was constructed for its use about 1851, but it has been replaced by the present large structure erected in 1885.

The Lancaster New Jerusalem Church (Swedenborgian) had a following among some of the highly educated and scientifically minded citizens of Lancaster, and in 1836 an association was formed. While never a large congregation, it survived throughout the last century and into the present one.

Universalist preachers visited Lancaster on numerous occasions in the 1830s and 1840s, and attracted large crowds that wanted to hear about universal salvation in a city where Calvinist thought was prevalent. One Universalist lecture held in Zion Lutheran Church in the 1830s erupted into a riot when someone remembered that the landlord's bylaws prohibited the use of the English language in the building!

Education of Lancaster's proper young ladies occurred at James Damant's seminary on West Orange Street east of North Prince Street. The antebellum structure is used today as a commercial building.

LADIES SEMINARY.

JAMES DAMANT'S SEMINARY.
FIRST GIRLS HIGH SCHOOL.

In cultural matters Lancastrians in the 1840s were flocking to lectures on every conceivable subject. Self-improvement was all the rage, and industrious mechanics patronized the Mechanics' Library, turning the precious pages with oil-stained fingers and devouring the information under flickering oil lamps. When the Fulton Hall was opened in 1852, entertainment and traveling shows were a pleasant diversion for the townspeople. In 1855 the Lancaster Philharmonic Society presented its first concert, but an alarm of fire in the town emptied the hall during the violin arrangement of the *casta diva* from Bellini's *Norma.* It must be presumed members of the Union Fire Company and their ladies were in attendance, hence the unseemly but obligatory departure during a cultural high point! The Philharmonic's repertoire was heavy on overtures to Italian operas, Gyrowetz's symphonies, and marches by the orchestra's own conductor, Maestro Keffer.

Another entertainment, the Lancaster circus, advertised "the most Grand, Rich and Rare Collection of Living Animals ever exhibited in America." Lancastrians were treated to the sights of two Arabian camels, one of each sex; a "real Red African Lion, almost full grown . . . and the keeper will kiss him," an African ape, and llamas from Peru, among other oddities. Adults were admitted for 25¢, children for 12-1/2¢.

Lancaster's children were being educated in public schools as early as 1809, if their parents did not mind being classed as paupers. By 1822 all children were to be educated at public expense in Lancaster. Even earlier, advocates of the teaching methods of Joseph Lancaster practiced their art in the city. The big day in the lives of many young Lancastrians occurred 28 July 1825 when General LaFayette visited the school to receive bows, curtsies, and poems recited by the youngsters. In 1834 the common school system was introduced, which provided an education for all, regardless of wealth and station in life. Lancaster's early schools were barrackslike structures often built in series along the streets. Black students were educated in a separate building. A night school functioned as early as 1840.

The population of Lancaster grew rapidly after 1840, as more recent European immigrants, mainly from Ireland and Germany, arrived. The surplus of females

One-stop service was offered in 1843 by Drs. Ely and James Parry for patrons in need of trusses, false teeth, and artificial eyes. When Dr. James was pulling teeth, Dr. Ely was busy selling horse powder, dyes, surgical instruments, and paints. The Parry Shopping and Professional Center was 150 years ahead of its time.

The Lancaster Fencibles, the community's elite military unit, stand for inspection before parading in 1857. Old City Hall is to the rear.

was an influential factor in attracting industry that could employ the women and girls at lower rates of pay. Nonetheless, the city's large middle-class population continued to thrive, with the German and Irish immigrants struggling to climb the ladder of upward mobility. By the 1850s the Germans had begun to cluster in the shadow of St. Joseph's Catholic Church on what is now called "Cabbage Hill," its name arising from the prevalence of cabbages grown for sauerkraut and other German dishes. The Irish tended to live along East King Street between Shippen Street and the prison.

Lancaster's black residents were to be found living among the unskilled whites in the southeast quadrant of Lancaster in what was to become the Seventh Ward. The borough had fifty-seven slaves in it in 1790, but there were only fifteen in 1800, and seven a decade later. All of these were household servants. The 1830 census shows fifteen slaves in the city, but if the entry is correct it is likely these were fugitives from the South. Many free black persons lived in Lancaster, owned property, and carried on small businesses. If one reads between the lines of the local newspapers of the period, it becomes obvious Lancastrians thought with two levels of standards. "Our colored folk" are fine, hardworking, law-abiding, Christian people; "other colored folk" are often lazy, intemperate, and quarrelsome. The ordinance that required visiting Negroes to register with the mayor upon arrival is a case in point. Moreover, the socioeconomic level of many members of the black community in Lancaster was fairly comparable to that of semiskilled white artisans. Little pressure existed in the competition for menial jobs. Bias generally was benign in white-black relations, open hostility being a characteristic of a severely depressed, unskilled, and disadvantaged white community. Despite the probable patronizing by the dominant white community, Lancaster's black citizens quite likely possessed ample self-respect.

The local Quaker influence, while not very strong in the city, made itself felt in antebellum days when questions of abolition, African colonization, and fugitive-slave laws were discussed. Lancastrians generally detested the institution of slavery; they were somewhat less enthusiastic about waging a crushing civil war to end slavery until the gauntlet was thrown down to them at Fort Sumter.

§ § § §

The 1818-1860 period saw Lancaster begin its existence as a city with serious economic problems, whipped by unemployment, inflation, speculation, and chaotic banking. During this period the first generation of industrial enterprise began, providing jobs for men and women, and encouraging new immigrants to settle among the old residents. Despite the general lack of sophistication and technological know-how, Lancaster saw trade unions and industries develop, first stumbling, then enthusiastic, and finally maturing into workable, practical instruments for a healthy economy. Then, as later, the salvation of Lancaster's economic being was its diversification. It ought to be admitted, however, that happy condition was more luck than design. Recovering slightly from the panic of 1857, the city was able and ready to serve the nation with its men, manufactured goods, and agricultural products in the approaching war between brothers, the sounds of which had reached Lancaster even prior to President Buchanan's arrival back home in Lancaster.

Chapter IV

The Roll of Drums and the Surge of Industry

1860-1900

Many drummer boys that served during the War Between the States were only fourteen or fifteen years old. Lancaster's best-known drummer boy was George W. Brientnall who joined the 77th Penna. Volunteers when he turned sixteen. He became, in reality, the "Drummer Boy of Shiloh." One of the experienced local drummers was Israel C. Landis who joined the Union Army to train combat soldiers, not beat a drum. Landis is shown here with his drum.

As Civil War clouds gathered on the horizon Lancaster was more concerned with disruption of southern trade and the nature of the incoming Lincoln administration. The Democrat organ, the *Intelligencer,* was filled with gloom and doom; Lincoln's election was a disaster that would destroy the nation! Lancaster's handsome Democrat mayor, George Sanderson, certainly did not sympathize with the pro-slavery Democrats, and he was respected by the city's Republicans and most of the dying embers of the Whig and Native American groups.

Thousands of Lancastrians responded to the call for volunteers. Professional soldiers from the city were to be found in command positions. General John Fulton Reynolds, an officer being considered for the command of the northern forces, would be killed on the first day of the Battle of Gettysburg. His brother, William, was an admiral in the U.S. Navy. Other local names holding high rank were General Samuel Heintzelman and Colonel John Hambright. Only a segment of the Pennsylvania German population in northeastern Lancaster County refused to cooperate with the military officials in the draft. They rioted at the courthouse until the sheriff deputized a goodly number of patriots and routed the "Dutchmen." Copperhead activity was rife in the Ephrata-Denver area.

Daily the mails brought letters from Lancaster's homesick soldiers at the front or in camp. Surviving letters and diaries furnish much evidence that the typical Lancaster soldier, whatever his personal feelings, was quick to laud the Union cause, a patriot

Maj. Gen. John Fulton Reynolds, son of a prominent Lancaster family, lost his life on the first day of the Battle of Gettysburg, but only after placing his units personally where they would be able to withstand the Confederate Army and take the offensive. He had been offered the command of the Army of the Potomac, but declined it in protest of command decisions being made in Washington by politicians, not by West Point professional soldiers.

beyond any doubt. The "bloody shirt" had its desired effect!

Lancastrians turned out in force to maintain the home front. The Patriot Daughters raised funds, rolled bandages, knitted socks and sweaters, and provided wholesome hospitality to the troops passing through Lancaster and in nearby military hospitals. The Sanitary Fairs benefited hugely from the work of Lancaster's women, among whom was the redoubtable Rosina Hubley, surely one of Lancaster's greatest and most resourceful leaders. Mrs. Hubley had the intelligence of a Ph.D., the energy of a dozen men, and the heart of a saint. When the war was over, the Patriot Daughters turned their vast efforts to building the Soldiers and Sailors Monument, which was dedicated on 4 July 1874 in Centre Square.

Local industries were not as prominent in furnishing materials for waging the Civil War simply because many northern towns and cities were industrialized by 1861. The cotton mills turned out sheetings by the mile, and the leather industries were put to work producing saddles and harness. The major material contribution of Lancaster County was in the provisioning and horse-dealing business. Army beef made many a countian wealthy, and stories of horses sold two and three times over to the army

tickled the cynics.

In late June 1863 the Army of Northern Virginia swept north to invade Pennsylvania. General Richard Ewell's forces moved quickly eastward to York County where food, clothing, horses, and other needed supplies were confiscated, and some property destroyed. General John Brown Gordon's advance unit arrived at Wrightsville on 27 June 1863, sending the home guard and other details hastily assembled into retreat across the long, wooden, covered bridge over the Susquehanna River. When the retreating forces reached the safety of Columbia, the bridge was set afire to prevent the Confederates from reaching Columbia. Lancaster was thrown into a panic. Valuable possessions, money, and public records were hidden, buried, or shipped eastward by wagons. Christopher Hager accosted Mayor Sanderson with an old pistol, threatening to shoot him unless His Honor promised not to permit the Confederates to take goods from the stores if they should invade Lancaster. Smoke from the burning bridge could be seen easily in Lancaster. Home guards had been dispatched to watch the river shore. Fortunately Lancaster was not invaded by the southern forces until July 1976 when the city gave a rousing warm welcome to the Bicentennial Wagon Train composed largely of southern state groups!

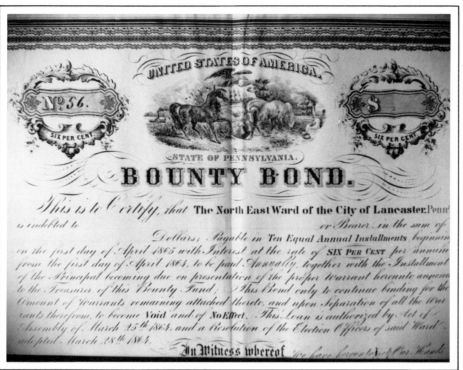

To raise funds to pay bounties to enlistees in the Union Army, bounty bonds were sold during the Civil War. This bond raised funds for the Northeast Ward — now the 2nd and 6th wards.

Below, a Civil War era diary page.

Sunday   June 28   1863
The Rebels have taken possession of York and are marching towards the Susquehanna. The bridge at Columbia was set on fire the night after our men retreated through it after fighting 45 minutes. We saw the fire from here. 'Twas awful. The whole bridge was burned. The excitement in town intense. Immense numbers of refugees came to town and hundreds of poor negroes walked from Columbia The roads are lined with them.

An 1861 drawing shows Lancaster women making uniforms for Union soldiers. It was reproduced in Harper's magazine.

On 28 June 1863 Lancaster Countians were alarmed when Gen. John Brown Gordon's Georgian troops started across the Columbia bridge preparatory to invading the county. As soon as the retreating troops, home guards, and refugees cleared the long bridge into Columbia, the bridge was set afire, driving the Confederates back to York County. The burning bridge could be seen in Lancaster.

Early nineteenth-century home in which Maj. Gen. John Fulton Reynolds was born. Located at 42-44 West King Street, the structure still has much of its original fabric and design. Reynolds was killed the first day of the Battle of Gettysburg.

Maj. Gen. Samuel P. Heintzelman was a native of Manheim, Lancaster County. Although he was considered a courageous and resourceful Union Army officer, he lacked much sophistication and polish in his social life. Heintzelman was a practical soldier, and acquitted himself well on the field of battle.

A big day in Lancaster's history was the dedication of the Soldiers and Sailors Monument on 4 July 1874. The monument marked the site in the center of the Square where courthouses had stood from 1737 to 1852, where the Continental Congress had met, and the Pennsylvania Legislature had assembled for a dozen years. Honoring the men of Lancaster County who had served in the armed forces, particularly but not solely in the War Between the States, the monument came into being through the exertions of the Patriot Daughters, Lancaster's "protofeminists." The photo shows the northeast corner of Centre Square in the background.

To obtain sufficient recruits for the Union Army many Lancaster County institutions and municipalities offered bounties to men who would enlist. This poster sought men to complete a company formed by Millersville State College students and faculty, then known as Millersville Normal School. An obelisk on the campus commemorates the valor of Principal John P. Wickersham and his scholar-soldiers.

87

In 1860 the city hall on Centre Square had its main entrance upon West King Street. Beneath Lodge No. 43 are the arches that supported the lodge hall and provided shelter for the farmers' market. To the rear of the city hall can be seen the market shambles which had been built in 1854. The city fathers planned to raze the city hall in 1876 because Georgian architecture was old-fashioned, but they lacked the funds to build a Victorian monstrosity. The building, now preserved and restored, is Lancaster's cultural gem.

42 and 44 W. King St.,
Lancaster, Pa.

Chief Harry N. Howell of the Union Fire Co. No. 1 was a stern commander. In the days before "walkie-talkies," the chief gave his orders through a speaking trumpet, an elegant metal version of today's cheerleader's megaphone. Chief Howell has one in his right hand.

The end of the war saw Republican strength in Lancaster increased, but not to the extraordinary degree found in the county. When Mayor Sanderson's term ended in 1869, he was replaced with William Augustus Atlee, a Republican, whose victory margin was twenty-three votes. Until 1900 the Democrats and Republicans regularly switched offices:

William A. Atlee, Republican, 1869-1871
Frederick Pyfer, Democrat, 1871-1873
William D. Stauffer, Republican, 1873-1877
John T. MacGonigle, Democrat, 1877-1884
David P. Rosenmiller, Republican, 1884-1886
William A. Morton, Democrat, 1886-1888
Edward Edgerley, Republican, 1888-1890
Robert Clark, Democrat, 1890-1894
Edwin S. Smeltz, Republican, 1894-1898
Simon Shissler, Democrat, 1898-1900

Nine wards were established, and the city charter was amended to provide one select councilman from each ward and two, three, or four common councilmen from each ward based upon population density, making a total of twenty-seven common councilmen.

On 1 April 1882, the city's volunteer fire departments, Union, Sun, Friendship, Washington, American, Humane, Shiffler, and Empire, were exempt from firefighting; and the professional, paid fire department commenced their duties, the second city in our state to make this modern improvement.

Constables kept the peace in Lancaster from the beginning, and by 1865 the police force consisted of ten uniformed constables and a special detail of twenty men called "night police." In 1867, when the charter was updated, a police department was established and staffed with seven officers for the nine wards. Councilmen played politics with the appointments, a sorry situation that lasted to 1925. In 1874 the first police station was built on Grant Street behind First Reformed Church, and the lock-up moved there from the basement of Old City Hall on the Square.

Strangers had difficulty in finding addresses, so an ordinance was adopted in 1871 that established a numbering system. The ordinance mentions "Centre or Penn Square," the first official use of the name recognized today.

As the centennial of American independence approached, the city councilmen came to the belief the old city hall on the Square, with its classic Georgian

Captain Thomas Thurlow, chief engineer of the Union Fire Co. No. 1, stands beside his steamer about 1870. Then, as now, fire apparatus received the most careful attention from the firemen, being kept polished and ready to run at a moment's notice. Captain Thurlow's trousers were gray, his shirt green, and the numeral "1" in gold. His belt was green and gold.

architecture, was hardly representative of the modern and bustling city. Bids were sought to demolish the structure, but the replacement costs were considered too great to carry out the plan to erect an elegant Victorian monstrosity to house the city government. Later, the Masonic lodge urged the city to cooperate with the lodge in removing both city hall and the equally handsome lodge hall, both to be replaced with a Victorian building. Again the city could not afford to tear down the historic and handsome buildings.

Lancastrians in 1876 were talking about the big affair in Philadelphia, the Centennial Exposition. School pupils were preparing artwork, penmanship, and other samples of their achievements for display. Local industries and farms were sorting over their best examples for exhibition at Philadelphia. Lancaster walked off with many prizes and ribbons.

By the end of the nineteenth century Lancaster was in full swing in its second generation of industrial development. The Penn Iron Works was rolling bar iron; half a dozen lock companies were busy producing many thousands of padlocks and other hardware; umbrella factories, including the famed Follmer and Clogg Co., largest umbrella factory in the world, seemed determined to protect the whole earth from raindrops; and carriage manufacturers rolled the buggies and wagons off the assembly lines in a steady parade of vehicles. Lancaster's breweries by now were called the Munich of the West, and the beer was shipped as far as Boston to satisfy discriminating tastes. The highly diversified industries turned out corks, combs, leather, furniture, watches, cigars, steam engines, cotton goods, and even microscopes. A center of the cigar industry, the city had factories and tobacco warehouses covering many acres and employing hundreds of women and children. Watches had been made in Lancaster in a factory predating the Hamilton Watch Company from the mid-1870s.

Labor unions kept pace with the development of industry. Among the trade unions were the ironworkers, weavers, brewers, cigarmakers, railroad employees, carpenters, printers and typesetters, foundry workers, and painters. A series of wage demands by the cigarmakers' union eventually caused the proprietors to move their operations from Lancaster, thus ending a major local industry.

Lancaster's letter carriers in the late 1890s were more mindful of the U.S. Postal Service slogan concerning rain, sleet, and snow when they reached newly opened streets with calf-high mud. Apparently the postmaster did not conduct dress inspections prior to the men going on their appointed rounds! The photo was taken on the steps of the Lancaster Post Office, now the City Hall.

Philip Lebzelter, a German immigrant, founded the Eagle Wheel and Bending Works in Lancaster in 1854. This plant became the largest establishment of its kind in Lancaster, and it included hardwood tree lands. When rubber tires were invented, Lebzelter became a Goodyear distributor, and today the firm, now owned by John Way, is the oldest Goodyear distributor in the nation. This photo of the Lebzelter employees was taken about 1892.

Like a sprawling red-brick Victorian sentry, St. Joseph's Hospital dominated Lancaster's western horizon during the 1880s, the community's first general hospital. During the mid-1950s a modern hospital plant was constructed along College Avenue starting at Walnut Street. Upon its completion, the old structures were demolished, and the space filled with more large buildings and the School of Nursing. Today St. Joseph's is the second-largest hospital in the county.

Catherine Long's residence at the southeast corner of North Duke and East Orange streets, about 1890. A few years later the house was demolished and replaced with the handsome stone mansion that now serves as the Hamilton Club. Mrs. Long was the widow of Judge Henry G. Long, prominent jurist and philanthropist.

The west-southwest corner of Centre Square in 1880 is bare of the trolley tracks that would come in 1890. The only track is that of the Lancaster and Millersville Street Railway, a horse-drawn service begun in 1875. Old City Hall is at the right.

As some Lancastrians prospered they built fine large homes along North Duke Street, and later along West Orange, West Chestnut, and West James streets. In the 1870s a North Duke Street address suggested opulence and gracious living with liveried servants easing the burden. From 1885 to 1900 the "right" address for wealthy Lancastrians was one of the west-end streets between Chestnut and James streets. St. Joseph's Hospital appeared on College Avenue in 1878, but was closed for some years owing to financial difficulties.

Flickering gaslights began to illuminate the houses of Lancaster on 21 February 1850 using rosin gas made by the Lancaster City Gas Company. In 1876 another gasworks was built by the Lancaster Gaslight and Fuel Company, and three years later the two companies merged. Organized in Lancaster in 1886, the Edison Electric Illuminating Company furnished the first

electrical power in the city. Smarting under the competition, the Lancaster Gaslight and Fuel Company bought the Edison company and combined operations. In 1900 control of the stock of the gas company passed to the Lancaster County Railway and Light Company which, in turn, was acquired in 1926 by the Lehigh Power Securities Corporation.

In the mid-1870s a horsecar line was constructed from the Pennsylvania Railroad station down Queen Street to the Square, then down West King Street to Prince Street, and west on Orange Street to Columbia Avenue. From this point it followed the Millersville Pike to Millersville. In the 1890s electric streetcar lines were built around the city streets and connected the city to the county boroughs. All trolley lines ended at the Square in Lancaster, then the hub of commerce in Lancaster County.

In this 1887 steel engraving of North Queen Street at the Pennsylvania Railroad Depot, F.W. Woolworth's 5 & 10¢ store can be seen at the right. Chestnut Street crosses North Queen Street just beyond the tracks. In the 1840s a railroad siding extended down West Chestnut Street. Careful observation will disclose a horsecar coming up North Queen Street towards the depot.

North Duke Street was the finest residential street in the 1870s but that didn't stop local drovers from driving their flocks of sheep down that street. This picture was made in 1893.

Behind the scenes in old downtown Lancaster, about 1885. This rear view of houses was taken along the second block of North Queen Street. The building at the right was one of Lancaster's many hotels.

Ten Hour House

Benjamin Mishler, a Lancaster businessman and huckster extraordinary, took a wager that he could build a house in ten hours. The colorful bitters manufacturer did precisely that, completing a house at 533 South Prince Street in 1873. Photos show progress of construction.

After winning a wager that he could build a house in twenty-four hours, Mishler accepted a bet that he couldn't build one in ten hours. The house shown in the photo at 533 South Prince Street won Mishler his wager, being completed in the required ten hours. Now a century old, the building is in excellent condition.

The second block of North Queen Street with the Orange Street intersection in the foreground, about 1888. The poles were laden with telephone wires.

Oyster saloons were numerous along the streets of old Lancaster. This ancient stone oyster house, located along Church Street near South Queen Street, was built prior to 1775 as a farmhouse. Fried oysters at six for ten cents have passed, but the building survived and has been restored.

A city ordinance required the power company to paint its poles white. The location of poles often was a serious political matter, and property owners occasionally extorted fat sums of money from the electric company for the privilege of planting poles. Street gas lamps gradually gave way to overhead arc lights.

As telephone service developed during the late 1880s, the streets of downtown Lancaster were darkened by hundreds of wires strung along clusters of cross-arms, each telephone having a wire. The Independent Telephone Company competed with the Bell Telephone Company in providing service. At one time the telephone exchange was on the top floor of Old City Hall, the wires to subscribers radiating out from an ugly boxlike tower sitting on the roof.

Lancaster's water supply continued to be the Conestoga River from which waterwheel-powered pumps sent raw water to the town's reservoirs located east of the prison between King and Orange streets. The ancient machinery, installed in 1837 when the original waterworks was constructed, no longer was capable of serving a city of thirty-five thousand persons, even when assisted with the steam pumps added in 1878. Lancaster was growing rapidly in the northeastern and northwestern portions, the most remote areas from the pumps and reservoirs. Late in 1888 a new pumping station was built along the Conestoga River near the railroad bridge at the Grofftown Road. Two large steam pumps operated with a daily capacity of eleven million gallons. These were placed on a reserve basis in 1929 when eight electrically driven and three gasoline-powered pumps were installed. This plant was removed in 1976, having been replaced by a small pumping station used to augment the city's water-treatment plant located along the Susquehanna River in Columbia. This was constructed in the 1950s. Lancaster's water was used untreated until 1907. A large reservoir built in Buchanan Park in the 1890s burst during its initial filling, flooding the west end. A small wading pool marks the site.

Of considerably greater interest to the water committees of the city councils than planning for replacement and expansion of the water facilities was how the water was to be used. After Jacob Demuth put a bathtub in his home in 1839, one of the first bathtubs in the Republic, the city was aghast when eight more

A northwest view of Lancaster about 1895 from the steeple of Trinity Lutheran Church. Central Market tower can be seen just left of center, and to its left the top of the Civil War monument in the Square and Old City Hall with the telephone-wire terminal box on its roof.

tubs appeared in city homes; and to make the well-washed citizens pay their proper share, each tub was assessed three dollars annually. Most physicians in Lancaster were not entirely convinced frequent bathing was healthy, but one doctor demonstrated the courage of his convictions by putting in his own tub in 1849. Dr. John Light Atlee, a leader in the healing arts, was the straw that broke the camel's back — the city charged him thirty dollars. Out came the tub and up went the protest. The city relented and lowered the annual charge for tubs to sixteen dollars.

Until the germ theory was understood in the 1880s, health care and sanitation were not critical matters to Lancastrians. Cholera deaths in 1832 and 1854 were attributed to fogs and misty clouds of putrifying organic matter decaying along the streams and canal. One Lancastrian, however, believed differently. Dr. John L. Atlee, owner of the bathtub and one of the nation's most distinguished physicians, thought some organic substance he could see in his microscope probably was the cause of cholera. Dr. Koch proved him correct about thirty years later.

The medical practitioners in nineteenth-century Lancaster were among the most innovative and skilled physicians in the nation; they created a pioneering tradition that continues to bring laurels to their professional descendants. The Pennsylvania Medical Society was organized in Lancaster by local physicians

In order to pipe water into Lancaster city, this water-pumping plant was built in 1837 along the Conestoga River downstream from East King Street. Originally the pumps were powered by waterwheels. Later, steam engines were added and a boiler house was built. The water was forced up to reservoirs along King Street at Franklin Street.

in 1848; the local society having been founded in 1844. When he was eighty-three years old, Dr. John L. Atlee was elected president of the American Medical Association. His brother, Washington L. Atlee, was a pioneer in surgery, having perfected the safe removal of ovarian tumors. When the Pennsylvania Medical Society refused to recognize women as physicians (it was not a proper task for the female!), the Lancaster group urged the state unit to change its policy.

Female physicians practiced in Lancaster without hostility from the local male chauvinists. Dr. Mary E. Wilson was practicing medicine as early as 1875. Other female physicians were Dr. Hannah Carter, Dr. Letitia Frantz, Dr. Adelaide Underwood, Dr. Marie Van Ness,

and Dr. Elizabeth Kendig, who opened her office in 1886 and was still treating patients at the age of eighty-eight! Osteopathic physicians numbered among their pioneering members in Lancaster Dr. Lillian Hartzler in 1896; at that time there were only two male osteopaths, Dr. Oscar Mutschler, the first such physician in the city (1894), and Dr. H.R. Kellogg. By 1907 Dr. Emma Purnell had joined her sister osteopathic physician in Lancaster.

Protestant churches formed new congregations as the city population grew. Lancaster's large Catholic population outgrew St. Mary's and St. Joseph's parishes, and in 1870 a new parish, St. Anthony of Padua, was established at Orange and Ann streets.

The new stone bridge, right, built in 1888 by the Pennsylvania Railroad frames the old Lancaster waterworks steam-pumping station along the Conestoga River. The wooden falsework still remains in place behind the new structure. Anticipating the addition of more tracks, the railroad company left the south side of the bridge unfinished so new stonework could be attached readily. The addition was not needed.

A Pennsylvania Railroad twelve-wheeler en route to Lancaster with two boxcars crosses the high stone bridge over the Conestoga River in 1895. The bridge, built in 1888, was left unfinished on its south side so that it could be widened to accommodate more tracks, if needed (they weren't). A short distance to the left was the Lancaster cut-off which handled trains stopping in the city.

The Pennsylvania Railroad solved a knotty problem in replacing its old wrought-iron truss bridge on the Main Line at the Conestoga River in 1888 by running the trains over wooden falsework during the construction of the high, stone-arch bridge that still carries the railroad's main east-west traffic. Hundreds of Lancastrians gathered to watch the "shifting over" operation.

Sacred Heart Academy for girls was located opposite the church. With the movement of the population into the northwest portion of Lancaster in the last quarter of the nineteenth century, a new parish, Sacred Heart, was formed at Walnut and Nevin streets in 1900. The last parish formed within the city was St. Anne, established on East Liberty Street in 1923.

From the earliest days until the late 1870s Lancaster's Jewish community was chiefly German. Temple Shaarai Shomayim was founded in 1855, and during the 1880s the congregation aligned itself with the Reform movement. In 1895 a new synagogue was built on the northwest corner of Duke and James streets, replacing the earlier building at Orange and Christian streets.

From the 1880s on, most Jews arriving in the city had come from Eastern Europe, mainly Poland and Russia. In 1887 they formed Congregation Chizuk Emunah, an Orthodox body. Some differences led to the founding of another Orthodox congregation, Hagudah Sholom, in 1892. In 1896 Degel Israel was formed, and in 1900 Chizuk Emunah merged into the Degel Israel congregation. The fourth Orthodox congregation, Kesher Torah, was formed in 1911. Hagudah Sholom merged into Degel Israel in 1920, and Kesher Torah joined in 1924, thus uniting the Orthodox congregations.

Between the Civil War and 1900 Lancaster's industry prospered in its diversity, but the business leaders were farsighted enough to realize new industries had to be brought in to replace those that would fall victim to technological progress. The first generation of industry had ended with the Civil War, and the second generation already was showing signs, albeit subtle, of decline, highlighted perhaps by the business depression of 1875. Business leaders met occasionally to discuss the future of Lancaster's economy. This concern led to the establishment of a board of trade in the 1870s. An early report of that body suggests the problems it faced:

Our city for many years has been the subject of ridicule by more earnest and progressive towns for our want of public spirit and energy in bringing around public improvements. Our want of sufficient and good hotel accommodations, our filthy streets, our poor public buildings for municipal purposes, our want of proper market accommodations, and in fact the want of public improvements of all kinds has been a great

Fountain Inn on South Queen Street was a famous hostelry in early Lancaster. It was replaced by the Lincoln Hotel in the late-nineteenth century. An organ-grinder completes the scene.

Graeff's Landing, now known as Engleside, was an important crossing of the Conestoga River. George Graeff built the stone tavern in 1784, and the structure is still used as a hotel. The covered bridge, one of the few "two-lane" bridges in this vicinity, provided advertising space for Rhoads Jewelry Store. Advertising revenues apparently went for county bridge maintenance. This photo, taken about 1896, shows the inn before it was "modernized."

disadvantage to our town. It is to the interest of every businessman to foster and encourage public improvements of all kinds. Good hotel accommodations attract strangers who, seeing our advantages as a manufacturing town, could be induced to locate here.

Lancastrians soberly studied that statement. Shortly afterward, in 1874, the Stevens House was built, and within a decade the Hotel Lancaster appeared next to the railroad station. Both had excellent accommodations for the traveler, but the Stevens House was a more elegant hostelry. Fulton Hall, already a venerable theater, in 1873 was remodeled extensively into a first-class opera house; its acoustical qualities and Victorian opulence made it a theater of widespread fame. Every actor, actress, and musical artist of note appeared on the stage of the Fulton during the nineteenth century. Before the 1870s had passed into history the Reading and Columbia Railroad extended a branch into Lancaster city. Another railway connected the city to Quarryville, with a station located in the Stevens House.

By the 1880s interest in the board of trade decreased, but downtown merchants retained a lively concern in the appearance of their shops. The early nineteenth-century storefronts, with windows of many panes, had begun to look dowdy, so new facades replete with every Victorian gimcrack known to the Gilded Age architects were built. The entire south side of the first block of East King Street went Victorian in 1883. Gaslights hissed and glowed where oil lamps so

As built in 1852 Fulton Hall was a large flat-floored meeting hall with a stage at one end. In 1873 the interior was changed greatly, making the structure a first-class small opera house, complete with sloping floor, balconies, boxes, and a large, well-equipped stage. The acoustics are most remarkable, being "tuned" especially for the human voice. During the conversion to the Fulton Opera House the exterior was mostly unchanged except for the addition of a large stage-house to accommodate the stage machinery. Although this photo is dated 1904, the appearance of the structure had not changed from 1873.

Emanuel Shober's Eagle Hotel, northwest corner of North Queen and West Orange streets, operated most of the nineteenth century. Later, Shober called the place the Columbian Hotel. It was razed in the early 1890s to make way for the YMCA building.

In the 1870s Lancaster's YMCA was established in the old Judge Charles Smith mansion at the northwest corner of West Mifflin and South Queen streets. The building to the right was the home of Paul Zantzinger, a prominent revolutionary war merchant, clothing manufacturer, and civic leader.

Lounging around the railroad depot was a favorite American pastime. This 1889 photo of the Pennsylvania Railroad Station at North Queen and East Chestnut streets portrays the dark and cavernous train shed coated with layers of soot. The object at the curb between the arc-light pole and the gaslight of the Globe Tavern is an old-fashioned fire hydrant.

East Chestnut Street looking west from Duke Street in 1885. The rear of the railroad station is at right, and the Hotel Lancaster is at far right.

The Orange Street Opera House, also known as Mozart's Opera House, was built at the end of the nineteenth century to provide some competition to the venerable Fulton Opera House. It is located at the southwest corner of East Orange and North Christian streets, and functions today as an office building. It was never successful as a theater.

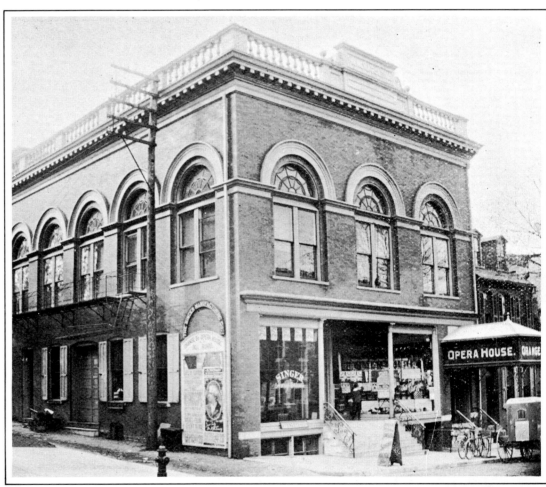

To the rear of Shober's Hotel, along West Orange Street, was Reitzel's Theatre. Market Street ran beside the dilapidated structure, to the left. Apparently the quality of the performances in the theatre was superior to the surroundings. This view was taken about 1890.

A famous old Lancaster inn, the Sign of the Benjamin Franklin, at 120-122 North Queen Street, as shown in this 1885 picture. The sidewalk billboard advertises The Hustler, *which would appear at the Fulton Opera House.*

The Relay House earned its name from the place where teams were changed on the railroad tracks before steam locomotives operated on the Columbia and Philadelphia Railroad. Located on the southeastern corner of Walnut and Prince streets, this old tavern catered to the drovers and mechanics. The tracks are behind the structure. The stone inn was razed in 1923.

recently had smoked and sent out dim illumination. Watt and Shand, two Scottish dry goods merchants, started their little store in 1878, probably little realizing that a century later their descendants would own the largest department store in Lancaster, growing with prosperity while others failed and closed their doors. Known as "The New York Store," Watt and Shand made a careful study of Lancastrians' needs and preferences in quality — and then set about to fulfill those needs. Leinbach and Company then opened "The Boston Store" on North Queen Street, suggesting New York may be brash and new, but Boston was the center of culture, learning, and traditional quality. Leinbach's store had a large, open court soaring up through five stories to skylights. Balconies enclosed the court like boxes in the opera house, while green shrubs, vines,

After the Swan Hotel was converted to stores, the south side of Centre Square took on a new appearance. In this 1872 photograph, the left corner property dispensed Benj. Mishler's celebrated herb bitters, which was good for all ailments. For those who needed a headier tonic, J.R. Watkins liquor store was right next door. The First National Store was a wholesale and retail dry-goods emporium. On the South Queen Street corner was the Inland Insurance & Deposit Co., which had a brief but checkered history, and above it the Anglo Arabia Horse-Powder Depot, purveyor of comfort for horses. The arrival of wine and liquor barrels may have attracted the crowd of men, but, in the quaint terms of mid-nineteenth-century writers, a "vast concourse of citizens" would always gather to have their pictures taken, as we see here. Watt and Shand store now is on this site.

The north side of West King Street at Market Street in 1880 shows Hager & Bro. dry-goods store at left (established 1821) and, on the east side of Market Street, Frank Ruth's grocery store. There was no excuse for Lancastrians to miss Logan and McCoy's lectures — unless the working literati preferred to read in the Mechanics' Library, east of Ruth's store. The Millersville horsecar track is in the street.

and ferns grew around the edges. On East King Street several large dry goods stores competed. Fahnestock's, later to be Garvin's; Williamson and Foster; and Hoar and McNabb attracted the folk that were suspicious of Boston and New York fashions. Hager and Brother continued to operate from the dingy little store begun in 1821, and would refuse to budge until the twentieth century. For those talented ladies that made their own stylish clothing there was Astrich's Palace of Fashion at 115 North Queen Street for the latest ribbons, bows, feathers, and hats.

The panic of 1893 made the businessmen jittery. The iron industry, based on anthracite pig iron and wrought-iron products, had become obsolete. The cotton mills were equipped with obsolete machinery, and the cigarmaking business was declining rapidly. On 6 November 1896 thirty of the most enterprising and progressive citizens of Lancaster met to establish a new board of trade. This organization became permanent and scored some definite gains. It set up goals and objectives to be met. Members were assigned specific tasks. The city government was involved, and businessmen took to the public rostrum to spread the gospel of economic well-being. Nine points — Lancaster's "acres of diamonds" — were stressed:

1. Lancaster is situated in a wealthy agricultural area where the cost of living is low and the standard of comfort is high.
2. Transportation facilities are unexcelled.
3. Closeness to coal fields for cheap fuel.
4. Lancaster's eleven banks and trust companies are as sound as the Rock of Gibraltar.
5. The water supply is pure, adequate, and inexpensive.
6. Lancaster has a first-class fire department and has been free of large, disastrous fires.
7. Many desirable factory sites available at low cost.
8. Availability of skilled and unskilled laborers, many of which own their own homes. Almost entire freedom from labor disputes.
9. Lancaster has an aggressive, progressive, and thoroughly interested Board of Trade.

It was added that "Lancaster presents a thousand attractions to the wage-earner, the student, the scholar, the man of leisure, and to that most practical of all philanthropists, the enterprising capitalist seeking safe investment. . . ." It cannot be said the new board of

This view of Centre Square, south side, about 1868, shows John Wise, Lancaster's famed pioneer aeronaut and inventor, preparing to go aloft in a balloon. An illuminating gas valve had been installed in the south side of the Square to furnish "lifting power." To a community unburdened by motion pictures, radio, television, and "riding the loop," balloon ascensions brought out spectators by the thousands. John Wise's studies and published reports on aerodynamics have brought forth from the U.S. Air Force Academy the suggestion that he was the father of scientific ballooning.

This commercial structure on the southeast corner of East King and South Duke streets was fairly typical of center city shops. Taken about 1890, this picture shows the steeple of Trinity Lutheran Church in the right background.

trade was guilty of hiding Lancaster's light under a bushel!

By the end of the nineteenth century the efforts of the board of trade had begun to bear fruit. Its officers welcomed new industries but, much to their credit, they discouraged enterprise of dubious quality. A good credit rating, a reputation for quality production, and a sound, conservative stability were the criteria by which the prospective businesses were judged. Lancastrians possessed the "work ethic," and incoming industries were expected to exhibit acceptable business ethics. The tradition of Lancaster was to be honored!

A pair of Lancaster businessmen took the local tradition for ingenuity, resourcefulness, and technical perfection a step beyond what the board of trade had in mind. During the 1890s a leaf-tobacco dealer and the owner of a cigar factory began making and using counterfeit revenue stamps. The perfection of the engraving and quality of paper, complete with the USIRS watermark, all executed in the finest tradition of Lancaster craftsmen, enabled the enterprising partners to fool completely the federal agents. Flushed with such success, they went into the production of paper money, applying the same skills in engraving and paper preparation. Again they were successful — until some clerk noticed the color of the seal was faded. The suspected bill was pronounced genuine by the Bureau of Engraving and Printing of the Treasury Department. The Secret Service was bothered, however, so the legendary detective William Burns was called in. Shortly after that it was found the "genuine" money was a Lancaster creation of Messrs. Kendig and Jacobs. To this day the federal government claims the Lancaster-made bills to be the most perfect counterfeits ever discovered! The state of the art had come a long way from Ann Toews's clumsy attempt to alter a shilling note!

§ § § § §

As the dawn of the new century approached, Lancaster was looking forward to increased and sustained prosperity. Conservative yet progressive, liberal yet cautious, wed to the profit motive yet wholly mindful of cultural necessities and humane considerations, Lancaster had reason to be optimistic and proud.

Poles and vast clusters of wires marked technological advancement in Lancaster, but the citizenry didn't think the newfangled contraptions did much for the scenery. Here a telephone pole frames Penn Square in December 1900. Christmas trees were sold in the Square.

King Street

The story of Lancaster visibly unfolds in pictures that demonstrate the significance of the camera as a historian's tool. In this series of ten photographs Dr. William B. Fahnestock and others confer immortality upon early King and Queen streets: the faces, the facades, the very footsteps frozen in time. Imagine the voices that echo the busy activities of Lancaster townspeople as they patronize Creswell's Restaurant, Frederick Cooper's Red Lion Hotel, and Samuel Williams's barber shop. Discriminating shoppers stroll down "department store row" amidst the hustle and bustle, while horse-drawn carriages clatter over uneven stones. Soon the stones, the carriages, the old familiar places are gone — to be replaced by the next step in the evolution of the city as it constantly renews itself.

Taken in 1845 by Dr. William B. Fahnestock, this view of West King Street looking eastward to Centre Square is the earliest photograph extant in Lancaster. It also is the only photograph that shows the old courthouse in the square. Dr. Fahnestock was a physician that had a scientific curiosity about both photography and psychiatry.

East King Street in 1858 was a sea of mud in wet weather and quite dusty at other times. Duke Street crosses in the middle of the photo. At the left side, above Duke Street, was a favorite stopping place for stagecoaches to county towns as well as to Philadelphia and other cities. Reigart's Old Wine Store is now the site of the Provident Book Store, Christian booksellers.

The north side of the first block of West King Street had two hotels. At the far left side was the Sorrel Horse, and in the middle of this 1860 photograph was Frederick Cooper's Red Lion Hotel. Along the curb may be seen a stone "mounting step" to help ladies climb aboard their carriages. Samuel Williams's barber shop was well advertised at the right side of the picture.

West King Street, looking into Centre Square in 1865, contained little traffic this day as local citizens gathered in the square to hear orations on the Union Cause. Wooden awnings covered most of the sidewalks, enabling shoppers to stay out of the rain, if not the mud. The inn sign at the left is on William Cooper's Red Lion Inn, later the St. George Hotel. Steinman Hardware Store occupied the three-and-one-half story building with two dormer windows at the right.

The northeast corner of Centre Square and East King Street as it appeared in 1870. One of the town pumps can be seen along the curb. The building on the corner housed a brush manufactory. The site is now part of the Fulton Bank.

Upper half of the first block of East King Street, south side, showing the newly remodeled Victorian storefronts in 1883. South Duke Street is in the background.

This panoramic view of Penn Square taken in 1905 shows West King Street at the far left. City Hall, Central Market, and Hirsh's Men's Store were in the northwestern corner. North Queen Street is in the center, and along its east side may be seen the towered Woolworth Building. From left to right in the northeastern corner were Zahm's Corner, Conestoga Traction Co. waiting room, Delmonico Cafe, Charles Grove's Liquor Store, Hendren's Cigar Store, and Dr. Richard McCaskey, dentist. The Western Union Telegraph Co. office occupied the corner under the dental office. Creswell's Restaurant and Gegg's Barber Shop were located in the basements along the east side of the Square. East King Street and the Watt & Shand Store are at the far right.

West King Street in 1888 was bumpy and dirty. The street was paved with blocks of stone that rose and fell with the spring thaws. Litter on the street and sidewalk suggests city dwellers were less tidy than country folk. Hager & Bro. dry-goods store occupied the same site since 1821.

East King Street in the early 1900s was "department store row." This view of the south side in 1905 shows the Victorian facades of 1883 that required the removal of wooden awnings over the sidewalks. Merchandise is still displayed along the walkway. At the far left, Benner's 3 and 9¢ Racket Store was one of many variety stores that competed with F.W. Woolworth's 5 and 10¢ Store. If a small object could not be bought at a racket store, it simply had not been invented.

East King Street in a snowstorm about 1900 was not jammed with snowbound automobiles. Periodically the trolley car snowplow would clear snow from the rails. Other than that cleaning, the streets remained packed with snow. Duke Street crosses in the foreground. The Courthouse is to the far right.

Chapter V

A New Sense of Interdependence

1900-1950

Fourth of July flags still flying, this 12 July 1926 photo of Penn Square shows life in center city. Along North Queen Street automobiles park diagonally. A traffic officer's box stands in the street near the Griest Building. An electric company line-repair truck is parked on the south side of the utility office building. East of the monument two motormen talk while an Amishman chats with the freightman waiting for the country trolley.

In 1900 Henry E. Muhlenberg, Republican, received about one hundred more votes than Simon Shissler for the office of mayor, thereby sending that gentleman back to his famous cigar store and marking the end of the Democrat-Republican alternation in the city's office of chief executive. William Walton Griest was in command of the Republican party, and his leadership — although he never served as chairman — forged the party into a well-organized institution for winning elections and maintaining low-cost government. After Shissler the next six mayors were Republicans:

1900-1902 Henry E. Muhlenberg
1902-1906 Chester W. Cummings
1906-1910 John Piersol McCaskey
1910-1915 Frank B. McClain
1915-1920 Harry L. Trout
1920-1922 Horace E. Kennedy

By 1900 Milton Thomas Garvin, owner of a department store, and a liberal civic leader, decided to wrest city control away from Mr. Griest. Garvin lined up formidable support from "all the nice people" living on College Hill, and along the upper-middle-class avenues. To reduce the threat to his organization, Griest ran the elderly, beloved educator John P. McCaskey, thus blunting the efforts of a reform ticket. McCaskey had small armies of "Jack's Boys" in influential positions in the city. To vote against McCaskey would be an act of sacrilege, and the voters once more stemmed the tide of the liberal reformers. By 1922 the reformers discovered they enjoyed several advantages. Business concerns that had established operations in Lancaster, such as the Armstrong Cork Company, were distressed by the reactionary philosophy of Mr. Griest's organization; some of these business leaders were influential in city life, and most of them were genuine card-carrying Republicans. City merchants were upset by the appearance of the center city, with its bumpy streets, antiquated lighting, and miles of telephone and electric wires festooning the streets. North Queen Street was compared to a shipping pier, with masts and rigging blotting out the daylight. Others were unhappy with the quality of the police department, and the Law and Order Society fretted over the rampant vice and prostitution. There were even rumors that hidden factions of the GOP were running their mayoralty candidate with less than appropriate enthusiasm. The outcome was a victory for the Coalition, a mixture of Democrats, reform Republicans, and persons that sympathized with the Coalition's standard-bearer who had lost an arm in his youth when struck by a broken cable on Mr. Griest's streetcar system.

Frank C. Musser became Lancaster's reform mayor in 1922. By the end of the decade the fatal flaw had afflicted the reform administration — they were human, after all, and in 1930 T. Warren Metzger was elected mayor on the Republican ticket. The victory of the New Deal carried James Ross, Democrat, into the office in 1934, only to be ousted by Dr. Dale E. Cary in 1938. The Republican organization by now was headed by Guy Graybill Diehm, and was extraordinarily successful. Dr. Cary retired in 1950 after a long, honest, and industrious administration during the war years.

In 1926 the city adopted the commission form of government. The councils were replaced by four commissioners elected as councilmen. Each commissioner plus the mayor comprised a board of operating department heads. It was a decided improvement over the cumbersome councils, but in time it proved difficult to assign responsibility owing to the dual nature of the respective commissioners' duties.

Lancaster has a reputation of being a city of churches. There are times when that sobriquet can be misleading. In 1913, for example, Dr. Clifford Twombley, rector of St. James's, discovered much to his horror that there were more than forty houses of prostitution within a few blocks of the Square, and that these enterprises were patronized by hundreds of men

President Theodore Roosevelt visited Lancaster briefly in 1912 where he greeted Lancastrians from the platform of his observation car. This picture was taken at the east end of the Pennsylvania Railroad station, along East Chestnut Street. Hotel Lancaster is to the left; it was razed in 1941, a decade after the station and tracks were removed. (Courtesy John J. Bowman, Jr.)

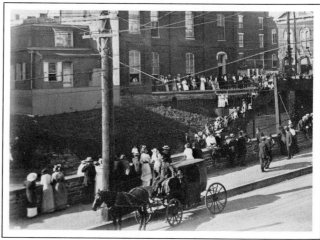

Early on 5 July 1915 Lancastrians gathered at the Duke Street bridge over the Pennsylvania Railroad tracks to be first to see the car bearing the Liberty Bell to the Midwest. The train paused in the "cut" to the left of the picture so that thousands of citizens could see the famous bell.

Theodore Roosevelt came to the Imperial Hotel in 1909 to help Lancastrians celebrate the 100th anniversary of Abraham Lincoln's birth. Lincoln spoke from this same balcony on Washington's birthday in 1861. The Imperial Hotel, later replaced by the Brunswick Hotel (original and its present-day successor), was the site of hotels from the earliest days. The Pennsylvania Railroad station was opposite the hotel on East Chestnut Street.

Lancaster's Iroquois Band takes time out to pose in front of the old Foltz Building on East Chestnut Street, about 1916. This band was one of Lancaster's best, in an era when parades and outdoor ceremonies demanded the most of skilled musicians.

Few persons have left their marks as indelibly on the Lancaster heritage as did G. Graybill Diehm who never lost his "Dutch" touch and dialect as he rose to the peak of Republican power and influence in state politics. A man of few words — most of them epigrammatic — Diehm was legendary in his tightfisted and scrupulously honest handling of taxpayers' money. Despite his *extreme frugality with public funds, Diehm personally was generous. He served as chairman of the Republican Party in Lancaster County for more than three decades, was a state senator, headed the Board of County Commissioners from the mid-1930s to 1960, and was the elder statesman of the Pennsylvania GOP. (Photo from author's collection)*

The Lancaster emblem did not come into existence until 1907 when it was discovered Lancaster had no flag to send to the Jamestown Exposition that year. The design was suggested by F.R. Diffenderffer, Benjamin C. Atlee, and S.M. Sener. Fred Mentzer drew the sketch embodying the suggestions. Thus Lancaster City's flag was born.

and boys weekly. One establishment was near the Boys' High School; it was suspected the location was not accidental. Lewd dances were commonplace, and vulgar shows were presented to mobs of howling men and boys at some of the town's theaters. Gambling was prevalent; youngsters were seen intoxicated; and the midway of the county fair was crammed with devices calculated to create lust and wonder, and to relieve naive persons of their cash. A Law and Order Society was started, and within a year or two Lancaster was nearly as clean as a "hound's tooth." Dr. Twombley bullied the district attorney and the police into closing up the worst places. It is not a facetious statement to say Dr. Twombley's quixotic adventures quite effectively put Lancaster in the advance guard of well-behaved cities, his influence being hard at work more than sixty years later. The Law and Order Society closed its books in 1973, satisfied that it had accomplished its objectives.

The liberal influence that M.T. Garvin sensed is an ancient Lancaster tradition, another of those confounding contradictions that abound in Lancaster County. In the 1870s professors of Franklin and Marshall College, Millersville State Normal School, and the Theological Seminary of the Reformed Church, along with enlightened townsmen and women, provided the humane coloration to the Lancaster tradition. With its pluralistic origins Lancaster never possessed the nearly monolithic culture of other Pennsylvania cities in which one group, class, or religious influence dominates. The reform impulse, as such, is foreign to the Lancaster heritage. It is, however, the other aspect of Lancastrians.

Lancaster's last execution occurred 23 May 1912 when Antonio Romezzo paid the penalty for murdering a fellow railroad laborer. Mr. Romezzo, who stoutly protested his innocence during the last rites, was hanged twice, the aged rope breaking on the first try. (With customary frugality the county chose not to buy a new rope for the last execution.) Romezzo is the young man standing sideways at the frame. Others are the soon-to-be-embarrassed sheriff, priest, warden, constables, and the physician. Some saw the mishap as divine intervention.

The Lancaster Agricultural Fairgrounds were along the old Harrisburg Pike, now the site of the Donnelly Printing Plant. Fairs were held annually from the early twentieth century until the early 1930s. The managers of the fair insisted on no gambling and clean, nonalcoholic entertainment, and the prospective attendees stayed home in droves, bringing an end to the fair.

Parades and speeches always brought crowds of people to the courthouse steps, downtown Lancaster's largest "bleachers." Flags and bunting were hung over the streets on all occasions. In this early twentieth-century picture the citizenry enjoys a good speech — usually an oration of not less than one and a half hours' duration!

127

Armstrong Cork Company's Closure Plant on New Holland Avenue in 1948. The central buildings adjacent to the stack were erected 1881-1882 by G.W. Dodge & Son, successor to the Lancaster Cork Co., Ltd. After some business reorganizations the firm was incorporated in 1893 as the Lancaster Cork Works by B.G. Dodge. Two years later the works were acquired by the Armstrong Cork Company for the manufacture of corks. Other local cork works were merged into the Armstrong operation. This plant was sold to the Kerr Glass Company in the late 1960s. (Courtesy Armstrong Cork Co.)

Armstrong Cork Company built the huge linoleum plant in Lancaster in 1905-07, providing employment for many Lancastrians, and exposing the community to a different culture. With the establishment of the Armstrong Cork Company corporate headquarters here in 1929, many well-educated, enlightened, and successful executives and their families became an active part of the community's social, civic, fraternal, and religious life. New experiences brought to Lancaster were shared with the native residents, and in time Lancastrians, old and new, profited immeasurably by the cultural exchange. Armstrong Cork Company's policy of encouraging participation by its employees in the civic life of communities facilitated acceptance of new ideas and outside influences as Lancaster came to respect, and then welcome,

Local businessmen were an imaginative lot around the turn of the century. When Joseph Schmitz wanted to call attention to his bedding emporium at 221-223 West King Street, he sent this little cart drawn by a mismatched pair of burros around the city. The signs were topped off with a fluffy mattress. Lancaster's own Herr Manufacturing Company is a major producer of fine mattresses today.

The diversity of Lancaster's business community is well illustrated by the producers of lesser-known items, such as soap. Charles Miller's soap works on South Prince Street at Seymour Street kept Lancaster very clean. In this 1905 view a load of Miller's naphtha soap is being shipped elsewhere by rail.

corporations that wanted to shoulder responsibilities rather than siphon off the city's assets.

At the turn of the century Lancaster experienced a sudden upsurge in the establishment of numerous small industries, partly as a result of boom conditions following the Spanish-American War of 1898. The city had nearly one hundred large tobacco warehouses and another fifty tobacco-packing houses, along with dozens of cigar factories. Despite the exodus of cigar factories from the county in the 1890s, there still were over one thousand cigar factories in Lancaster County in 1900. Some were quite small factories; others employed hundreds of workers.

Printing and publishing had developed into a major industry, a heritage from Lancaster's pre-revolutionary days. The New Era Press handled many book- and

The watch industry began in
Lancaster in 1874 with the Adams
and Perry firm. After five
bankruptcies the Hamilton Watch
Company emerged in 1892.
Becoming the renowned "watch of
railroad accuracy," the Hamilton
Watch Company has pioneered
many technological developments,
including the electronic watch. The
Hamilton plant is now owned by
HMW Industries, and its divisions
manufacture precision
instruments, military fuses, and
rolled metals. What had been the
watch-manufacturing subsidiary is
now owned by a Philadelphia
jewelry firm. This 1904 photo
shows the machine shop of the
Hamilton company.

periodical-publishing contracts. Now known as the Lancaster Press, the company shares with many competitors in the county a huge amount of high-quality printing, publishing, and binding work, much of which is done under contract from the nation's leading publishing houses.

Descendants of those hearty saddlers and shoemakers of 1777 were busily producing leather goods in 1900, much of it as belting for industrial machinery. By 1900 Lancaster's Union Stockyards were handling approximately sixty thousand head of cattle annually in facilities said to be the largest east of Chicago. This business received its impetus during the Civil War when Lancaster was called upon to supply thousands of tons of beef for the Union forces.

Rising out of a series of bankrupt firms dating back to 1875, Hamilton Watch Company soon earned the slogan, "the watch of railroad accuracy," with the dawn of the present century. The plant covered the two entire blocks bounded by Columbia, Race, Wheatland, and North West End avenues. Hamilton Park, a residential development south of the plant, became home to many watchmaking employees.

Other businesses that were built in the city near the turn of the century included an elevator works; a large plant for manufacture of brickmaking machinery patented by Lancastrian Henry Martin; the Follmer and Clogg Umbrella Company, which kept the nation drier than the Eighteenth Amendment; the Stehli Silk Mill, the longest in the world; and numerous steel-product and hardware factories. The candy industry was very

Ruins of the Reilly Bros. & Raub hardware store after a major fire on 10 February 1910. The first block of North Queen Street was filled with fallen wires and debris. A Hayes ladder truck, coated with ice, pours water down on the ruins.

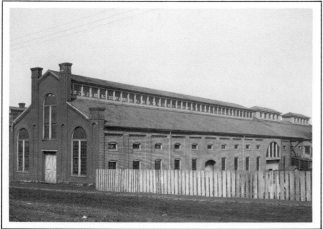

The inventive genius of Lancaster's mechanics is typified by Henry Martin who developed brickmaking machinery to replace the tedious old method of handmade bricks. Martin's machine factory, located north of Frederick Street on Charlotte Street, is shown in this 1905 view.

Formerly the home of the Washington Volunteer Fire Co., this city firehouse on North Queen Street served the industrial north end. Equipment in 1910 included a steam pumper and a chemical wagon. The firehouse disappeared in the early 1960s.

The massive plants of Follmer, Clogg and Co. umbrella works made Lancaster the umbrella capital of the world. The main plant at West King and Mulberry streets employed many Lancastrians in the making and assembly of the large, black-silk, family-size "bumbershoots." This factory is now a Van Sciver Furniture Store.

large in Lancaster, with Hershey Chocolate Company and its successor American Caramel Company (1899), Lancaster Candy Company (1901), R.F. Keppel & Bro. (1902), Elias Candy Company (1908), and R.E. Rodda Candy Company (1908) churning out the sweet stuff for children and lovers. In 1902 the Kunzler Meat Packing Company started operations, an outgrowth of the many slaughterhouses on Cabbage Hill, which in turn resulted from the cattle yards that used as feed the spent mash of local breweries.

Lancaster's iron heritage in earlier years spanned the entire process from production of pig iron to secondary manufacture of cast- and wrought-iron items. The blast furnaces of Lancaster County now lay cold and silent, having been supplanted by the modern furnaces attached to the vast steel mills then being built far from Lancaster. Iron and steel products continued to be made in many plants such as Lancaster Iron Works (1910); New Process Steel Company, a wire-drawing and treating works; Bearings Company of America (1910); Lancaster Steel Products Company; and Carbon Steel Castings Company.

A survey of 1909 showed that Lancaster ranked fourth in Pennsylvania for manufacturing — behind Philadelphia, Pittsburgh, and Reading. The city had three hundred establishments employing ten thousand workers.

A concerted effort to attract new industry to Lancaster was launched by the Lancaster Improvement Company, a group of businessmen affiliated with the Board of Trade. Industrial sites were made available to new businesses at reasonable terms.

If Lancastrians were disposed to celebration of the new century in a nightclub atmosphere, they could have achieved that feat in the new roof garden of the Woolworth Building, the city's tallest commercial structure in 1900. Built by Frank Woolworth to honor the city in which his first successful five-and-ten store was established in 1879, the first level contained a large sales floor of the five-and-ten store chain, while the six upper floors were offices. Later a rear addition was built, and the roof garden with its twin ornate golden towers was converted to office space. This building was razed in 1948 and replaced with a standard Woolworth store of fairly nondescript design.

132

The Rossmere mill of the Stehli Silk Corporation was the largest in the nation and the second largest in the world. The huge plant, shown in this 1931 aerial photograph, is now used as a warehouse. More than two thousand workers produced miles of broad silks and dress goods in this mill. Silk growing dates back to 1839 in Lancaster County.

Generations of Lancastrians gratified their "sweet tooth" at G.W. Gibbs Confectionery at 339 West Orange Street. Gibbs' ice cream was said to be the best in Lancaster. This picture made in the 1910 era caught part of the George Gibbs' family.

North Queen Street during a gala celebration and parade during the early 1900s. Two of Lancaster's "finest" guard the northeastern corner of Centre Square, now beginning to be called Penn Square. The Woolworth Building looms above the policemen and to the rear of the clock.

Some adventurous photographer braved the dizzy heights of Trinity Lutheran Church steeple in November 1919 to take this view towards the northwestern part of Lancaster. The courthouse is right of center with North Duke Street running to the upper right. The major building to the right, with the towers, is the Woolworth Building designed by C. Emlen Urban in 1899. To its right is the new reinforced-concrete building of the Lancaster Examiner which would be demolished in 1928.

Woolworth's success in Lancaster attracted competition, among them McCrory's 5 and 10¢ store. This 1920 vintage show window made the mouths of Lancaster shoppers water. Every square inch of display space was used in old-time window dressing.

A Sunday afternoon in the lives of many Lancastrians was a "voyage" down the Conestoga River aboard the Lady Gay or one of the other steamers in the Lancaster "navy." Named for the civil engineer that built the Conestoga Navigation Canal, Edward Gay, the boat was a favorite attraction at the amusement parks along the river between East King Street and South Prince Street. Photo about 1905.

Lancaster businessmen enjoyed a day away from the store or office occasionally. Their organization was called the Pirates, and excursions were known as "cruises." One early event was this 1902 outing called The Shad Choir Club. The sober-faced gentlemen are on Henry S. Williamson's porch steps at Upland Lawn. The host is the second man from the right, last row. The two characters in "drag" are Scott Leinbach, merchant, and T. Wilson Dubbs, jeweller.

Culturally, Lancaster was furnished with a public library in 1909, housed in the old mansion of former congressman A. Herr Smith. The invention of the phonograph was celebrated in center-city music stores with a nearly constant pandemonium of Caruso, Tin Pan Alley compositions, and *Amazing Grace.* With literary hyperbole rarely surpassed, Kirk Johnson & Co. advertised:

If music hath charms to soothe the savage breast, the establishment of Kirk Johnson & Co. harbors enough of it to tame every aboriginal from here to Timbuctoo. It is preeminently the music emporium of the Conestoga Valley. If you hunger to let loose your soul by elbowing over the cat gut, there are violins of every timbre and tone of sweetness.

Rocky Springs Park along the Conestoga River was one of three large amusement resorts to which Lancastrians flocked during the summer months. A roller-coaster thrill ride may be seen at the left.

The first automobile built in Lancaster was this handcrafted horseless carriage made at the Safety Buggy Works about 1903. The "assembly line" is in the blacksmith shop of the buggy factory then located near Rossmere. Later the Rowe Company built trucks in a factory on Fountain Avenue. Others built cars and trucks in small numbers from time to time without enduring success.

Later, when radio broadcasting was begun in the city, the music store opened a studio on its top floor and beamed to Lancastrians the programs of WKJC. The other pioneer radio station was WGAL, now bearing call letters WDDL.

Summer days and Sunday afternoons were spent at Conestoga Park, operated by the Conestoga Traction Company and served by its trolleys; Captain John People's Resort on the opposite side of the Conestoga River; Rocky Springs Park just southeast of the city along the Conestoga River; or Maple Grove Park west of the city. Hikers could stroll in Gable's Woods or climb the rocks near Rock Ford. More adventurous souls could cruise up and down the Conestoga on one of the three steamboats of the Lancaster navy, the most famous being the *Lady Gay*, named to honor Mrs.

Edward Gay, the wife of the canal engineer.

The twentieth century ushered in the automobile age. Milton S. Hershey announced his candy factory would have the first motorcar in town in 1900; it was a Riker Electric Vehicle. By 1904 Samuel K. Landis was selling and repairing autos in a garage at 126 East Orange Street. He sold Reo, EMF 30, Premier, and Haynes motorcars. Three years later S.G. Roth established the National Auto Company, Inc., at Duke and Vine streets, which later was the home of the Conestoga Truck Co. Lancaster had hopes of becoming the Detroit of the East when Samuel Rowe built his motor-vehicle factory in this city in 1918, just in time to land — and lose — a contract for building army trucks. The plant went into receivership in 1925, and one of the surviving buildings is now part of the DeWalt

Lancaster's curb market was an old institution that existed along the downtown streets until 1 January 1927 when they were abolished by law. In this 1926 scene along South Duke Street just south of East King Street several Amish women tend a stand along with their more worldly neighbors. The demise of the curb market promoted greater activity in the market houses — and created roadside stands outside the city.

A 1900-era character in downtown Lancaster was banjo-playing Jake Parks. He died in 1928, aged 92. His living was earned gathering old newspapers and rags.

Hiram Kroom was a colorful character in the early 1900s. A Scot who loved to sing in St. James's choir, Kroom was a scissors grinder by trade. His voice was the best in town, it was said.

Chief Strong Wolf came to Lancaster 13 September 1924 to help the Lancaster County Historical Society dedicate a marker at the site of the Conestoga Indian town. Few indians visited Lancaster after the massacre of the Conestogas in 1763.

"Blind Johnny" Shindle played his accordion at the northwest corner of the square for pennies dropped in a tin cup. He was a fixture there for many years at the beginning of the twentieth century.

Lancaster's vitrified brick streets were quite an improvement over oiled, packed earth or stones, but the age of the motorcar soon made that advance obsolete. In this April 1921 view is seen the southwest corner of North Queen and West Orange streets, with the traffic officer tending the semaphore. Most of the buildings in this picture are still standing. The bricks, wires, and semaphore are gone.

Cassius Emlen Urban was Lancaster's first native architect, earlier architects being commissioned from Philadelphia or located here for terms of their commissions. Urban began designing churches, hotels, commercial structures, and homes in the 1890s, and continued practicing his profession until retirement and death in the early 1930s. Among his larger structures are the Griest Building, Reformed Theological Seminary, and buildings at Hershey. He was a classicist in his art; he disdained engineering detail work, which often was left to the building contractors.

When Frank Woolworth opened a five-and-ten-cent store at this location in Lancaster in 1879, it became a success and started Woolworth on his road to millions. The first successful Woolworth store was located on the southwestern corner of North Queen and West Chestnut streets.

Division of Black and Decker Co. Industries supplying the auto trade sprang up in Lancaster, chief among them the K-D Manufacturing Co.

In 1902 the Lancaster General Hospital moved to a new structure on North Lime Street after operating nine years in an old building on North Queen Street. Lancaster Osteopathic Hospital broke ground for its building a fortnight before the stock-market crash in 1929; the steel skeleton and foundation stood unfinished until 1941. Educational buildings constructed early in the twentieth century included Stevens High School for Girls in 1904, and Boys' High School in 1916. Both were converted to elementary schools in 1938 upon the completion of the ultramodern coeducational J.P. McCaskey High School, a stunning monument to the architectural genius of Henry Y. Shaub.

Cassius Emlen Urban, Lancaster's most distinguished architect from 1900 to 1932, was busy designing new structures for modern Lancaster. Among the buildings were the Hotel Brunswick (1914, 1922), Griest Building (1924), Grace Lutheran Church (1895), Unitarian Church (1908), Woolworth Building (1898), Watt and Shand Store, and the Stevens House Annex.

The financial strength of the community was expressed in optimism as local banks were organized or expanded. The Fulton National Bank, founded in 1882, built a large new structure in 1928 on the northeastern corner of Penn Square, as old Centre Square had become known. Northern National Bank put up a

A view of Penn Square taken from the top of the Griest Building in August 1926. The south side of the square is at the top. Double trolley tracks in north half of square served passengers from the north, east, and west portions of the city and county. Passengers mingled with motorcars, trucks, and trolley cars in the square with amazingly few tragic encounters.

Traffic moved both ways in 1928 on South Queen Street, and even then the "tin lizzie" had not displaced entirely the faithful old horse. Built in the 1890s to dispense Sprenger beer, the Lincoln Hotel featured huge terra cotta capitals and heads of Neptune on its facade. The hotel was dry, naturally, during Prohibition, when this picture was taken.

The busy commercial hub of Lancaster County appears in this 1929 picture of Penn Square. The new Griest Building (1923) at the left and the just-completed Fulton Bank building in the center (1929) were designed by Lancaster architect Cassius Emlen Urban, who also did the Woolworth Building (1890) to the rear of the bank, farther north on Queen Street. In the distance may be seen another Urban structure, the first Hotel Brunswick (1914).

*Lancaster's oldest bank, the
Farmers National Bank,
established 1810, has been a
fixture on the southwest corner of
King and Duke streets. This photo
made in 1922 shows the Victorian
facade before the front was rebuilt
into its present Georgian style in
1928. Now the Trust Department
of the National Central Bank, the
old bank was merged into the
Lancaster County National Bank.*

classical-style banking house on North Queen Street in the 1920s. Peoples National Bank on East King Street, organized 1887, replaced its Victorian house with an Art Deco structure in 1927. The venerable Farmers Bank demolished the front portion of its banking house at East King and South Duke streets in 1928, and constructed a handsome late-Georgian-style building that now serves as National Central Bank's Trust Department. Lancaster Trust Company, established in 1889, rebuilt its house on North Queen Street in 1911. The Union Trust Company was organized in 1902 at 26 East King Street. In 1912 the Guaranty Trust Company started doing business in the rear of the courthouse on North Duke Street, and in 1919 the Agricultural Trust and Savings Company was chartered, a successor of the old Agricultural Trust Company at 45 North Duke Street. Alas, the financial conditions of the early 1930s saw the closing of many of the newer banks. Following the "bank holiday" and reorganization, Lancaster was left the Farmers Bank and Trust Company, Lancaster County National Bank, Fulton National Bank, Conestoga National Bank, and the Northern Bank and Trust Company.

Church congregations in Lancaster tended to settle somewhat in the early 1900s, with the most visible changes occurring among the denominations not previously represented. As the Greek community grew around 1900-1905, its members sought means to worship in their tradition. Services were held in the Eastern Orthodox mode at various meeting halls, and in 1921 the group purchased the old building of St. Paul's Methodist Church on South Queen Street. The

After the removal of the Pennsylvania Railroad station from downtown Lancaster in 1930, the city took up the floor of the Duke Street bridge and filled in the former railroad cut. The task required bracing up the heavily used Duke Street trolley tracks. In the background is the old fire headquarters and the miniature garden maintained by the firemen.

community expanded rapidly over the years, contributing heavily to the business and professional life of Lancaster. In the 1960s the Hellenic Orthodox Church erected a large new building on Hershey Avenue.

The Conservative movement in the Jewish tradition organized Temple Beth El in 1945, and began worshiping in its synagogue at the northeast corner of Lime and Grant streets.

Lancaster's Italian community started slowly in the 1880s, and became quite large and active in the early 1900s. Like the Greek community, they have taken an active and most worthwhile role in adding to the fabric of Lancaster's heritage.

Liberal religious thinking in Lancaster combined forces to establish the Unitarian Church in 1902. By 1908 the congregation had built a beautiful church at the southwest corner of Chestnut and Pine streets. Its impact on the intellectual life of Lancaster has been great.

Lancaster's congregation of First Church of Christ, Scientist, traces its beginnings to the early 1900s. They built a handsome church in traditional Georgian style in the 1950s at Columbia and President avenues.

World War I created ideological problems in many Lancaster families in which several generations of German immigrants lived. Few had much regard for Kaiser Wilhelm II, but their hearts sank at mention of the "Krauts" and the "bloodthirsty Huns." Emotions brought about the renaming of German Street to Farnum Street, and Freiburg Street to Pershing Avenue. Liberty bonds were sold in Penn Square (old Centre Square) in a small version of the old courthouse that was in the Square. Lancaster industries produced for the war effort, Lancastrians observed meatless Mondays and heatless Tuesdays, and the city's matrons rolled bandages for the Red Cross. Lancaster's young men and women enlisted in the armed forces or waited for their draft notices from President Wilson. A total of 5,238 men and women served in the armed forces from Lancaster County, of which 100 were members of the black community, and 47 were women commissioned as nurses. Of those who died in the service of their nation, 201 were army men, 11 were navy personnel, 14 were Marines, and 2 were nurses: U.S. Navy nurse Amy Treichler and U.S. Army nurse Anna E. Kemper. When the armistice was announced, Lancaster's factory

Washington's Adjutant General was Lancaster's General Edward Hand. Pershing's Adjutant General in World War I was Lancaster's General Robert Courtney Davis. He was born in Lancaster in 1876, the son of Thomas J. Davis, Esq. A graduate of West Point, Davis distinguished himself in the Spanish-American War and World War I. He was awarded the Distinguished Service Medal, and numerous honors by the British, French, and Belgian governments. He died 2 September 1944.

Men of the Company A, 109th Machine Gun Battalion of the 28th Division were given a hero's welcome home on 5 May 1919 after valiant service in France during World War I. The company was commanded by Lancaster's Captain W.C. Rehm, later to become a major. West Orange Street is the scene of this parade.

Lancaster's worst train wreck occurred 17 November 1919, where the Lancaster station tracks left the main line southeast of New Holland Avenue. A freight train engineer and fireman lost their lives when the freight disobeyed a signal and converged into an express passenger train. Six boxcar loads of meat destined for war-ravaged nations were scattered widely, earning the tragedy the name "kidney wreck."

Lt. Gen. Daniel Bursk Strickler is Lancaster County's highest-ranking military officer. The much-decorated and honored officer was the youngest combat officer in World War I; and during World War II, in the Battle of the Bulge, he was able to hold off the enemy for days and eventually extricated his troops from their perilous position. From 1947 to 1950 he served as lieutenant governor of Pennsylvania. A native of Columbia, General Strickler is a practicing attorney in Lancaster.

whistles blew continuously for hours and the population went wild.

During the Roaring Twenties Lancaster's breweries were hit hard. Beer could not be brewed legally. Outside mobs moved into the city and operated one of the breweries and a number of stills. The Rieker Brewery transported its unlawful product through a hose line strung through the West King and North Water streets' sewers. Police raids were infrequent and disobedience was rampant. Finally the corruption and disregard for the law moved the city to take action. A police lieutenant was murdered by an outside mob for refusing to cooperate. Colonel Daniel Bursk Strickler, a much-decorated officer of World War I, and a Lancaster attorney, was persuaded to assume temporary

command of the police department. In less than a year Commissioner Strickler was able to return to his private life and profession after cleansing thoroughly the police system. To the great credit of the city police, Colonel Strickler's work has remained an object of integrity that is followed faithfully.

The depression of the early 1930s affected almost every Lancastrian in some manner. Banks closed, savings were lost, jobs disappeared; but, on the whole, the city was better off than most communities in the nation. Local industries found ways to function, and the stronger banks remained solvent and useful. Churches and private charities helped unemployed persons over personal crises. Although local citizens cooperated with the regulations handed down by the New Deal

administration, Republicanism in Lancaster County survived quite well. Henning W. Prentis, Jr., president of Armstrong Cork Company, was one of the most influential spokesmen for the National Association of Manufacturers in attacking the New Deal, which he saw as destroying the freedoms of Americans.

When the guns started blazing in 1939, Americans were divided on the issue of remaining neutral or taking sides in the war then beginning in Europe. Lancastrians discussed the matter earnestly, but when Pearl Harbor was attacked they hastened to the armed forces recruiting offices to enlist. Local industries swung into war production, with Armstrong Cork Company making shells, airplane fuselages, bomb racks, camouflage netting, and other articles of warfare.

German prisoners of war found Lancaster a congenial place to work despite the ever-present guards. Those men captured in southern Germany found the Pennsylvania German dialect fairly easy to understand. Here POWs are at work in a Lancaster tobacco warehouse. (Lancaster New Era photo)

During World War II Lancaster's McCaskey High School students served in Victory programs. While young men learned the rudiments of military drill, girls tended young children of women war-plant workers or sold war bonds and stamps, as these McCaskey coeds are doing in 1942.

Hamilton Watch Company turned its heritage of precision timepiece production to making marine chronometers, air-force watches, and map-measuring tools. The U.S. Navy established a plant operated by RCA to make electronic devices, and this plant, now owned by RCA, continues to be one of Lancaster's major industries. A modernistic glass-and-wood structure was built in Penn Square to sell war bonds and stamps. J.P. McCaskey High School created a Victory Corps program in which most of the students participated, doing their part to win the war. Air-raid tests, civil-defense wardens, and victory gardens became the order of the day. Earl F. Rebman, a local merchant and candy manufacturer, was put in charge of gathering salvageable materials for the war effort, and he was so successful that other communities across the nation were urged to imitate Lancaster. Thousands of local citizens unable to serve in the armed forces served on numerous government boards, helping with rationing, housing, and civil defense. Lancaster's volunteerism tradition had its finest hour.

In 1942 Lancaster celebrated its two-hundredth anniversary, but the clouds of war hung heavy, and there was little festivity. The citizenry did take enough time out to help the Lancaster County Historical Society place a plaque in city hall, by now occupying the old federal building on North Duke Street.

By the time the war ended, Daniel Bursk Strickler had many more decorations and soon would be wearing three stars, the highest-ranking officer in Lancaster. An immense victory parade was held 14 June 1946, giving Lancastrians a festive time to express their gratitude.

Leading the parade were General Strickler, Commodore William Behrens, Colonel Harold Hogg, Lt. Col. William Blank, Lt. Col. Harry E. Balmer, Lt. Col. Benjamin Kendig, Captain Edward Jaeger, Lt. John Milton Rank, Captain James Trost, Captain William Chapman, and Lt. Harold W. Budding.

The war over, Lancaster turned its attention to conversion of wartime industries to peacetime production. Temporary unemployment resulted when all government contracts were canceled at once, but local businesses had planned for that eventuality and the distress did not last long.

With the end of the war, Lancaster had time to celebrate — but not the past. It was time to look forward. The world would never be the same, and Lancaster was determined to be a significant part of that new world to come.

Those who remained behind to serve during World War II worked in war plants, guarded electrical and communications installations, and looked after the safety of the civilian population. The hometown ''soldier'' was the Civil Defense warden. Here a warden and his young assistants help a family find shelter along East Clay Street during an air-raid drill. (Lancaster New Era *photo)*

Young Lancastrians also were caught up in the joy that swept the city as Germany surrendered in 1945. These carrier boys would be seeing older brothers and fathers returning home as soon as the war in the Pacific ended. (Lancaster New Era *photo)*

Several blocks of downtown Lancaster were cleared in the 1960s as an urban renewal project. After years of discouragement, the project, under the direction of private interests, blossomed into a fine-looking, taxpaying, job-providing series of structures. North Queen Street runs from the right to the gap between the large buildings. The large building to the left is part of the Armstrong Cork Company office complex. The ground floor features sample rooms used in national advertising of Armstrong's products for building and furnishing homes. The structure to the rear is the Hotel Brunswick, replacing on the site an older hotel of the same name. Concrete walkways remain as part of a large and costly complex that originally filled Lancaster Square following urban renewal.

Chapter VI

Change and Renewal

1950-1978

Before victory was won in World War II, Lancaster began planning for the future. A postwar planning commission studied the needs of the city and came up with a number of sound recommendations. The "Greater Lancaster" concept was developed as a recognition that sprawling suburban communities were physically adjacent to Lancaster, and that, therefore, the problems of each were intertwined and mutual. Cooperation was required if solutions were to be found and implemented. Unfortunately, the suburbs had grown as an alternative to city life, while using the expensive educational and cultural assets of the city. The suburbs seemed isolated and immune from the problems of the aging city with its increasing population of disadvantaged persons. Decaying neighborhoods and slums, with attendant crime and need for expanded social services, placed an ever-increasing burden on the city taxpayer, making continued home ownership in Lancaster less attractive.

A comprehensive municipal plan — the Baker Plan — resulted from the planning efforts of the citizens and their governmental leaders. Slum clearance began with the removal of blocks of deteriorating housing, while public-housing programs tried to provide homes for the displaced residents. In the public's eyes the gap between destruction and rebuilding was intolerably long. Complaints about destroying restorable structures were common. Within three years, however, much of the worst slum area, including the notorious Barney Google Row, was removed. Public housing developed such projects as Hickory Tree Heights in the southeast

151

section near the Conestoga River.

The environmental and recreational concerns of the city were given public attention by the Conestoga Valley Association, another project of the indefatigable Earl Rebman, who previously urged the creation of a parkway along the Conestoga River. Mr. Rebman envisaged the construction of cultural and recreational facilities in the area being beautified. General Edward Hand's historic mansion, *Rock Ford,* was included as one of the highlights of the parkway project. Although the project did not unfold quite as anticipated, the major portions of the plan materialized. County Park and *Rock Ford* are magnificent realities and are tributes to the dreams and efforts of Earl Rebman and the enlightened county commissioners during the 1960s and 1970s. *Rock Ford* has been preserved through the efforts of the Junior League of Lancaster and the nonprofit foundation the league created to preserve and maintain General Hand's plantation. In the late 1930s President James Buchanan's mansion, *Wheatland,* was acquired and has been maintained under similar auspices.

Zoning, housing, traffic control, school expansion, crime, recreation, decreasing tax base, and modernization of the police and fire departments continued to attract public attention and criticism as the city fathers wrestled with the problems. A city planning commission with a professional staff was appointed. Renewal of slum housing and deteriorating commercial properties was placed under the control of the Lancaster Redevelopment Authority. In order to preserve the more deserving buildings of architectural and historical merit, as well as to conserve the human setting of the city landscape, a historic district ordinance was enacted, and a board of review was set up to administer the policy. Every step taken by the city government was roundly criticized by its opponents and just as vigorously praised from friendly quarters. Planning, as a concept, never was popular to Lancastrians; it smacked of governmental control over one's life and property. Yet, Lancastrians were orderly; they were dismayed by threats to their lives and property caused by haphazard growth, crime, increasing taxation, and the rapacity of those who saw opportunities to enrich themselves from publicly funded efforts to rebuild the city.

Upon the retirement of Dr. Dale E. Cary as mayor in 1950, an elderly physician who had steered the city through the trying war years with integrity and fatherly devotion to its heritage, Kendig C. Bare was elected mayor on the Republican ticket. An enthusiastic, imaginative, and highly articulate young man, Bare quickly caught the interest of the citizenry and proved to be an exceedingly popular mayor. But during his term he was recalled as a reserve officer to serve in the Korean conflict. His brother Howard, an attorney, was appointed to serve as mayor during his absence; and in 1954 Kendig Bare was elected to another term.

The mid-1950s saw much new construction in the city. In 1954 a new library was built for the Lancaster County Library, replacing an obsolete facility on the same site. During the same year a public safety building was erected at the northwest corner of Duke and

Closing night at the Boyd Theatre at Queen and Chestnut streets prior to demolition of the theatre district in the mid-1960s. The Boyd had been the Colonial Theatre, largest of the many downtown theatres and motion-picture houses. Having seen the film, "The Sandpipers," the patrons sadly leave the neon-lit lobby which soon will crumble under the wrecking ball.

Lancaster's notorious southeast quadrant contained most of the slum housing. Lancaster city council and Redevelopment Authority members tour the area to be cleared in the 1960s. Mayor George Coe, with paper in pocket, leads the inspection party. The late W. Hensel Brown, Jr., is on the sidewalk at left.

The classic facade of the Northern Trust & Savings Co. in the second block of North Queen Street made it the most handsome building in that area. Its solid, stone Corinthian columns suggested great strength, a solace to timid depositors. The bank later was merged into the Lancaster County National Bank, now known as National Central Bank. This structure, although as sturdy as the day it was built in the 1920s, was demolished for urban renewal.

In the last moment of glory before decline and demolition, the second block of North Queen Street in this 1953 picture shows the various ages and styles of architecture so much a part of the downtown scene. A part of late-eighteenth-century Lancaster survived in the dormered shop next to the early twentieth-century Capitol Theatre building.

When the Stevens House, Lancaster's most venerable hostelry, was to be closed and torn down, a farewell party was held in the Toby Tavern for the celebrated "old lady" that had catered to Lancaster gentry and the Fulton Opera House prima donnas since 1874. Hosting the party which mingled tears with good spirits were the proprietors, Robert and the late Mabel Shoemaker, standing in rear.

The southwest corner of Chestnut
and Queen streets was home to the
Colonial Theatre and the Imperial
Drug Store since 1912, although
the Colonial became the Boyd
Theatre, and the pharmacy a bar
room. F.W. Woolworth started his
first successful five-and-dime store
on this site in 1879. When all the
buildings along North Queen
Street were razed, the Imperial Bar
stood alone until 1967, pending a
court battle.

Chestnut streets. The chaste structure with elements of contemporary design pleasingly integrated with traditional style by its architect, H.C. Kreisle, houses the police and fire department headquarters and the city council chamber. It is the first building constructed for the city government, the municipal building having been the Federal Building-Post Office from 1894 to 1932, and Old City Hall having been a hand-me-down from the county, 1854 to 1932. Other major construction included Lancaster's three hospitals. Between 1952 and 1978 Lancaster General Hospital took form, replacing its half-century-old facilities and becoming in the process the largest single mass of structures in the city. St. Joseph's Hospital's obsolete Victorian brick pile was replaced entirely by a vast new complex between 1950 and 1977. Lancaster Osteopathic Hospital, in a series of building projects, has a large modern facility adjacent to the city in Lancaster Township. All three hospitals have the highest accreditation possible, and are justly famed for the extraordinary quality of their service and facilities, not least of which are the skills and personal attention of their personnel.

The center city was losing ground in its struggle to survive despite the efforts of Lancastrians to breathe new life into it. Eventually the city government concluded local property owners and businessmen either did not have faith in revitalization by private initiative, or they lacked the means to grasp and solve the problem. The response to that indicated the failure of Lancastrians to understand fully the dimensions of the matter. They wanted something done, and done quickly, but it had to be accomplished within the structure and philosophy of the Lancaster tradition — the heritage, if you please. Outside entrepreneurs and the camp followers of federal and state projects were suspect. The city administrations, one succeeding another, found themselves immobilized as urban renewal plodded along, leaving acres of cleared land strewn with broken bricks and sprouting wasteland weeds. It seemed as if Lancaster had lost its faith, imagination, and spirit.

Mayors came and went, battered and bruised, saddened and wiser, but inwardly satisfied they had fought the good battle even as victory eluded them. The sequence of administrations is:

Kendig C. Bare/Howard Bare, Republican,
   1950-1958
Thomas J. Monaghan, Democrat, 1958-1962
George B. Coe, Republican, 1962-1966
Thomas J. Monaghan, Democrat, 1966-1974
Richard M. Scott, Republican, 1974-

In April 1966 the city adopted a new charter that would replace the commission form of government with a strong mayor-council scheme. The mayor would be a full-time executive and the council would be a legislative body.

The east side of the second block of North Queen Street prior to all the buildings pictured being razed for urban renewal in 1965. Between the Hotel Brunswick and the Grand Theatre were a number of pool and billiard parlors, night clubs, and small retail firms.

Mayor Richard M. Scott poses with
Tom Ratza, president of the Old
Town Lancaster Corporation,
which is restoring an area with
seventy historical structures in the
downtown area.

This scene on North Queen Street
was taken just before the buildings
were razed in 1965. The Hotel
Brunswick, with its celebrated
Baron Stiegel Room, is at the far
left. The site is now occupied by
the new Brunswick Hotel and
Lancaster Square.

Once part of Lancaster's slums, these early houses are being restored along South Duke Street near Vine Street. The entire neighborhood around this view is being rehabilitated by private enterprise — not by state and federal funds from taxpayers. A prominent attorney now occupies the completed building with the wooden railing. (Photo by the author)

Between 1967 and 1970 the first tiny fruits of urban renewal began to ripen with the completion of the Hilton Inn and the Hess department store along the east side of the second block of North Queen Street. The Hilton Inn replaced the old Hotel Brunswick. After several years of operation the large Hess store closed owing to what was described as insufficient business downtown to warrant continued investment.

Joining the hotel and the department store was a gigantic concrete monstrosity that enclosed "Lancaster Square," an enlargement of Queen Street. The concrete thing rose several stories and contained walkways and fountains, all subject to constant vandalism. The decor complemented the design of the hotel. Atop the structure, often referred to by natives as the "concrete jungle," was a road planned to connect

the Prince Street parking garage with the Duke Street parking garage. Octagon-shaped bricks paved North Queen Street where it passed through the "jungle," keeping motorists alert as the bricks flew up against the undersides of automobiles.

The election of 1973 swept Richard M. Scott, a former Air Force brigadier general and onetime fighter pilot, into office on the Republican ticket. Voters had grown impatient with the empty spaces and bureaucratic inaction. Mayor Scott was able to enlist a number of community leaders and business interests in solving Lancaster's problems. This approach was not new. But a new dimension emerged. With all the planning and demolishing and publicly funded programs there had been a missing ingredient: humanity. The mayor announced there would be a halt

When the children of the "first families" on East Orange Street became prosperous merchants and lawyers, they built their townhouses along North Duke Street. These lovely old houses built in the 1840s and 1850s, between Chestnut and Walnut streets, shelter a men's club and numerous professional offices. Block after block of substantial early townhouses are being cared for by appreciative owners as Lancaster pride manifests itself.

to tearing things down — except for the "concrete jungle" — until there was something worthwhile as a replacement. The emphasis was put on rehabilitation, conservation, and on doing what people, not bureaucrats, wanted accomplished. The results were stunning.

The empty spaces filled up with the large new National Central Bank corporate headquarters and the immense design center and office building of Armstrong Cork Company. The concrete thing came down for the most part, and people-oriented improvements were installed. The Hilton Inn became the Brunswick Hotel, reviving an honored name, warm memories, and, it was hoped, profitable operations. Plans were announced for the creation of shops between the hotel and former department store

building. And in 1978 Richard Scott took the oath of office for his second term.

The center city was turned into a place of great beauty, with Penn Square and adjacent streets made both modern and traditional, and above all, a place for people rather than for motorcars and impersonal bureaucratic contrivances. While owners of commercial structures were urged to retain the worthwhile "old" aspects of their buildings, conformity to one age or style was out. Meantime, residential neighborhoods throughout the city were getting spruced up, partially through a publicly funded cooperative program (Neighborhood Improvement Program) and through private initiative of the property owners. John A. Jarvis spearheaded the program to encourage residents to bring out the beauty of their neighborhoods by their

Now enlarged and covered by clapboard, this well-maintained home between Slackwater and Rock Hill was John Postlethwaite's tavern in 1729 when the first court of Lancaster County met here to name the original townships and mete out justice. To the rear of this structure is a valley through which flows the Conestoga River. The ancient Great Conestoga Road passed the tavern-courthouse.

own efforts, and thus generate much pride. This development has been extremely successful in converting block after block of dingy homes into neighborhoods of great charm and awakened pride.

In 1977 a seven-story annex for the courthouse was completed at the southwest corner of Duke and Orange streets.

During the 1960s the old Fulton Opera House, the queen of Prince Street at one time, now shabby and disreputable, was acquired by the Fulton Opera House Foundation and restored lovingly to its early elegance. The house has been returned to its cultural function and is the home of the Lancaster Symphony Orchestra, one of the finest symphonic bodies to be found in the nation's smaller cities. Celebrating its thirtieth

Built about 1785, the log house at 113-115 Howard Avenue (formerly Middle Street) was in a blighted area and in danger of being razed when an enlightened Lancastrian decided to acquire it and have it restored. In the photo, restoration is under way. The building was insulated with a straw and mud mixture. (Lancaster New Era photo)

During the Vietnam War, Lancaster's selective-service draft board offices often were the scenes of demonstrations by young men and women protesting the war. This group was present on South Duke Street in 1967 to urge draftees not to serve. The signs refer to the demonstrators' frustrations at not being permitted to deliver anti-war speeches to the inductees.

anniversary in 1977, the Lancaster Symphony attracts as its guest musicians the leading artists of the nation. From its inception Dr. Louis Vyner has been permanent conductor and musical director.

Music always has been a significant part of the Lancaster heritage, stemming from the emphasis placed on man's ability to create beauty in praise of God, characteristics of the Lutheran, Moravian, and Reformed churches in Lancaster. Pro Musica Sacra, a choral and instrumental group directed by Dr. Carl Schroeder, performs sacred music of the Baroque period for Lancastrians. The Lancaster Opera Workshop, under the direction of Dr. Frederick Robinson, has earned a reputation well beyond Lancaster for the professional quality of its performances. Although the bands so prevalent in Lancaster in the 1870-1915 period have disappeared, the Malta Band has continued to provide music for the city's ceremonies and performs with rare musicianship. The Musical Arts Society and its junior group play important roles in the serious musical life of the community.

Art also is a major ingredient in our heritage. From the days in the early nineteenth century when Jacob Eichholtz and Arthur Armstrong painted portraits of prominent citizens, to Charles Demuth in the present century, the visual arts have been celebrated in Lancaster. A list of Lancaster artists would fill a directory! The Lancaster County Art Association, after a period of activity in the 1930s, was reorganized in

Black demonstrators at Rocky Springs swimming pool in the 1960s seek equality and an end to discrimination in admission to the pool.

1948 and its many activities continue to serve well the artistic community. Other art groups, some oriented more to the abstract or nonrepresentative modes of visual art, flourish in Lancaster. The arrival of spring always brings out sidewalk art shows that are strung along the downtown buildings.

The Lancaster County Historical Society, founded in 1886 as a successor to the Historical, Agricultural, and Mechanics' Society of 1857, occupied its new fireproof building adjacent to *Wheatland* in 1956. Recognized throughout North America and Europe for the quality of its research, publications, and holdings, the Society attracts scholars and historians to its library and archives. Incorporated in 1971, the Heritage Center of Lancaster County has acquired the Old City Hall and

Masonic lodge buildings from the city and, with the support of the county commissioners and the James Hale Steinman Foundation, has converted the structures to an unusually high-quality museum of Lancaster's finest creations in the arts and crafts. The late nineteenth-century buildings have been restored in exterior appearance, and this work will continue in years to come. The North Museum of Franklin and Marshall College operates in a new building, and is an outstanding natural-history museum and planetarium.

During the 1950s Lancastrians discovered a new ethnic group arriving in their midst. Hispanics — usually from Puerto Rico — had been migrating northward to work as agricultural laborers, and many chose to remain. Problems arose when the new

162

Lancastrians, many with dark skins and speaking an unfamiliar language, settled in the densely populated areas of the city.

Human rights was a subject other minorities in Lancaster were examining with renewed interest. Public swimming pools did not exist in the 1950s, and privately owned swimming pools had the custom of not admitting black persons. Black civil rights groups protested and held demonstrations. When it appeared the pools would be obliged to admit Negroes, the pool owners formed private membership clubs and controlled the membership. Lancaster city and county then built large public pools that are open to everyone. The war in Vietnam prompted many marches and demonstrations by students and religious pacifists.

Lancaster's Democracy turned out in September 1960 to welcome John F. Kennedy to the Red Rose City. Despite the traditional Republicanism of Lancaster Countians, the Democratic presidential candidate received a warm welcome as he spoke on the northern side of Penn Square. Pennsylvania's Governor David Lawrence is listening intently to the right rear of Kennedy. (Lancaster New Era photo)

Both major party candidates visited Lancaster during the 1960 presidential campaign. In October Richard and Pat Nixon received the enthusiastic greetings of a vast crowd estimated to be in excess of forty thousand. Mrs. Nixon was presented with a bouquet of Lancaster red roses. At the far right is former Congressman Paul B. Dague. The old Hotel Brunswick is in the background. (Lancaster New Era photo)

Other demonstrations took place, all of them relatively peaceful, and Lancastrians soon learned to live with a changing society, as had their ancestors.

To facilitate harmonious relations, the Lancaster City-County Human Relations Committee was established under joint sponsorship by the two governmental units. The committee, capably administered by Patrick Kenney, Jr., operates with a low profile, solving many potentially thorny problems with dispatch, intelligence, and good humor. Mr. Kenney makes use of the local heritage rather than attacking it.

Women always have been a great deal more important in Lancaster than their sisters in many other communities, despite the heavily Germanic culture that traditionally relegated women to a lower status. Among the more prominent women in Lancaster's heritage were: Alice Appenzeller, Hannah Brown, Mercy Shreve Brown, Mary McIllvane Dickson, Charlotte Heinitsh Eichholtz, Marie Ferree, Susan Carpenter Frazer, Eleanore Fulton, Ann Scott Galbraith, Hannah Gibbons, Ann Wood Henry, Rosina Weaver Hubley, Mercy Johnson, Harriet Lane Johnston, Ann Bonnetable LeTort, Ann Moore, Susanna Rohrer Muller, Hetty Esther Parker, Anna Carpenter Reichert, Elizabeth Smedley, Lydia Smith, Abigail Bailey Steele, Elizabeth Cameron Whitehill, and Susannah Wright. Among contemporary women active in Lancaster are Julia Brazill, city councilwoman; June Honaman, assemblywoman, ninety-seventh district; Jean Mowery, county commissioner; Doris Moyer, chairman, Republican Committee of Lancaster County; and Sarah Ann Stauffer, former national GOP committeewoman. Others recognized for their outstanding work are Ruth Grigg Horting, former state welfare secretary, and vice chairman, Democratic State Committee; Dr. S. June Smith; Shirley Watkins; Geraldine Inez Funk Alvarez; Christine Gruber Kreider; and Mrs. Harold Fischer. There are hundreds of others who have made worthwhile contributions to the heritage of Lancaster.

Women's suffrage in Lancaster made men snort but, when the inevitable happened, the ladies received recognition from the gentlemen, self-consciously at first, but wholeheartedly when the women had proved themselves capable. The Republican County Committee promptly created a vice chairmanship to be filled by a woman, and among the holders of that office has been the grand old lady of Lancaster, the spry and sharp-witted Louise Sauder who would have been able to vote at the beginning of this century had present laws been in effect at that time! It is customary to include women on the county office tickets, and all of them have served with distinction.

It seems fitting to end *The Heritage of Lancaster* on a comment about tourism, the most rapidly growing major industry in Lancaster County. About 1960 the businessmen engaged in servicing tourists formed an association, the Pennsylvania Dutch Visitors Bureau, to coordinate efforts and encourage a businesslike, ethical approach to the task. Tourists for the most part want to see the Amish because they are quaint, and of another age and world. The Amish are a part — but only a small part — of the Lancaster heritage. More in keeping with traditions of Lancaster enterprise would be the development of standards by which example our visitors might learn from and about the heritage of Lancaster — all its people in the proper context.

EPILOGUE

When all is said, the heritage of Lancaster has been created by, with, and for people. All else is accident or luck. Lancaster does not have a distinctive architectural style, it is not known for a single institution that is unique, and it had no one citizen in its history who stands above all others. Diversity, reasonable tolerance, compassion tempered with common sense, pragmatism, and independence are traits that best characterize Lancastrians. Just as the human personality is a blend of the rational and the irrational, so Lancastrians are a blend of Calvinism and humanism in their approach to life. The material community of Lancaster is but an extension of the Lancastrian personality. Its heritage has been and will continue to be people — those whose privilege it is to be called Lancastrians.

John Ward Willson Loose

The Surviving Past

Despite the many physical changes to Lancaster's appearance over the years — the disappearance of the beloved old buildings and the construction of fresh, new structures boldly displaying an unfamiliar architecture — the community has never looked better. It literally bursts with pride, and for good reason. It is a handsome city.

Much that the average Lancastrian passes daily on the street has become so familiar to him that he misses the little changes, the nuances in sound and color as he steps upon a new brick sidewalk or passes a freshly planted shrub growing along the street curb. Architectural geegaws pop up at every turn, delighting the visitors, and amazing longtime residents who never before took a close look.

For example, how many Lancastrians ever looked up at the eave of the old William Bausman building at 121 East King Street? There, staring down at passersby, is an impish face that belongs to an eavesdropper, a face that probably amused Lancaster's barristers a decade before the Revolution. Or look at the symbols worked into the frieze of the Griest Building, or the faces of Neptune that glare down from the facade of the venerable Lincoln Hotel. Animals abound in terra cotta ornamentation throughout the city. Lions guard the professional offices at 126 East Chestnut Street, and marvelous horned creatures embellish the facade of the Southern Market, adding a bucolic touch to that Queen Anne-revival structure.

The heritage of Lancaster is everywhere. Set into a niche above the entrance to the Fulton Opera House is

Eavesdropper peers down from the Bausman Building.

a statue of Robert Fulton, although his presence is largely ignored. And speaking of statues, who can locate the six around Penn Square? How many Lancastrians can identify the statues in Buchanan Park and on the Franklin and Marshall campus?

To document the evidence that Lancaster is a distinctively beautiful and charming community, and that much of the past has survived to the present, scenes from the city and the surrounding countryside have been captured in color by the photographers' skill. Mere words often do not express much that is the heritage of Lancaster as subtly as do lines, shadows, tints, and moods in color. Through the color photograph the reader can see for himself that Lancaster not only has preserved its charm, but that the 250-year-old community has become, without doubt, what H.L. Mencken had in mind, concerning home, when he wrote:

> . . . its essence lies in its permanence, in its capacity for accretion and solidification, in its quality of representing, in all its details, the personalities of the people who live in it.*

*Quoted from H.L. Mencken, *Prejudices: Fifth Series* (1926), p.11.

Lions guard the professional offices at 126 East Chestnut Street.

A ram adds a bucolic touch to the facade of the Southern Market.

Fulton Opera House, built in 1852 by Christopher Hager, has been in continuous use as a theatre, making it one of the oldest in the nation. The ornate interior shown here dates from 1873. Now owned and operated by a cultural foundation, the historic building has been restored and refurbished. Its acoustical qualities are near-perfect. The home of the Lancaster Symphony Orchestra, the Fulton Opera House also features many musical and dramatic presentations by outstanding repertory companies.

A product of the inventive Lancaster mind, the Conestoga wagon became the "truck" of early America. It developed in the Conestoga Valley of which Lancaster city is the center. The front wheels are small, to permit turning under the body. The undercarriage was built of heavy timber and painted red. The wheels were wide, and tended to pack rather than rut the dirt roads, which resulted in a lower toll for using the turnpikes. The body or bed of the wagon usually was arched slightly like a boat to prevent the freight from shifting on steep hills. Myths persist that the boatlike body was to permit floating across rivers. The wagons could ford streams but they could not float. The bodies were painted bright blue, and a canvas top stretched over hoops protected the freight. Blacksmiths were proud of their artistic abilities in making the hardware for the wagon. The vehicles were drawn by four or six horses — also bred in the Conestoga Valley.

The 208-year-old Demuth
Tobacco Shop was established in
1770 by Christopher Demuth, son
of a Moravian immigrant from
Karlsdorf. The quality of snuff and
other tobacco items sold by
Demuth soon made the shop a
gathering place for the town's
gentry. Snuff for the king's men,
revolutionaries, and lawmakers of
the young Republic was furnished
by the enterprising Demuth family.
A token of President Buchanan's
esteem usually was one of
Demuth's superb cigars. No
meeting of the Union Fire Co. was
official without the Demuth cigars.
Since 1870 Demuth's Golden Lion
cigars have been shipped around
the world to discriminating
smokers. Fifth-generation
descendant Christopher Demuth, a
tall, lanky 79-year-old, presides
over the memento-filled shop in its
third century, now the oldest
tobacco shop in the nation.

Center city Lancaster has preserved and "recycled" many of its sturdy old buildings, creating a complementary setting of rare charm for the contemporary architectural forms. This quaint window display of wares is reminiscent of early Lancaster shops with their great profusion of wares exhibited inside, outside, and all around the salesrooms. Shoppers that have grown tired of plastic and printed plywood are returning to the quality merchandise and substantial charm of downtown Lancaster.

The apothecary's mortar and pestle decorate a Lancaster windowsill today. More than a century ago Lancaster was a highly important pharmaceutical center, with the Heinitsh Apothecary Store being one of the oldest in the nation. The first U.S. Pharmacopeia was written in nearby Lititz during the Revolution. Today the vast Warner-Lambert plant is located in Lititz, while the Wyeth Laboratories manufacture vaccines and serums at Marietta.

The Amish farmer is not permitted
by his religion to use self-propelled
vehicles or farm machinery. A
curious sight is the Amish farmer
driving his shiny new New Holland
harvesting machine drawn by as
many as a dozen horses and mules
while a gasoline engine perched
atop the huge machine operates
the processing equipment. Here is
a farmer driving his mule-drawn
hay rake past a herd of holstein
cows. While the Amish farmer has
vast assets in land and equipment,
he has a low cash-flow economy
and no outlay for employees.
Property and inheritance taxes eat
deeply into the Amish economy.

Every season is beautiful in
Lancaster County, but many
visitors come to see the
magnificent colors of the autumn
foliage. Winter is only a few
months away, and the Amish
farmers are completing their
harvests. With the harvesting
completed, the Amish wedding
season begins.

Lancaster County, often called the "Garden Spot of America," has the most productive farmland east of the Mississippi River, and the best non-irrigated agricultural land in the nation. Though by no means the only Lancaster County farmers, the Amish farmer seems to typify the renowned agriculturists of this county. When the dawn comes up and the cock crows, the rest of the world may be asleep but in the Amish land the smell of wood smoke from cast-iron kitchen stoves means fried potatoes, scrapple, and other Amish breakfast food being prepared for the men and boys who will be milking the cows and hitching up the horses and mules to farm equipment. The Amish family blows out its kerosene lamps and goes to bed early so that they can be up and busy at the crack of dawn. The Pennsylvania German mind looks upon late awakenings as not quite moral and closely related to the deadly sin of sloth.

A covered carriage, or Amish buggy, means the occupants are married. Here a horse pulls a carriage along a country road. Suspicious eyes of man and beast watch the photographer, because it is not proper to allow one's picture to be taken with any degree of willingness. Carriages today must have electric lighting and reflectors for highway safety. The favorite carriage horse is a "pacer," whose gait is fascinating to watch. The Amish are excellent judges of good horseflesh, and young Amish lads are just as proud of their steeds as their more worldly neighbors are of their customized sports cars.

Lancaster County is the birthplace of the famed Pennsylvania rifle, erroneously called the "Kentucky rifle." Melchoir Fordney was among the finest of the city riflemakers, until he was brutally hacked to death in 1846 by John Haggerty, a "madman." The case that resulted was a landmark trial over which the eminent jurist, Ellis Lewis, presided. At issue was the legal responsibility of a defendant who was judged insane. Every physician in Lancaster had his say during the trial, with spectacular clashes of opinion. Haggerty was hanged, and Judge Lewis eventually became Chief Justice of the Pennsylvania Supreme Court.

Franklin and Marshall College's Old Main, a brick Gothic-Romanesque jewel, was built in 1856. This structure is flanked by a pair of matching buildings for the Diagnothian and Goethean Literary Societies. Franklin College (1787) was founded in Lancaster under the auspices of the German Reformed and Lutheran churches. Marshall College began in 1835 at Mercersburg under the control of the German Reformed Church. When the two colleges were merged in 1853, the Lutheran interest in Franklin College was transferred to the college at Gettysburg. The quality of German scholarship present at the merged college compared favorably with the English scholarship as represented at Harvard and Yale.

Wheatland, *the home of James Buchanan, Pennsylvania's only U.S. President, has been preserved in all its restrained elegance and is open to the public. Owned and operated by the James Buchanan Foundation for the Preservation of Wheatland, Inc., the mansion and its beautiful grounds have been a major attraction for visitors since the late 1930s. Costumed hostesses receive the visitors and conduct tours of the rooms, all furnished just as when Buchanan lived there.*

James Buchanan's skill in foreign relations, and particularly in negotiating commercial treaties, is an oft-forgotten highlight of his administration. Despite a hostile Congress, "Old Buck" managed to open the Far East for trade. A grateful Japanese delegation visited Washington in May 1860, bringing with them a personal gift, a handsome bowl, from the Mikado to Buchanan. The lovely piece occupies a position of honor at Wheatland.

A curiosity in the Wheatland collection is this desk from Buchanan's law office. Designed for doing research while preparing legal briefs, the desk features two side shelves for reference works and court reports.

The study in Wheatland where James Buchanan frequently pondered the affairs of state, interviewed prospective cabinet officers and ambassadors, and found solace in the classical literature of which he was fond. Buchanan's well-stocked wine cellar always contained the finest Madeira wine, a favorite of Lancaster's aristocracy.

Wheatland's "door-knocker" thumped overtime after James Buchanan's election to the U.S. Presidency in 1856 as office-seekers sought out the laird of Wheatland. The country estate, two miles from center city, afforded Buchanan the necessary privacy to entertain prominent visitors without undue fanfare. With the outbreak of the Civil War, Buchanan received threats on his life and property. He refused the services of detectives, but his Masonic brethren (Lodge 43) took it upon themselves to guard Wheatland around the clock until he retired from the White House.

General Hand's desk and portrait. Hand was an Irish-born physician that responded promptly to the Revolutionary cause. He participated throughout the Revolution and became one of General Washington's most trusted confidants and friends. After the war Dr. Hand served as burgess of Lancaster and, later, tax collector for the federal district. Hand was an aristocrat. He married well and was a respected leader in Lancaster. Hand is buried in the St. James Episcopal Church graveyard.

Rock Ford, *country home of General Edward Hand, is maintained in its original 1784-era beauty by the Rock Ford Plantation Foundation. The completed furnished rooms are open to the public. Located just southeast of the city along the Conestoga River, the plantation features restored outbuildings, lovely gardens, and a fine museum of early tools, hardware, and domestic equipment.*

The Rock Ford *sitting room represents a restrained, country elegance. When the old mansion was acquired for preservation in the 1950s, most of its woodwork, ornate mouldings, and interior fabric were intact, despite previous use as a tenement house.*

Old City Hall, built in 1798 as the County Office Building, and used 1799 to 1812 as the State Office Building when Lancaster was capital of Pennsylvania, has been converted along with the adjoining Masonic Lodge Hall into the Heritage Center of Lancaster County, a museum of the finest Lancaster County arts and crafts produced in the eighteenth and nineteenth centuries. Old City Hall faces Penn Square on its west side. The third story was added in the late 1830s.

When Trinity Lutheran Church steeple was completed in 1794, marking the completion of the church begun in 1761, Lancaster had the tallest structure west of Philadelphia in 1800. The strikingly handsome Georgian tower contains a full chime of bells, and is decorated with statues of the four evangelists. In 1854 the central main entrance on the west side of the church was moved south, where vestibules were built as extensions to the building flanking the tower. The Trinity congregation is Lancaster's oldest, and this building is the longest surviving church in the city.

The red rose is the symbol of Lancaster County. This beautiful flower of antiquity was used by the English House of Lancaster. The rival House of York adopted the white rose as its symbol. During the War of the Roses, that long and acrimonious dispute between the two royal families, the House of York won the right to the British Crown.

John Wright, the primary magistrate of the newly established county, chose the name Lancaster for the county, to honor his English birthplace. The red rose, however, did not become the local symbol until the beginning of the present century, when the city discovered it did not have a flag. Today the red rose is found blooming in all its elegance in Lancaster, and the flower has official status.

By coincidence, Henry William Stiegel, the colorful ironmaster-glassmaker of Manheim, loved the red rose so much that he specified the payment of "one red rose forever" annually as ground rent for the Lutheran Church he gave Manheim.

Chapter VIII

Partners in Progress

Lancaster is an investment — it began as an investment for James Hamilton, and it has been the economic stage upon which countless Lancaster entrepreneurs, from the builders of Conestoga wagons to the technicians assembling space-age instruments, have earned their living. Whatever the enterprise, Lancastrians have plied their skills in an economic environment that has encouraged realization of each individual's potentiality.

It will be recalled from an earlier chapter that the first settlers came here primarily for economic reasons. Pennsylvania — especially the inland area — was indeed the land of opportunity for those willing to work hard to convert the wilderness into fields of grain, and harness the flowing waters for the manufacture of flour, lumber, paper, pig and wrought iron, and flaxseed oil. Initially this activity was for self-sustenance, but later, as surpluses developed, the economic effort was directed toward the marketplace. With increased population and a more highly specialized division of labor, Lancastrians began establishing businesses that depended on others for labor and material.

Economic survival here has never depended upon one major employer. By the mid-nineteenth century, with the advent of the factory system, economic diversity was encouraged by the many needs of such factories. Diversity of industry continues today as one of Lancaster's healthiest qualities.

As in the days of old, Lancaster businessmen are meeting the challenges of the times by investing heavily in the community, often through the rehabilitation of older commercial properties, and in the process are enhancing a traditional aspect of Lancaster — honesty. The bricks are real bricks, the wood is not plastic, and business ethics are practiced routinely. When asked to explain their heavy investment in creating an irresistible shopping atmosphere, Lancaster businessmen generally sum it all up quite simply: "We have faith in Lancaster's future!"

No business succeeds in a vacuum, however. Without customers or patrons, the doors would close and employees would lose jobs. Supporting businesses would move away, and banks would be distressed. Taxes would be left unpaid, and ambitious residents would leave the city. Crime and social degeneration would increase rapidly. Governmental costs would mount astronomically. It should be apparent, therefore, that economic success — the keystone of our heritage — depends heavily on two factors: businessmen and businesswomen willing to risk their faith in Lancaster, and Lancastrians willing to match that faith with their own by sustaining the local businesses.

Lancaster as a cultural center depends upon the support of those who believe that such activities spell the difference between living and mere existence, between civilization and barbarousness. The inherent nature of cultural affairs requires that large amounts of financial aid be given to our museums, libraries, symphony orchestras, opera houses, theatres, art galleries, historical societies, and private educational institutions. Public or private support is needed for all cultural activities, whether presented to sophisticated audiences in white ties and tails or blue-jeaned masses clustered around Penn Square listening to the Brown Bag festivities twice weekly. Lancastrians expect their elected officials to exercise a frugal stewardship over tax funds. That means enlightened officials carefully appropriate representative sums to cultural activities, fully expecting the private sector to come forward with major financing. Here, again, the Lancaster business community has responded magnificently. Considerably more than half of the support for most cultural activities — particularly those events that have no membership basis — comes from area businesses, including the banks. Truly, Lancaster's heritage arises from its economy, the partnership of Lancaster business with Lancaster employees and consumers.

In acknowledgment of the many important contributions of the city's business community, on the pages that follow are the histories, the biographies, the success stories of many of the area's leading businesses — companies where you may be employed, services that you may patronize, familiar places that you see in your daily travels. They form — in partnership with their employees and their customers — the very foundation of the community. They are, in the most basic sense, the strength and continuing source from which arises the heritage of Lancaster — today and tomorrow.

American Bank and Trust Co. of Pa.

Persistence, optimism, a little chaos — building a successful business has always been the same, whether it's the 1790s or 1970s. It's hard enough to do it once, but when you do it a second time by earning the confidence of new customers in a new region — you're part of a real American success story.

Tracing its roots to the decade before the twentieth century, American Bank was already a highly successful bank when it took its first step out of Berks County in 1963. That step was into neighboring Lancaster County, where a branch office was established, via merger, in Reamstown. Other carefully planned mergers and new office openings followed in Lancaster city and county. Solid links were established in the bank's network of community banking facilities.

Overcoming its "Reading bank" image was not easy, and gaining acceptance in Lancaster city proved to be the toughest challenge of all. A group of four American Bankers, including William E. Snell, Jr., vice president of the region, recall working out of the trunk of their car while laying the groundwork for the bank's regional headquarters here in the early 1970s. In those days, their office was in a basement, their desk was a lunch table, and their briefcases and files traveled with them in the car.

A view of the area a block south of Penn Square that is being transformed into elegant town houses in Old Town Lancaster.

Initial construction and mortgage financing was provided by American Bank.

An artist's rendering of one section of Old Town Lancaster looking south on the corner of Duke and Vine streets.

The bank started, literally, as a "bank on wheels." But it worked. And it grew. It continues to grow in Lancaster because of American Bank's basic philosophy that a bank can be "big" enough to service corporate needs yet "little" enough to give highly personalized attention to families and small businesses. Providing customer convenience, the bank has been a pioneer in modern drive-up units and electronic banking. American Bank surpassed the billion-dollar mark in assets and deposits in 1976 but continues to stake its reputation on its network of local community banking offices.

The bank is committed to reinvesting customers' deposits back into the community. The "Old Town Lancaster" project is an outstanding example of this commitment to community betterment. The bank initially provided over $3 million in construction financing in what used to be a blighted area of boarded-up, condemned housing. Additionally, nearly $1 million in American Bank mortgage funds sparked the initial impetus for this residential development — combining the best of the past with the needs of the present in Lancaster's historic district.

The regional headquarters of American Bank are at 42-44 North Prince Street, Lancaster. Because of its location in the heart of the city and its commitment to the improvement of life here, American Bank has blended its successful operations into the fabric of Lancaster's continuing development.

APBA Game Company, Inc.

"I'm proud of my business, proud because it promotes worthy use of leisure time and keeps kids out of trouble," says J. Richard Seitz, creator and president of APBA Game Company. It all began with a tabletop game of baseball he invented and played with a handful of high school friends; they called themselves the American Professional Baseball Association, APBA for short.

J. Richard Seitz, president of APBA Game Company, with some of the games he has created.

For years the baseball game was a hobby as Dick Seitz updated it regularly, incorporating new statistics each year as players aged, retired, and new faces, new facts were introduced. He was intrigued to see how his game caught the imaginations of those playing it, as well as the spectators. By 1955 he was devoting full time to the game company in the basement of his home.

Other games followed: football in 1958; golf in 1962; basketball and horse racing came later. The game concept remained the same — a dice-activated game using individual player cards that relied on complex play charts. APBA individualizes the players and attempts to re-create the player's real-life performance. New cards are issued every year (every three years for golf) based on the preceding season's statistics and calculated by a formula that no computer could touch. The magic ingredient is human judgment.

Variations include mythical teams, historic teams, all-time great golfers, Hall of Fame horses — absorbing pastimes for the tens of thousands of sports fans who subscribe to APBA games. By and large, it is a direct-mail-order business, but retail outlets are on the rise all across the country. It is the only baseball game sold at the Baseball Hall of Fame in Cooperstown, New York.

By 1962 APBA moved into its own building on Eastman Avenue. Still more space soon was needed, and Dick Seitz found an ideal location on Millersville Road. APBA now commands a sweeping view of its surroundings that provides a blend of contemporary homes, old farmhouses, and an historic mill. The panorama is typical of Lancaster County at its best; the Old World making room for the New because the people are flexible enough to respect the past and accept progress.

Dick Seitz is a native of Lancaster County and his roots are deep in an area he knows and loves. He and his staff cater to customers they refer to as fans. And those fans come in all age groups, representing every background imaginable. Often they become good friends. Such is the case with David and Julie Nixon Eisenhower who entertained the Seitzes one entire day at the White House. "The most thrilling day of my life," says J. Richard Seitz. And an exciting way to be thanked for many satisfying hours of playing APBA Baseball.

Commonwealth National Bank of Lancaster

The Commonwealth National Bank and its predecessors have had a corner of Lancaster since the 1800s when the business of banking was just starting to grow with our nation. Coal-oil lamps lighted most homes, city streets were cobblestone; but the changes to be created by electric lights, electric street railways, and the telephone were near.

During 1888 leading men of the community saw the need for a new bank in Lancaster. They agreed to rent two rooms on the first floor of the Black Building at South Queen Street and Center Square. (The upper floors were occupied by the *Daily New Era*).

The Conestoga National Bank was formally opened for business in March of 1889. The event was described in the *Daily New Era:*

> "Fully $35,000 was placed on deposit and the clerks did not get through with arranging their books and their papers until 10:00 o'clock Monday night. The Conestoga certainly starts under auspicious circumstances."

By December of the same year business was going so well that the board of directors felt it was necessary to have a telephone placed in the bank.

Two years later the Conestoga merged with the private banking firm of Reed, McGrann and Company and moved to its present location on the southwest corner of Penn Square. With growth came mechanization: the first primitive adding machine, called an Arithmometer, was purchased in 1897 to help with the bookkeeping, though it was noted that the machine was used only when a very large number of sums had to be totaled.

December 2, 1967 — a devastating fire gutted the bank building. Its origin was finally traced to an electrical failure in the basement.

The Conestoga Bank building was destroyed by fire in 1967, and subsequently rebuilt on its traditional corner. It opened as the Commonwealth National Bank on January 1, 1970, following the consolidation of three of the oldest banking institutions in Central Pennsylvania — the Conestoga National Bank, the Harrisburg Bank and Trust Company, and the First National Bank of York. The new bank was formed so as to be in a better position to handle increased credit demands from the expanding economy of the community. Commonwealth National Bank serves residents in Cumberland, Dauphin, Lebanon, Lancaster, Perry, and York counties through forty-two banking offices, and with assets of $807,172,000 (1977) — a very long way from two rooms and $242,000 that Conestoga Bank worked with in 1890.

◄Following the merger of the Conestoga National Bank with Reed, McGrann and Company, the new bank moved to its present location on the southwest corner of Penn Square in 1891.

Commonwealth National Bank▶ has sponsored six free outdoor concerts on the Square. Here, Fred Waring draws a bring-your-own-chair crowd of approximately four thousand as part of the Summer Arts Festival in 1974.

Dutch Wonderland

An overview of Lancaster County heritage is beautifully displayed at the Wax Museum, a part of Dutch Wonderland on Route 30. Scenes from the 1600s to the present are depicted in lifelike poses; the effect is as startling as imagining "you are there" in a dream sequence. And indeed the museum, like the entire Dutch Wonderland complex, is the result of the founder's dream.

Earl Clark was among the first to spot a trend toward the county's appeal as a vacation spot. Having traveled widely himself, he appreciated comfortable lodgings and good food on the road. That observation led him directly to the building and operation of the Congress Inn Motel in 1959. As he talked and listened to his guests at the motel, he noted a recurrent theme in their conversation: they enjoyed their trip to Lancaster, but after they had toured our lovely countryside and seen our historic sites, the question was "What's fun for the children?" When a fourteen-acre tract of land came on the market, Dutch Wonderland began to take shape.

There were just four main attractions offered in 1963: the Wonderland Express train, the *Lady Gay* riverboat, a sample-sized turnpike with miniature 1910 Buicks (later changed to 1916 Mercers), and whaleboat rides (since metamorphosed into Freddie's Log Ride).

As the park has grown in popularity, more attractions such as the Sky Ride and Double Splash Flume have been added each year. Now Dutch Wonderland is an amusement park, but much more. For instance, the botanical gardens, a seven-acre island, is landscaped to represent different regions around the world: it's here that you can imagine you're in France with the Eiffel Tower, or London with Big Ben, or Holland in the spring, with the flowering of ten thousand bulbs. The area is colored by 275,000 annuals in the summer, and the whole display can be enjoyed from a tugboat ride on a canal that surrounds the gardens. An Indian village has been recreated with tepees, and Chief Halftown, a Seneca Indian chief, greets guests on the weekends. Attractions include a miniature animal farm, a dolphin and sea lion show (the first in the Northeast), puppet shows, and special weekend entertainment in the amphitheater. A mile-long monorail train circles the park for a spectacular bird's-eye view. A different view is provided by a trip in the *Lady Gay,* a replica of an old-fashioned paddlewheel riverboat.

Above, *Earl E. Clark, owner, founder, and president of Dutch Wonderland Enterprises.*

The Dutch Wonderland Castle is a gateway to a world of make-believe on Route 30. The park and varied attractions are planned to appeal to the whole family — from "one to eighty-one."

Scenes from the National Wax Museum of Lancaster County Heritage: A huge diorama depicts a typical Lancaster County Amish farm scene on the day of a barn-raising.

Hans Herr led a colony of Mennonites from Switzerland to Lancaster in 1710. His home, built as a combination dwelling and meetinghouse in 1719, has been restored as a historical Lancaster County landmark.

In 1969 the Wax Museum opened and has gained national attention for the accuracy and excellence of its presentations. It has been called "the best internationally" by authorities in the field. Some of the tableaux chosen are William Penn receiving his grant to "Penn's Woods," the life of early settlers, Hans Herr, the "Witness Tree" ceremony at Donegal Presbyterian Church in 1777, General George and Martha Washington being hosted at Rock Ford by General Edward Hand, and present-day representations of Amish life, including a barn raising and dinner. The museum also houses a $42,000 custom-built 1924 Brewster. It is of particular interest locally because the first owner of the Brewster was F.W. Woolworth who opened his first successful 5 & 10 in Lancaster.

From its inception the park has been planned with great care and attention to detail. The attractions are designed to appeal to the whole family — from toddlers to grandparents. Fun and make-believe take precedence over teeth-jarring thrill amusements. Bring-your-own picnickers are welcome, though a cafeteria and snack bars are available for convenience. A notable example of the care with which the park was planned is the inclusion of accommodations for the benefit of those in wheelchairs. Ramps and especially wide passageways make a welcoming atmosphere, as does the fact that it always has been a policy to admit the handicapped without charge. A staff of over three hundred is needed to keep all the varied activities humming smoothly.

The Dutch Wonderland complex now includes fifty-four acres, a camping ground (the Old Mill Stream Camping Manor), three theaters, and the Wax Museum.

The very lovely Castle Gift Shop, located at the entrance of Dutch Wonderland, is rated one of the largest retail gift shops in America. Once inside the shop, one can browse through the vast selection of items ranging from the unusual and the elegant to souvenirs of Lancaster County.

The Weavertown One-Room Schoolhouse (in Bird-in-Hand) is also a part of Dutch Wonderland. Here, authentic old-style desks are filled with lifelike animated figures to recreate the original atmosphere and purpose of the school as it was for nearly ninety years. Word of Dutch Wonderland has been spread by pleased customers and by an extensive promotional effort both individually and in conjunction with the Lancaster Information Center. Representatives of each travel throughout the mid-Atlantic states, Midwest, and up into New England with display booths to participate in vacation, travel, and sport shows. The results can be noted by the steady increase of visitors to the area.

Each year, more and more people have been attracted to Lancaster by Dutch Wonderland. Pleasing guests has always been a specialty here, as exemplified by the many visitors who return each year. This experience has been both rewarding and gratifying to the management of Dutch Wonderland.

DeWalt Stationary Power Tools

A Division of the Black and Decker Manufacturing Company

The DeWalt radial-arm saw, the saw that revolutionized building techniques: made in Lancaster.

Like most successful ideas, this special saw derived from a need. Raymond E. DeWalt spotted that need in 1922 while he was managing a woodworking mill. A major production bottleneck was the cutting of lumber to specific dimensions efficiently. It was a cumbersome job because it was necessary to move the lumber through a stationary saw. DeWalt conceived of rigging the blade so that it could be moved up and down, back and forth, and at any angle. He braced the lumber in a fixed position. The result was the ability to cut wood with reproducible accuracy and do it faster than before. The DeWalt "Wonder Worker" that could perform twenty-nine different cutting operations was thus invented. As word of the invention spread, DeWalt became so busy making saws for his friends that he left the construction business and set up his saw company in 1923. He began production in a two-story frame building in Leola, and established a reputation for the high-performance standards that are still synonymous with today's version.

DeWalt's shop in Leola, where ▶ each man built a complete saw from scratch and signed his output.

◀*Raymond E. DeWalt's "Wonder Worker," the first radial arm saw, patented in 1925. Versatility, reliability, and accuracy led to quick success.*

Selling the "Wonder Worker" ▶ — the first mobile unit.

Two local businessmen, Paul Gardner and Israel Rutt, bought out DeWalt in 1928, changed the name to DeWalt Products Corporation, and moved to a larger building in Grandview Heights, Lancaster. American Machine and Foundry, Inc. of New York purchased the business and operated it as a wholly owned subsidiary from 1949 to 1960, when it was acquired by the Black and Decker Manufacturing Company.

The exceptional versatility of the DeWalt saw was appreciated by the armed forces and, during World War II, the government bought almost the entire output of the company for the building of army depots, barracks, etc., at home and abroad. DeWalt employees (some of

whom have been with the company for forty years) still remember the sixteen-hour days, seven-day weeks, trying to fill the government's need. They recall making saws with special wiring to fit power generators in the Pacific islands, and special packing so the saws could be floated ashore from submarines. The exposure of the DeWalt radial-arm saw among those serving in the armed forces accelerated the growth of the company and fame of the product.

Up until the war DeWalt primarily had been concerned with industrial and construction markets. In 1953 they turned their attention to the consumer market with the introduction of the Powershop, a multipurpose tool that is designed to be used for all facets of woodworking.

Nineteen seventy-eight — and the radial-arm saw is still the core of the business, though the Lancaster plant also produces nineteen kinds of woodcutting saws,

three types of metal cutters for ferrous and nonferrous metals, panel saws, power miter-box saws, and bench grinders. Now operated as a division of the Black and Decker Manufacturing Company, the local DeWalt plant has its own marketing, administrative, financial, engineering, manufacturing, and quality control functions, as well as its own sales force and distributor network for industrial and consumer products.

Educators Mutual Life Insurance Company

Educators Beneficial
Association. All financial
functions were conducted from
one office in the Woolworth

Building, downtown Lancaster,
in 1910.

A master salesman, L.C. Reisner, helped spread the word of the fledgling insurance company in 1913. He presented an imposing figure at 260 pounds, wearing a Prince Albert coat, striped trousers, and black derby. One of his favorite sales tactics was to sell his insurance to a public school principal, then pay the principal ten dollars a day to drive him in a horse and buggy to call on teachers. The principal would recommend Educators, and most teachers would enroll: disability insurance for the teachers, one dollar commission for Mr. Reisner. Though he personally disliked the idea of automobiles, he realized that faster transportation meant more earnings. His compromise was to buy an auto and employ a driver. Mr. Reisner became sales manager in 1916 and served until his death in 1940.

Educators Beneficial Association (the forerunner of Educators Mutual) was formed in 1910 by a small group of teachers and other professional men, to provide teachers with adequate health insurance. The company had a series of addresses in downtown Lancaster, including 548 West Walnut Street, the home of its guiding light, Mr. E.W. Strickler. Mr. Strickler was a city high school teacher and then part-time secretary of the organization. The company built and moved to its present modern home office at 2490 Lincoln Highway East in 1961.

The thrust of the business also has changed over the years as the company moved from teacher disability insurance to health insurance for people of all occupations. Then, in 1943, the company broadened its product line and offered group insurance to teachers. Through group insurance, more persons can be insured at a lower cost due to administrative savings and spread of risk. Non-teacher, or commercial, marketing began in earnest in 1946 and gradually an entire product line of health insurance was offered in addition to disability insurance: hospital, surgical, medical expense, major medical, credit, campers, sport-team, and college-student insurance. Educators rode the wave of growth in the late 1940s and 1950s of the fastest growing product line in the insurance business — health insurance — and spread throughout its present territory. Realizing the need to offer life insurance as a natural companion to health insurance, the company was rechartered as a mutual life insurance company in 1956, and several years later began seriously to sell both group life insurance and a complete line of individual, ordinary-life insurance and annuities.

As a mutual insurance corporation, Educators is operated for the benefit of its over 225,000 policyholders. An elected board of eleven directors guides the officers who manage the company.

Educators is licensed to operate in sixteen states and the District of Columbia. With 129 home office employees, 90 full-time agents, and many group-insurance brokers, it operates through four company sales offices located throughout its territory. With a 1977 premium income of over $34 million, the company ranks 131st in health-premium volume and 253rd in life-insurance premium volume, out of over 1,800 insurance companies in the United States writing health and life insurance.

Educators Mutual Life
Insurance Company. In 1961
Educators built and moved into

this modern facility on the
Lincoln Highway East.

Emtrol, Inc.

Emtrol-designed process control systems are used in a wide variety of industries; here, a lime-processing plant in Bellefonte, Pennsylvania, mining lime from nine hundred feet underground.

Above, a sand-processing plant in Bristol, Pennsylvania.

An abandoned auto garage waited on Bridge Street in Mountville, Pennsylvania.

In 1961 two men changed the character of the place drastically with the founding of Emtrol, Inc. Joseph L. Grahek and Harry F. Moore combined their chemical and electrical engineering talents to form the company that designs and builds specialized control systems. Two years later they moved into larger quarters on Loop Road, Lancaster, Pennsylvania, the company's present location.

Emtrol is another example of a Lancaster firm doing business all over the world — in South America, Ireland, Germany, Poland, Australia, Canada — as well as throughout the United States. Each customer presents a new problem, frequently a new field, and always a new challenge.

"Keeping business under control" has a special meaning to Emtrol. It means skillfully engineered and manufactured control systems in a fascinating variety of applications. A sampling of electronic, electrical, and mechanical control systems designed by Emtrol includes controls for positioning the large refractor telescope at Swarthmore College with the timing exposure of photographic plates plus a printout of the time each photograph is taken (and a companion unit for fine positioning); controls for automatic stacker cranes and inventory control in warehouses; and for monitoring and safe disposition of dust in large grain elevators. Other systems are manufactured for roller hearth operations as well as tempering and hardening in basic steel manufacturing processes; for chemical-

process temperature monitoring, recording, and alarm systems; and for instrumentation systems built to test helicopter motor blades under simulated flight conditions. Emtrol engineers have designed a device to reclaim metal from slag piles, and controlled a process to dispose of fly ash by compaction and mixing to produce lightweight stone aggregates. They also have designed a control system for automatic production of consistent paste batches for corrugated paperboard fabrication.

Any size project, from a simple feed controller to complex batching and mixing systems, is an interesting job to Emtrol. They're organized to do the total job, from on-site analysis to monitoring initial operations, or to help with a single aspect of a particular project.

Emtrol engineers have a broad base of experience in a variety of construction and industrial operations. They specialize in continuous process systems but their abilities include the design of mechanical, electrical, electronic, pneumatic, and hydraulic control elements. H.F. Moore and Associates, a division of Emtrol, provides consulting engineering services for electrical and mechanical systems.

Emtrol Inc: H.F. Moore, president; Raymond J. Anater, vice president and secretary; Phillip L. Grahek, vice president and treasurer.

Holder Decker Brisson, Inc.

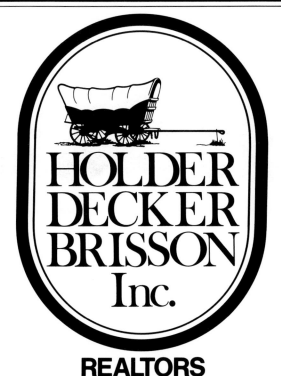

REALTORS

The symbol of the Conestoga wagon is a reminder that Holder Decker Brisson, Inc., evolved from the Conestoga Realty Company.

Holder Decker Brisson, Inc., prominent Lancaster Realtors, has had a close view of the changes that have affected both Lancaster and the real estate business over the years. From two employees in 1964, they now operate with a staff of twenty, and are the second-largest real estate firm in Lancaster County. Located at 439 North Duke Street, the corporate offices have been moved three times — to three different addresses on North Duke Street. The company chose not to take part in the flight to the suburbs, and has been a significant

force in the population movement back toward downtown Lancaster.

After a long period of drift away from city-living, the trend was reversed about four to five years ago. More and more home buyers are interested in renovating and restoring older properties. And the effect has been contagious. As whole city blocks participate in the improvement effort, our city is becoming more than an object of civic pride: it is becoming a model for other cities to emulate. Currently, Holder Decker Brisson is working with three major developers for the restoration and development of downtown Lancaster.

The real estate business itself is vastly different from the days when an individual could hang out a shingle and be in business. Today's agent must be familiar with zoning laws, financial arrangements, and the legal aspects of property changing hands. Today's buyer has become more knowledgeable about the intricacies of home buying. To accommodate the specialized needs of the present business, Holder Decker Brisson operates as three divisions: Residential Sales, Commercial Investment, and Property Management. The company offers the full cycle of real estate service.

The three corporate principals, Grover (Bud) C. Holder, Lloyd M. Decker, and Leon J. Brisson, have been active members of the real estate professional groups, and served as directors and presidents of the Greater Lancaster Board of Realtors. It was during Leon Brisson's tenure as president that the multi-list system was computerized in 1975. Though the multi-list system had been in service for fifty-two years and is one of the oldest in the nation, the computer broadened the service dramatically. An up-to-date listing of all available properties is issued every two weeks. Each member broker (over seventy in the county) has a computer terminal in his office to receive instant information on each property by every imaginable category: by location, size, price, number of rooms, municipal services, tax structure — all the details that are important to the buyer.

Holder Decker Brisson is justly proud of its contribution to the growth of Lancaster and is dedicated to the goal of emphasizing integrity and quality over bigness in the services it provides.

Hamilton Technology, Inc.

This early group of employees is pictured in 1893 at a time when the meticulous skills of the watchmaker were proudly passed from father to son.

"Hamilton — the Railroad Time Keeper of America." Pictured here, the first railroad watch, now preserved in the company's vaults.

"From the train age to the space age" aptly describes this community landmark, Hamilton Technology, Inc., that continues at the famed location on Lancaster's Columbia Avenue.

The fine watchmaking skills developed by its predecessor company, and the research and development of ordnance devices and in metals technology have made a unique combination of talent. HamTech manufactures precision components and assembles fuze mechanisms, safety and arming devices, sensing devices and timers that are used for military applications and guidance systems. Its metals operation is a specialty re-roller of pure metals and alloys in the form of close-tolerance strip and ultra-thin foil. HamTech's industrial customers reads like the list of the *Fortune* 500.

The development of the skills that make all of this possible go back to the very beginnings of a watch company on the same location. But not the Hamilton Watch Company itself! In 1874 the Adams and Perry Watch Company was responsible for bringing watchmakers to Lancaster. And it was they who recessed the building back from the Lancaster turnpike for practical, not esthetic, reasons. At that time Conestoga wagons plied the turnpike, creating a continuous blanket of dust. The watchmakers needed daylight and open windows. The solution was the move away from the road so that the distance would serve as a natural filtering system — air-pollution control, 1874 style!

Two other watch companies followed and failed. Then in 1892 the Hamilton Watch Company came into existence through the efforts of a group of leading Lancaster business and professional men. Included were J.W.B. Bausman, John F. Brimmer, Harry B. Cochran, Frank P. Coho, C.A. Fondersmith, George M. Franklin, John C. Hager, J.P. McCaskey, H.M. North, Martin Ringwalt, J. Fredrick Sener, William Z. Sener, James Shand, Peter T. Watt, and H.S. Williamson.

What made these men think they could succeed where others had failed? Hindsight suggests a correct assessment of the times. The demand for accurate timepieces was about to explode.

In the year 1880 every town and hamlet in the United States had a different time standard determined by the "sun time" of its particular location. There were fifty different "times" in use by the various railroads. Amidst all this confusion, faulty timing caused a series

The original Hamilton Watch factory as it looked when the newly organized company took it over in 1892. Built for the Adams and Perry Watch Co. in 1874, it also housed the Lancaster Watch Co. (1877-1885) and the Keystone Watch Co. (1886-1890).

Aerial view of the fourteen-acre HamTech facility.

of disastrous railroad accidents. A serious wreck in Ohio on April 18, 1891, was highly publicized. Witnesses testified that "the watches of the engineers and conductors of both trains were of the cheapest kind and in bad condition." Precise timing was of utmost importance for the safe completion of switching trains from one track to another because many single-track railroads at the time used switches to accommodate trains traveling in different directions. The national publicity given to these findings resulted in the adoption of official Railway Watch Inspection services that required employees in charge of train operations to have a watch of approved quality and subject to frequent inspection. Thus was created an enlarged demand for rugged, accurate utility watches.

The Hamilton Watch Company set out to serve the railroad market with accurate timepieces.

In 1893 a large railroad watch was built to meet the specifications of the Time Inspection rules that the railroads had established. By the turn of the century Hamilton watches had become a favorite of the. growing army of railroad men. Unsolicited letters of praise led to the well-known advertising campaign based on the success of the railroad watch. In 1908 Hamilton's first national advertising was placed in the *National Geographic* and was the magazine's first advertiser. The new slogan: The Watch of Railroad Accuracy.

During World Wars I and II, Hamilton was a major supplier of vital instrumentation to the government. As a matter of fact, in 1941, the factory's total output was devoted to military production for marine chronometers, sturdy chronometer watches for torpedo boats, and navigation master watches for bombers.

Just as the old Hamilton Watch Company began by fulfilling a need in the railroad industry, HamTech continues to meet its customers' needs with fabricated piece-parts and a variety of complicated precision assemblies and devices. The shift of the business from consumer to government and industrial markets reflects the changes wrought by the times. The space age has had a powerful impact with its emphasis on high technology, advancements in micro-miniaturization, and breakthroughs in electronics, as has the commitment by the United States to maintain a strong national defense.

Hamilton Technology, a subsidiary of HMW Industries, Inc.: a magnificent heritage and promising future — "a great small company."

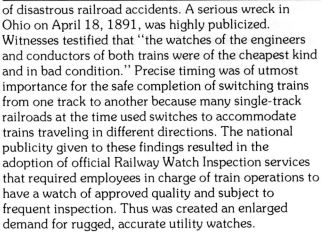

Harold A. Horn Agency

The Harold A. Horn Agency at
15 North Lime Street.

The Harold A. Horn Insurance Agency is as new as 1952. But the service it provides to clients is timeless: security and protection for family and business.

At first Harold Horn worked alone from an office in the Fulton Bank Building on Penn Square. He sold life, accident, and health insurance. But clients kept asking for fire and casualty coverage also. The repeated question led the company into a full line of insurance, as it is today.

More business soon required more staff, which was added gradually. There are now seventeen full-time employees and ten part-time brokers, with real-estate capability complementing the insurance business. The professional staff is committed to providing well-planned, comprehensive insurance plans for health, home, and business.

Additional staff meant additional space requirements and, in 1972, the company moved to its present location in a handsome restored townhouse at 15 North Lime Street. From all appearances, another move to still larger offices may be near.

"One thing is for sure," Harold Horn emphasizes, "our offices are always going to be in downtown Lancaster. No matter where you live in the area, downtown Lancaster must be recognized as the hub of our county. It certainly is the center of our government, banking, and legal communities."

The Harold Horn Agency owes its success to the service it provides its clients. Responsive, careful, conservative service. The same attributes apply to Horn himself, for he has served his country, commonwealth, and community with distinction. He is a retired colonel, U.S. Army Reserves, and a former state legislator. As president of the Rock Ford Foundation he presides over a community board that oversees the preserved plantation of Edward Hand, George Washington's Surgeon-General. He is vice-president of the YMCA board of directors.

Horn is a United Way board member, past chairman of 1977's successful United Way campaign, and holds positions with the Lancaster Association of Commerce and Industry, Boys' Club, and Blind Association.

Harold A. Horn is a dedicated community servant who, personally and professionally, is committed to a cause — a greater Lancaster.

International Signal and Control Corporation

International Signal and Control Corp. was born April 1, 1971. It was no April Fool joke then and certainly is not one now, since ISC has gained an international reputation as a major competitor in the fields of electronics, electro-mechanical products, optical and laser systems, as well as in domestic turnkey know-how and manufacturing capability.

In only nine months' time, ISC outgrew its first home, a converted garage on Route 501 north of Lancaster where James H. Guerin, founder and president, with his talented group of enterprising engineers had to share space with their landlord's horse. They subsequently moved to Hempfield Industrial Park, which presently serves as corporate headquarters. A number of separate divisions function autonomously here in their respective design and production fields, while key marketing and support offices are located strategically throughout the world.

Based in Lancaster are Electronics Systems International (ESI), offering overseas access to the most advanced United States systems technology; International Signal and Control Electronics Division (ISCE), offering state-of-the-art engineering, electronic systems, and control components; ISC Special Products Division (SP), with a full line of commercial electronic and related products; Novatec, with a full span of commercial marketing and technical services; the Micro Precision Tool and Die Division (MP), offering fine tools, dies, and fixtures, as well as precision small parts manufacturing and sheet metal fabrication. The Micronics International (MII) subsidiary is located in Anaheim, California, offering the West Coast a similar range of the engineering, electronics, and control capabilities that are available here.

ISC started with a nucleus of ten people, and grew rapidly. By the end of the first year there were thirty-five employees occupying ten thousand square feet of floor space on Hempland Road. All facilities are modern steel and concrete structures now totaling over 150,000 square feet and accommodating 750 employees.

Being hired as problem solvers often requires ISC to assemble unique talent. The corporation is capability-oriented rather than product-oriented. A full twenty percent of its personnel hold advanced engineering degrees from the nation's leading colleges and universities. ISC has assembled a roster of engineers and scientists with experience in many diversified areas, and skills at all levels, that is dedicated to the challenges of modern electronics technology. To complement the engineering team is a production staff where more than forty percent can claim ten or more years' experience in exacting design or assembly work.

Intense growth of the corporation is indicative of what's been happening in computer technology and the electronics industry. Whereas in its infancy ISC was often contracted to provide one component of a system, today ISC is contracted to provide the entire system. The technology-oriented operation has expanded to include business and marketing facilities so that an overall, balanced growth company is the result.

ISC does fifty percent of its business abroad, in seventeen countries, five continents. Twenty-five percent of its business is domestic. Another twenty-five percent is in government and related contracts. The measure of ISC's success is indicated when you read sales charts registering one-half million dollars for the first year, escalating to $30 million in 1978. That's what you call keeping pace with dynamic customer requirements.

No matter how far afield ISC's operations stretch, strength at the root level is of first importance. ISC's roots are in Lancaster. Without support of local financial institutions, specialized vendors, and key professionals, ISC might still be in the stable. But the corporation's main strength is its highly competent people whose industriousness and loyalty are legion. Matched by an aggressive, outgoing management team, ISC wants to tell its story — at home and abroad — that it is a leading contender for front-runner position in the systems and electronics engineering field. And it's here to stay.

Howmet Aluminum Corporation

William Hume, first president
Thomas H. Zimmerman

Raymond Buckwalter
Josephine Kirchner

Albert H. Charlton
John R. Keene

Can an abandoned freight station in Leola father a fifty-seven-acre, fully integrated aluminum plant on the Manheim Pike? The record indicates yes — if the name is New Holland Metals Company; Quaker State Metals Company; Howe Sound Corporation; Howmet Corporation; and Howmet Aluminum Corporation, sequentially.

Five visionaries joined forces in 1946 to lay the foundation of today's enterprise. The newly formed New Holland Metals Company in Leola began with William Hume (President), Albert Charlton, John Keene, M. Josephine Kirchner, and Thomas Zimmerman; with one piece of equipment (a sheet corrugator); and with an abundance of enthusiasm and hard work. The initial product line consisted of corrugated aluminum sheets for farm and industrial siding. In just two years the freight station was outgrown, and manufacturing was moved to Mountville in 1948. The larger quarters housed fifteen employees

This is the group that not only started the company, but was responsible for the "people-

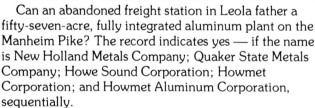

oriented" corporate style that still exists among today's one thousand employees.

and more equipment, and the product line was expanded to include rain-carrying systems. This was the first of a series of plant and product-line expansions during the past thirty-two years.

The sixth visionary, Raymond Buckwalter, came on the scene and provided the financial support to reorganize the company as Quaker State Metals. In 1953 (with its one hundred employees) the company moved to a site on the Buckwalter Farm along Manheim Pike, the present location of Howmet. A used rolling mill was purchased and installed, one that is still in use today. A mobile-home products firm, acquired in 1967, helped diversify the company and is now a division of Howmet. In 1968-69 the Manheim Pike operations were separated into two functional divisions: Mill Products and Building Products. The

The New Holland Metals Company opened for business in an abandoned freight station and grew to become Howmet.

A fifty-seven-acre tract along the Manheim Pike is now the Mill Products Division. The current $40 million expansion program assures Howmet's leadership in aluminum production.

Building Products Division, with additional facilities in Atlanta, Georgia; Bedford Park, Illinois; and Los Angeles, California, is the direct continuation of the original New Holland Metals Company and produces siding accessories, rain-carrying systems, flashing, and soffit systems. Similar but different, the present operation bears little resemblance to the original building and its minimal equipment; to the time when the company's single forklift truck was nearly as indispensable as the aluminum-processing equipment.

Today, with fifteen acres under roof for the manufacturing operation, Howmet's fifty-seven-acre plant with high-speed rolling mills provides the experience, up-to-date technology, and expertise needed to meet any semifabricated aluminum sheet and coil specifications. Howmet is fully integrated in aluminum, and, since 1975, a member of the Pechiney Ugine Kuhlmann Group, an international metals, chemicals, and nuclear-fuel organization. This latest transaction provides the framework for easy interchange of technology, management skills, financial resources, and manufacturing expertise between the three Lancaster-based Howmet Divisions and Pechiney — one of the world's one hundred largest industrial companies, and the world's fourth-largest producer of aluminum.

Millions of pounds of aluminum ingots are rolled into Howmet coil each week. Three hundred million pounds of aluminum sheet and coil and blanks are produced per year. Literally thousands of products are manufactured from Howmet sheet and coil: electrical

parts, patio covers, gutters and downspouts, cooking utensils, hubcaps and auto trim, recreational vehicles, air conditioners, light-bulb bases, light reflectors, and embossed parts in hundreds of colors. And that's just a sampling.

The Mill Products Division of Howmet is well into the largest expansion program in the company's history. In June of 1977 plans for a five-year building program were announced. The new 140,000-square-foot plant and mill are to be built and installed on three acres adjacent to the present operation to accommodate the fast-paced increase in the demand for aluminum.

Building Products Division, Hempfield Industrial Park.

Mobile Home Division, Conestoga Valley Industrial Park.

Kunzler and Company, Inc.

Christian F. Kunzler, right, stands with his helpers at his new butcher shop at 652 Manor Street, in 1902.

This familiar old Lancaster landmark started by chance, a seven-hundred-dollar investment, a bull, and a hog.

Chance played its role when a recent German immigrant, Christian F. Kunzler, came to Lancaster from New York to visit a relative. A weekend visit turned into a new way of life. He stayed as a butcher in the Gunz Meat Market at 652 Manor Street, then invested his life savings of seven hundred dollars in the business. The purchase, the twenty dollars rent money, shop equipment — he barely had enough money left over for a bull and a hog. But the famed sausage maker was in business: from the stockyards to the abattoir, then to the butcher shop and residents of Cabbage Hill.

In 1901, business literally started at the Lancaster stockyards. Every day a mini-cattle drive followed a two-mile path along the outskirts of town to the Kunzler plant on Manor Street. Imagine householders along the way, well accustomed to the sight, interrupting their sidewalk sweeping to prod an errant steer with the other end of the broom. That's the way it was.

Christian Kunzler had learned his trade as an apprentice butcher in Germany, finally receiving the degree of Master Sausage-Maker. His delicately spiced sausages were a hit with Lancastrians and the business quickly prospered. Always the ingenious businessman, he devised a refrigerated case and displayed his wares in the shop window, a novel and tempting sight to passersby. Within five years he had a stand at Central Market and opened two branch stores on Queen and Water streets. A major event in company history occurred in 1908 when the Kunzler Meat Wagon made its first trip to York, a journey that took from dawn until dark.

When it became difficult to accommodate both the wholesale and retail trade, Kunzler went all wholesale in the early 1920s and so it is today.

Much of the past is incorporated into today's operation: a modern, expanded plant stands at the same spot on Manor Street; the old twenty-stall horse stable has been remodeled and is used for storage; the original sausage recipes are still used; and the company is managed by the third generation of the Kunzler family.

Kunzler products now include all kinds of fresh meats as well as hams, bacon, luncheon meats, and sausage.

One thing hasn't changed over the years and that is the dedication to producing a quality product. The old hand butcher tools (now retired and polished for display) have given way to modern stainless-steel automated equipment in spotless kitchens. The hand operations that once produced elegant sausages from start to finish are performed by a custom-designed processing unit that can smoke, cook, and chill 120,000 frankfurters per hour — that's eight miles of franks! And that's probably more franks per five minutes than the founder could make in his ten-hour, seven-day workweek.

The first delivery to York in the old Kunzler meat wagon was a dawn-to-dark trip in 1908.

Lancaster Association of Commerce & Industry

Organized commerce in Lancaster is as old as the town itself. This plaque marks the original site of the Central Market, first established in 1730. The market is now housed in the building at center rear.

The industrial development of Lancaster dates back at least to 1847, when the first real factory, the Conestoga Cotton Mill No. 1, began production. The building is now used as a warehouse.

For more than a century, the Lancaster Association of Commerce & Industry and its "ancestors" have been representing the interests of the Lancaster business community.

Lancaster already had a long tradition as a center of industry and commerce when a group of local businessmen organized the Lancaster Board of Trade in 1872. Despite organizational difficulties — there were two reorganizations of the group during its formative years — the Board of Trade actively pursued programs intended to promote retail trade and attract new businesses to Lancaster.

In those early years, the affairs of the business community were of paramount importance to the organization; the 1896 charter of the Board of Trade summarized the Board's purpose as "generally, by united and well-directed efforts, to advance the interests and promote the commercial integrity of the business community."

In 1910, the Board of Trade consolidated with the Retail Merchants Association to form the Lancaster Chamber of Commerce. The new organization continued the activities of the Board of Trade, but — setting a most important precedent — it also added projects for the welfare of the community-at-large to its program.

The Manufacturers Association of Lancaster was chartered in 1912 to promote more directly the interests of the industrial community. Over the years, the Chamber and the Manufacturers Association cooperated on many projects of importance to both groups.

By the mid-1970s, the two organizations had both relocated into the same office building. With a considerable number of activities — as well as members — in common, consolidation of the Manufacturers Association and the Chamber was a logical next step. After thorough study, the two organizations joined together on 1 January 1977 to form the Lancaster Association of Commerce & Industry.

Representing the interests of, and serving as spokesman for, the business and industrial concerns of Lancaster City and County, LACI's leadership position in the community is backed by more than one hundred years of tradition.

Today, the thriving industrial and commercial interests of Lancaster are represented by the Lancaster Association of Commerce & Industry.

Lancaster Federal Savings and Loan Association

The new offices of the Lancaster Federal Savings and Loan in the Griest Building, Penn Square, Lancaster.

The first savings and loan association in the United States, the Oxford Provident Building Society, was formed in Philadelphia in 1831. That was a time when banks were geared to commerce and had no provision for lending money for long-term payment in small monthly amounts. The first association required a five-dollar initiation fee and dues of three dollars per month from each member. In return, members were issued dividend-paying shares, and when enough money accumulated to enable a member to purchase a home, the right to borrow the money was offered to the highest bidder. The original intent was to disband the group after all members had purchased homes. However, it took so long to accumulate enough capital for everyone to buy a home in a reasonable length of time, the association began accepting savers into the society and the savings and loan idea was established in more or less the same form in which we find it today.

The idea spread quickly and by 1890 there was a savings and loan association in every state of the union. Then known as building and loan associations, they were relatively loose-knit neighborhood-type organizations with no formal headquarters. Monthly meetings were rotated among the homes of different members. At one time there were hundreds of such small groups operating in Lancaster County.

As a result of the 1929 depression, the federal government imposed new regulations on the associations. They were required to establish headquarters (frequently rented corners or a teller window at a bank) and to carry insurance on the savings. In 1962 the government decreed that a savings and loan association must have ground-floor, independent office space. At that point, Lancaster Federal Savings and Loan moved to 134 East King Street in Lancaster, the same year that it was incorporated as a federally chartered and federally insured mutual organization.

Increased business activity dictated another move, and in a masterful display of moving technique, Lancaster Federal finished business as usual on Friday at East King Street and on the following Monday (August 5, 1977), opened for business as usual in new offices on the ground floor of the Griest Building. They are now in the middle of the "new-old Lancaster" — next to the renovated Central Farmers Market and Lancaster Heritage House. The main thrust of their business is the same now as in the beginning: to encourage thrift and home ownership. They note an ever-increasing rise in the number of applications for mortgages on city homes.

Lancaster has great faith in the future and will continue to reinvest Lancastrians' savings in Lancaster home mortgages.

Lancaster Newspapers, Inc.

The Sunday News *was conceived and published by Steinman and Steinman, September 16, 1923.*

Saturday, April 28, 1877, the New Era *was first published.*

The 1794 Lancaster Journal *was the forerunner of today's* Intelligencer Journal.

Few newspapers in the nation can trace their origin back as far as the *Intelligencer Journal.* Starting as a weekly in 1794, today's *Intelligencer Journal* can lay claim to being the seventh-oldest daily in the United States.

The Lancaster *Journal,* as it was known then, was founded by Wilcox and Hamilton, but unlike its issues of today, the old paper did not think local news was of enough interest to print. The records show only one exception when on the Fourth of July of the year 1794 the details of the local celebration were recorded in the news.

Following the *Journal* came an opposition weekly known as the Lancaster *Intelligencer and Weekly Advertiser.* In 1839 these papers merged and became known as the Lancaster *Intelligencer Journal.*

The daily *Intelligencer* came into existence on August 19,1864. It was in 1866 that Andrew Jackson Steinman, then one of the foremost members of the Lancaster Bar, became the editor and publisher, and he never gave up his duties until his death in November, 1917.

Charles Steinman Foltz, who died in 1941, was part-owner and editor with Mr. Steinman from 1887 until he sold his interest in 1921 to Mr. Steinman's sons, James Hale and John F. Steinman, who several years earlier had acquired their father's interest.

The *New Era* first appeared in 1877, founded by John B. Warfel, who had been a Republican state

senator for ten years, and J.M.W. Geist, who had risen from printer's devil to become a colorful figure in local journalism. They published the *New Era* until 1897 when it was taken over by the founder's son, John G. Warfel, and B.S. Shindle, Andrew H. Hershey, and James D. Landis. Mr. Landis later succeeded Mr. Geist as editor.

After being sold and later merging with the *Examiner,* the property was bought by Paul Block, a chain publisher, in 1923, and it remained in his possession until 1928 when the present alignment of the Lancaster Newspapers was effected.

On April 16, 1928, the *Intelligencer,* which was then an afternoon paper, was merged with the *News Journal,* a morning edition, and resumed its old name of the *Intelligencer Journal,* starting the morning publication which continues today. The Lancaster *New Era* continued afternoon publication.

Seeing the need for a Sunday newspaper, the publishers founded the *Sunday News* on September 16, 1923, and since that time it has made rapid strides in growth and development in Sunday newspaper circles.

The *Intelligencer Journal,* Lancaster *New Era,* and *Sunday News* are three distinct newspapers. The editorial policy of each of the three papers remains as disparate as the views of its editor and individual staff. In each case the editorial policy of the paper is directed by that paper's editor.

Lancaster Surgical Supply and Apothecary, Inc.

One of a collection of mortar and pestles, the time-honored symbol of the pharmacist, housed at Lancaster Surgical Supply and Apothecary, Inc.

Before Luther L. Wertz and Arahlee Wertz, R.N., opened their surgical supply store on March 27, 1941, there was no such service in Lancaster. He had been a practicing pharmacist in Reading, where he also had learned the surgical supply business. The deeply ingrained work ethic so characteristic of this area powered his success: he had sold newspapers at age six, lugged ice blocks at age twelve, and he approached the new business with the same tough singlemindedness.

The store was moved from 148 North Duke Street into the former American Legion building after an extensive remodeling job in 1961. Here the products displayed on the first level belie the extensive services offered by the business today. The twenty-three-foot ceilings of this four-story building create space — and all that space is being used, as is additional storage on

Walnut Street. The huge building houses a complete line of sickroom and convalescent equipment for sale and rent: wheelchairs, walkers, manual and electrical hospital beds, as well as an extensive inventory of supplies for hospitals and medical personnel. Where once the business served mainly physicians and hospitals, now Emergency Medical Technicians (EMTs), including crews for the fifteen ambulance services around the county, nurse practitioners, school and industrial dispensaries in a six-county area, are included. From individual requirements to the complete needs of establishing a new medical laboratory or office, Lancaster Surgical Supply is prepared.

With the move to the present location at 214 North Duke Street, Lancaster Surgical Supply opened its pharmacy department. There have been enormous changes in this field over the years as the pace of discoveries has accelerated: 1831 — chloroform; 1889 — aspirin, still the remedy of choice for myriad complaints; 1901 — adrenalin; 1936 — cortisone; 1941 — terramycin; and on to a bewildering proliferation of synthetic drugs, antihistamines, vitamins, etc. No wonder a layman can be confused. And no wonder that the training of a skilled pharmacist has increased from the three years of college required for Luther Wertz to the four years required of his son, Robert L. Wertz (president and owner since 1975), to the five years required of today's pharmacy students.

"Choose your druggist with the same care with which you choose your physician" is the advice of the modern pharmacist. His role in today's health service has assumed greater importance than ever because his prime concern is to be thoroughly knowledgeable about all the new drugs and their possible interactions. One of the pharmacist's most valuable services is the keeping of medical records for those customers wishing this double check. Acute awareness of the potential for abuse of controlled substances motivated Robert Wertz to be among the first of a group formed in 1968 to alert our community to the dangers. "Contact," the hospital drug program and, subsequently, Manos House evolved from their efforts in behalf of our entire community.

In a business where emergency and crisis are all a routine part of the twenty-four-hour day, seven-day week, Lancaster Surgical Supply and Apothecary is a valued community asset.

Penn Dairies, Inc.

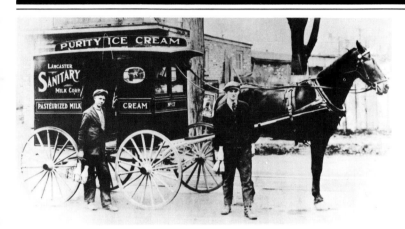

Here's "Charlie," with drivers J. Paul Bowman and John Eberly, about to leave the barn at Frederick and Prince streets for daily round of deliveries in 1923.

A long, dusty road. A man bent to the task of pedaling his bicycle from Stevens to Emigsville with $3,000 secured in his money belt. The man was Eli Garber on his way to buy a small creamery at the end of the forty-four mile, overnight trip. The year was 1890, and it marked the beginning of the Garber-Reist creamery, as well as Penn Dairies, Inc.

The Garber-Reist creamery operated in Stevens for three years, then began a series of mergers and name changes. By 1929 the firm was incorporated as Penn Dairies, a combination of three companies in Lancaster and York, Pennsylvania. Penn Dairies' Lancaster plant was first located on North Queen Street, the present site of the YMCA, then moved to its modern processing facility on Hempstead Road in 1964.

From Eli Garber to J. Ferry Garber and John F. Garber, Jr., president of Penn Dairies, management of the company has remained in the same family. It has grown from the initial five employees to nearly one thousand, who made possible sales of more than $50 million in 1977. Because of its long history in the dairy business, Penn Dairies has both witnessed and implemented dramatic changes in the processing and delivery of milk and milk products. Penn Dairies was one of the first milk companies to pasteurize milk in 1900 by a primitive, yet effective technique. Milk was poured into bottles which were set in a horse trough and covered with scalding water. The essential function of heating the raw milk and killing the bacteria was accomplished.

Today raw milk is pumped from tank trucks directly into a maze of seamless stainless-steel piping, through completely automated pasteurization and processing equipment and packaged for distribution — all untouched by human hands. Twenty-six million dollars' worth of milk was purchased and processed in 1977. Eighty percent comes from local farms.

In the 1900s milk and ice cream were delivered in horsedrawn wagons. Custom service was a specialty: two quarts of fresh ice cream delivered? No problem. The order was placed in a covered returnable tin container and set in a tub of salt and ice on the customer's porch. Penn Dairies was also among the first to introduce the freezing tunnel for use in ice cream manufacture, a technique that is now standard practice in the industry.

Home delivery of dairy products slowed with the introduction of supermarkets. In the late 1960s, following the trend of customer preference to buy in a store, Penn Dairies started opening the Pensupreme Grocerettes. These convenience stores make up an important segment of the company's business.

Penn Dairies' Lancaster processing center is supplemented by three branches. Pensupreme ice cream products are distributed in an area bounded by Boston, Norfolk, and Pittsburgh while Pensupreme milk products are distributed in southeastern Pennsylvania, Maryland, New Jersey, and Delaware.

Penn Dairies also operates a bulk dairy manufacturing plant in York, Pennsylvania, which manufactures and processes fresh and frozen cream, skim milk, sweetened skim condensed, skim and whole condensed, and blends for ice cream manufacturing. Customers of this plant include Penn Dairies' Lancaster processing center, as well as other large dairies, ice cream manufacturers, bakeries, and candy companies.

Pennsylvania Dutch Visitors Bureau

The Amish community attracts many visitors who wish to learn about their way of life.

The Visitors Bureau is an association of approximately 350 tourist-related businesses and attractions which was formed to tell the world what Lancastrians have always known: Lancaster is a "garden spot" in many ways.

The services of the Bureau and the interest of tourists in coming to Lancaster have grown hand in hand. Starting in 1957 as a division of the Lancaster Chamber of Commerce, the Visitors Bureau split off as a separate group in 1967. From their newly expanded headquarters at 1799 Hempstead Road, they assist travelers to find their way to the many attractions of the county. Their spacious new quarters feature a large oval information counter manned by a knowledgeable staff. The perimeter of the room is filled with racks of over four hundred different information pieces from local attractions, nonprofit organizations, and industries that welcome visitors for tours of their premises. An exceptional film, *The Lancaster Experience,* was produced to give newcomers an overview of the county and its people and is shown hourly in the 150-seat theater.

Impetus for the development of this relatively new industry came from the Broadway production of *Plain and Fancy.* Set in Lancaster County, the play drew widespread attention to the county and its Amish community, one of the three largest in the United States. People come to observe and learn about the ways of the Amish, to discover famed Pennsylvania-Dutch cooking, specifically requesting the shoofly pie and pretzels that have come to symbolize the area. Now Lancastrians find themselves sharing their county with five million visitors a year; in 1977, five hundred thousand of them contacted the Visitors Bureau. The county ranks among the top ten family recreational and resort areas in the country. And as the popularity of camping has grown, Lancaster County has kept pace and is prepared with over four thousand campsites.

Early this summer the Visitors Bureau opened a second office downtown in the Brunswick Mall. The Downtown Visitors Bureau provides descriptive material for points of interest in the county and city as well as displays of local arts and crafts. It also schedules walking tours in conjunction with the volunteer group that provides costumed guides. The rich architectural variety of historical Lancaster is viewed firsthand. Highlights of the walk include two-hundred-year-old homes, many freshly renovated in keeping with their former elegance; Trinity Lutheran Church which dates from 1730; Old City Hall in Penn Square, now housing circulating collections of early county memorabilia; the Fulton Opera House, stage for major theater stars since 1852; and the Central Farmers Market, an integral part of Lancaster life since 1744. Early risers can still watch the farmers unload their fresh, home-grown meats and produce on market days at 5:00 a.m. The market remains an important and delightful shopping place for Lancaster residents and visitors.

While agriculture remains Lancaster County's number-one industry, tourism fills the number-two spot. The Visitors Bureau is responsible for directing the growth of this important segment of the local economy.

Visitors are welcome to view the collections of early county memorabilia in the Lancaster Heritage Center housed in Old City Hall in Penn Square.

Permutit Company

Subsidiary of Zurn Industries

PERMUTIT — The name derives from the Latin verb *permutare* meaning "to interchange," and was first used to describe the ion-exchange process that removes hardness from water.

The familiar blue water tower on the Old Philadelphia Pike has signaled the Lancaster location of Permutit since 1954. But the company itself goes back to 1913 when it was incorporated in New York. An imaginative sales technique was used to introduce the public to the benefits of softened water. The first water-softener installations were made in commercial laundries at no obligation except an agreement to pay to Permutit half of the monthly savings in soap costs as determined by tests before and after installation of the Permutit Softener. In every such installation, the laundry purchased the softener after having made a few monthly payments. The concept of water softening was quickly established.

Where once the customer was a venturesome commercial laundry or homeowner, and the product was a water softener, Permutit now designs and manufactures equipment for complete water-treatment systems. Customers range from small businesses to corporate giants, and from villages to the greatest cities. Service includes study and analysis of a water-treatment problem, through equipment design, fabrication, test, and installation. Permutit does it all. Working closely with their research center in Princeton and engineering group in Paramus, New Jersey, Permutit can produce a complete line of process equipment, the facilities for manufacturing it, and the ability to fuse all of these elements to deliver a working system to solve water and waste-water problems.

The Lancaster plant manufactures and assembles all critical machined parts, valves, and control systems, as well as skid-mounted and packaged equipment. Local craftsmen include machinists, pipefitters, fiberglass applicators, assemblers, welders, wiremen, instrument makers, and finishers. An entire treatment system can be fabricated, skid-mounted, and tested at the plant, or the components can be shipped from the plant for on-site assembly. The main products leaving the Lancaster plant are components for nuclear reactors, standard water-treatment products, and waste-treatment equipment, including the DCG and MRP, units that press water out of waste in order to create disposable sludge.

Once *water treatment* meant the removal of minerals from water to soften it. Now Permutit *water treatment* includes: aerators, degasifiers, deaerators, central control systems, chemical feeders, precipitators, chevron tube settlers, dealkilizers, spiractors (clarifiers for softening clean hard water containing primarily calcium), filtration units, softening and demineralizing units, and on to the newest advances in process systems including reverse osmosis — its line of equipment is virtually unsurpassed in completeness and its process engineers have designed and built treatment systems for every known industrial and municipal application.

Above, *a Lancaster-built demineralizer, mounted and ready for shipment.*

Below, *the factory's machining capabilities range from turning rough castings to meeting exact tolerances required in equipment for nuclear service.*

RCA Corporation

*Worldwide headquarters for the
RCA Picture Tube Division,
and the Electro Optics and
Devices, Solid State Division.*

*Products from the Lancaster
plant are shipped all over the
world, as well as "out of this
world" in space missions.*

The RCA Lancaster plant location, originally a ninety-acre farm, was purchased on January 28, 1942. RCA and the Navy needed a site for a new electron-tube plant to manufacture specialized military tubes. In March 1942, ground was broken for the plant, and initial production of radio transmitting, radar, and oscilloscope tubes was started in December of the same year.

The year 1946 was a period of transition from wartime production under the Navy to peacetime operations by RCA. In May 1946 RCA purchased the plant from the Navy. Over the years the Lancaster plant has been the major base for RCA television picture tubes, as well as specialized industrial tubes and devices.

Lancaster was the birthplace for television picture tubes and television camera tubes for both black and white and color. In 1946 RCA Lancaster began large-scale black-and-white TV picture tube production, and by 1949 more than one million TV tubes had been manufactured. The original shadow mask color TV picture tube was designed and developed at Lancaster in the 1948 to 1953 period. In 1953 initial color-television picture tube production was started in Lancaster. Throughout the years, Lancaster has been

the center for RCA television picture tube engineering. The vast majority of new color picture tube types introduced to the industry were first demonstrated to the worldwide TV set manufacturers at the Lancaster plant.

In addition, the Lancaster plant has been, and is, the headquarters for RCA's many electro-optics products and special purpose tubes. Over the years, RCA has engineered and manufactured a wide variety of color television camera tubes, special photomultiplier tubes for medical and scientific applications, AM/FM and television transmitting tubes, high-resolution display tubes, and many others. Subsequently, super power tubes, small pencil tubes, and sophisticated storage and microwave tubes were added. Recent products include closed-circuit TV cameras, solid-state light-emitting diodes (LEDs), and image sensors (charge-coupled devices), plus solid-state transcalent power devices.

Products from the RCA Lancaster plant are used all over the world in a variety of ways: in communications, space exploration, photography, industrial and medical applications and, in the home, from TV to smoke-detection alarm systems.

Today the RCA Lancaster site comprises over one million square feet of floor space and houses two company divisions: Electro Optics and Devices, Solid State Division, and the Picture Tube Division. Since 1975 Lancaster has been the headquarters for the worldwide operations of the RCA Picture Tube Division.

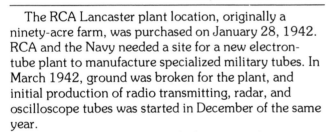

RM Friction Materials Company

The United States Asbestos Company was founded in 1906 in Manheim.

A small canning-company building in Manheim — a smoldering rubble — an industrial island frequently surrounded by water — RM Friction Materials Company has been all of these.

In 1906 five local businessmen got together and formed the U.S. Asbestos Company for the purpose of "mining asbestos and the manufacture and sale of merchantable products thereof." The mill was established in the building previously owned by a short-lived canning company. The location of the plant, near the Chickies Creek in Manheim, then as now, has led to regular flooding over the years, in varying degrees of intensity. An early wit suggested that there should be a tidewater table posted at the entrance so they could tell when it was going to be high water at the plant. On June 22, 1972, "Agnes" left from eight inches to four feet of water throughout the offices and factory: instead of manning the machines, manning the brooms and hoses was in order for three days of shoveling mud.

The company's products in 1908 consisted of spun yarn, tape, cloth, wick, fiber, sheet packing, gasket cloth, and gaskets. By 1910 the woven brake lining was reinforced with metal wire and organic fiber. Other product improvements and industry firsts rapidly followed, and by 1921 the mill was the largest producer of asbestos textiles in the United States.

The original offices for the business were at 47 North Duke Street in Lancaster. In 1922 the offices were moved to Manheim to consolidate the greatly enlarged operation. In 1929 the company joined with the Raybestos Company and the Manhattan Rubber Manufacturing Company to become Raybestos – Manhattan, Inc.

A realignment of the corporation by product followed in 1973, and RM Friction Materials Company was created. The local company makes friction materials (brake linings and clutch facings), mechanical packings and gasket materials, as well as textiles and plastic products for structural, mechanical, and insulating requirements. The friction material products are marketed to original equipment manufacturers in the automotive, farm implement, earth-moving, and general industrial fields, as well as to the replacement market. Friction materials sales represents over three-quarters of corporate sales. RM Friction Materials Company has twenty-two manufacturing operations in the United States, Canada, and overseas — in West Germany, Ireland, Australia, Japan, and Venezuela — and sells their products throughout the world. Intensive research and development effort continues in pursuit of new and improved friction materials.

Today, RM Friction Materials Company, Manheim, is one of the largest employers in the county.

Ross Engineering, Inc.

Ross Welding. Ross Engineering, Inc. Safe Walk, Inc. Wright-Hibbard. And Dexco. Dexco is the name to remember. What started as a well-respected local welding shop on East Main Street in Leola has burgeoned into a steel fabrication business capable of vertical plant improvement for heavy industry; the transformation is taking place under the irrepressible entrepreneurial leadership of Donald E. Speicher.

The old weld shop was basically a job shop. Reginald R. Ross and D.E. Speicher combined forces in 1962 to incorporate as Ross Engineering. By 1966 Ross had become a manufacturer by making specialty parts for the trucking industry, such as add-on frame pieces for the truck body. Expanded fabrication facilities for the steel work led to the design and production of hot-rolled steel racks for warehouses, designed and built on a custom basis. Their success led to a line of high-quality, heavy-duty structural steel pallet and cantilever racks, and on to the design of complete steel storage and handling systems. The versatile "Rugged Racks" are manufactured under the Dexco name and can be loaded from trucks, side-loaders, overhead cranes, or sophisticated computer-controlled storage-retrieval systems.

The 1973 acquisition of Wright-Hibbard Industrial Truck Company, Hamburg, Pennsylvania, was a logical extension of Ross's service to industry. Wright-Hibbard dates from 1917 and was a pioneer manufacturer of industrial electric trucks, the forerunner of today's forklift. They remain an important force in the field.

The company's close working association with heavy industry made it aware of the importance of safety flooring, such as "Algrip." Ross bought the rights and manufacturing equipment from a now defunct steel company, and markets this safety flooring under the name of Safe Walk, Inc. The special nonslip tread is

As a part of the integration of its materials-handling systems, Ross Engineering bought the Wright-Hibbard Industrial Truck Co. in 1973. Pictured is an early electric truck, circa 1925.

made of steel that has hard grains of aluminum oxide hot rolled right into the steel. A Ross plant in East Greenville is geared for preparing the steel for hot rolling, then shearing and finishing it into Algrip floor plates cut to customer specification. Algrip walkways are safe even when coated with oil, water, grease, chemicals, or slick lubricants. Installations over thirty years old are still reliable after constant foot traffic and abuse from wheeled vehicles.

From flooring to steel fabrication and materials handling systems for industrial plants, Ross engineers have done it; Dexco does it all.

Serta Mattress Company

John K. Herr, Sr., founder of Herr Manufacturing Company (now Serta Mattress Company).

What better way to demonstrate a quality product than to have circus elephants tramp around on it? That's what the Herr Manufacturing Company did back in the 1930s, and their mattresses survived unscathed. Another sales-promotion idea that was sure to draw a crowd was to subject a Serta mattress to an ironing by a steam roller. After being thoroughly pressed, the mattress was raffled off to one of the onlookers — destined for a long life serving its original purpose in the home of the lucky winner.

The idea for making mattresses started with John K. Herr, Sr., in 1907. Following the idea came a lot of hard work. The regular work week was fifty-nine hours (ending at 5 p.m. on Saturday), and the work force consisted of only three people. The location was the third floor of a small building on the second block of South Christian Street in Lancaster.

The bedding business progressed from the straw and corn-husk mattresses in the old days, through the cotton felt, hair, and kapok mattresses around 1920, then to the innerspring and foam mattresses of the present. Recently retired Richard Herr and John K. Herr, Jr., recall how they used to help their father stuff mattresses by hand before World War I with such things

as cotton felt, straw, and even sea moss. Horsehair was the stuffing of choice, however, because it resisted packing down like cotton.

The local company was a pioneer in the sale of innerspring mattresses, and later, latex mattresses. They were one of the first factories in Pennsylvania to manufacture these modern mattresses.

The Herr family has been deeply involved in both the business and cultural tradition of Lancaster. The Serta Mattress Company has been continuously owned and managed by three generations of the Herr family who trace their heritage to Hans Herr, the leader of a small Mennonite colony who came to Lancaster from Switzerland in the early 1700s. Mr. William F. Herr, President of Serta Mattress Company, was instrumental in the restoration efforts of the Hans Herr House, reputedly the oldest house in the county, dating from 1719.

In 1929 John K. Herr, Sr., became one of the fourteen founding members of what is today Serta, Inc. He was on the first board of directors and also served as president. Today William F. Herr serves on the board of Serta, Inc., which has grown to more than forty individually owned and operated factories located in the United States, Canada, and Puerto Rico. Each factory has its own manufacturing territory and all pool their national advertising, purchasing power, and ideas.

The company built and moved into its present home on Fountain Avenue in 1953, the same year that the company was reorganized into the present corporation, Serta Mattress Company.

Serta Mattress Company demonstrates confidence in its product by subjecting it to a pressing by a steamroller on the streets of Lancaster.

The Sico Company

From horsedrawn wagons hauling wood barrels of kerosene and gasoline to modern 1927-style chain-drive trucks, SICO delivers.

SICO was one of the first gasoline dealers in the area to install curb pumps, 1914. ▶

Clarence Schock is the one to be credited for making the decisions that have shaped the SICO Company. Yet the seeds of the business go back to 1830 — to a struggling coal, grain, and lumber business run by his father.

They entered the oil products business by chance. A Mount Joy dealer in kerosene had become a competitor for their anthracite coal customers, and Schock's company retaliated by going into the oil business. At that time the oil business meant buying and selling kerosene in wood barrels.

The beginning of the enterprise that came to be known as Schock Independent Oil Company is dated from the addition of kerosene to its product line in 1876, the first of the oil products for the company. Kerosene was used only for lighting purposes. It was received in barrels from the producer, and sold in barrels to dealers only within a ten-mile radius from headquarters in Mount Joy. The business from its inception was entirely wholesale.

In those early days the only use for gasoline was in gasoline stoves, and it was sold by a limited number of dealers who were primarily interested in the sale of the stoves. Gasoline was cheaper than kerosene, and the supply exceeded the demand. Market conditions were to be changed abruptly by the advent of the internal-combustion engine and automobile in the late 1890s.

In 1895 Clarence Schock became the company's sole proprietor. By 1898 he realized that the public could be served more economically and efficiently through the medium of tank wagons, rather than the old barrel distribution system. At that point a basic decision was made: to remain an "independent" dealer in oil products rather than become part of marketing organization of a major oil company. He did business as the Independent Oil Company. With characteristic farsightedness, his was the first company to install curb pumps for gasoline in 1914, and first in its territory to use large automotive trucks.

In 1921 the Independent Oil Company became the Star Independent Oil Co., and in 1924 the oil business was incorporated as the Schock Independent Oil Company. The SICO Company is a combination of several businesses merged in 1941.

SICO has become one of the largest independent oil companies in the eastern part of the United States. They employ over three hundred people in peak season, and handle over 170 million gallons of product each year. Customers are served from bulk plants in a thirteen-county area in Pennsylvania, Maryland, and Delaware.

Clarence Schock formed the SICO Foundation, administrator of the SICO Foundation Scholarship Plan. The scholarships provide assistance to those who otherwise might not have the opportunity to pursue their quest for higher education, a fitting memorial to the man who left Franklin and Marshall after one year of college in order to pursue the family business.

Slaugh-Fagan and Associates

In the year 1861 Widmyer-Prangley Company opened its real estate business in Lancaster, an uncertain adventure in a critical time for our country. The Civil War overshadowed the joy Lancaster expressed in welcoming home her adopted son, President James Buchanan.

Six generations later, "welcoming home" is a tradition still followed by Slaugh-Fagan as they pursue their goal of providing quality real estate services. The company traces its origins to the old Widmyer-Prangley firm, though the scope of their services has increased many times over.

Dorothy Slaugh joined Widmyer-Prangley as an accountant in 1929, at a time when the firm concentrated on insurance and property management, plus some agency rentals and sales. Mrs. Slaugh kept the name and business going for nine years after the death of the last principal. In 1964 Paul H. Slaugh, Jr. (Pete) joined the firm. He was responsible for relocating the firm to 635 Columbia Avenue and for opening the residential division of the company. Lawrence P. Fagan joined the firm in 1973, and the corporate identity became known as Slaugh-Fagan and Associates. It is Lancaster County's largest and best known real estate service organization. Soon sales and staff required new corporate offices at 150 Farmington Lane. Branch offices have been opened in Elizabethtown, Ephrata, and Millersville, with two more in the planning stages. There are now over one hundred people on the staff.

Success stories are never an accident, and Slaugh-Fagan's is no exception. They revolutionized the industry by offering a real estate institute to the general public. Completion of the concentrated course prepares individuals to successfully pass Pennsylvania State examination. Intensive on-the-job training further familiarizes associates with every phase of real estate service that clients expect. Another first for the industry came when Slaugh-Fagan introduced the twelve-month warranty protection to the buyer of a used home. Some other agencies have since followed their lead.

Further creative innovations include the establishment of Realvest, division of Slaugh-Fagan. Realvest, staffed by six graduates of a newly developed college-level real estate course, handles real estate investment, commercial real estate, and industrial sites. Property management service is available as a natural adjunct to the sales operation.

Slaugh-Fagan is a member of Electronic Realty Associates (ERA), a coast-to-coast network of over two thousand independent Realtors. The firm provides land developing, an affiliated title company, mortgage service, and construction by representing twenty different builders and developers in the Lancaster area.

Slaugh-Fagan and Associates — corporate headquarters at 150 Farmington Lane, Lancaster.

H.M. Stauffer & Sons, Inc.

The staff of H.M. Stauffer and Sons, 1920, at a time when the foreman (seated) earned $15 weekly, the others, $12.

The Pennsylvania Railroad encouraged H.M. Stauffer to establish a coal, lumber, and feed business in Leola to stimulate growth in the area. That was in 1890, and the same two acres adjacent to the railroad line serve today as the hub of H.M. Stauffer's diversified industry.

The first warehouse and coal trestle were put into operation before the turn of the century; then a new feed mill and warehouse were erected. In 1902 an elevator capable of storing two thousand tons of coal was constructed in the yard, the first of its kind in the county. By 1910 the needs of the many local farmers were well taken care of by offering for sale "tobacco shooks" (knocked-down tobacco cases). Cob crushers, attrition mills, and feed mixers were added to the feed warehouse in 1925.

Throughout the years, H.M. Stauffer has bought coal yards, trucks, and inventory of various forms from other businesses as they became available. In 1946 they entered the oil business, and that now requires its own Lancaster headquarters, fleet of trucks, and the "Compt-fuel" computer system to control oil deliveries.

Where once the H.M. Stauffer trucks went up and down Lancaster city streets delivering coal to every house for a stretch of fifteen or twenty blocks, one now sees a fleet of yellow fuel-oil trucks doing the same. Coal deliveries, while still a part of Stauffer service, are now just three thousand tons versus the eighty thousand tons delivered in 1946.

In 1955 one large building replaced several sheds used previously in storage of building materials so that thirty-five railroad cars of material could be placed in one location. Pallet manufacture began a year later, and was so successful that the first plant was outgrown within two years. In 1960 the Leola Supply Company building, a wholly owned subsidiary of H.M. Stauffer, was completed and fully equipped with woodworking machinery.

The firm did all of its business in Lancaster County for the first fifty years. Now, however, forty percent of its business is spread throughout the Middle Atlantic States and into New England. From the original coal-lumber-feed business, Stauffer's has grown to include pre-manufactured wood products for homes, farms, and industry. More work done at the factory means an important reduction in labor costs on the job site.

The language of the business has changed, too. President Robert B. Wentz and Vice President Raymond A. Bures speak of trusses or trim, pre-engineered farm buildings, package homes, pallets, and pressure-treated lumber — all new products reflecting the growth and imagination of the firm and its officers.

Fire is a major hazard to a lumberyard, and H.M. Stauffer has survived two such disasters: first, in 1969, at its facility in Maryland, and again in 1970 with a sizable loss in Leola. Yet the feeling of flexibility and growth is the predominant theme recounted by Stauffer's.

This third-generation, family-owned enterprise is a prime example of Lancaster County industry at its best; proud of the past, prudent about the present, and undeniably confident of its place in the future.

WGAL TV

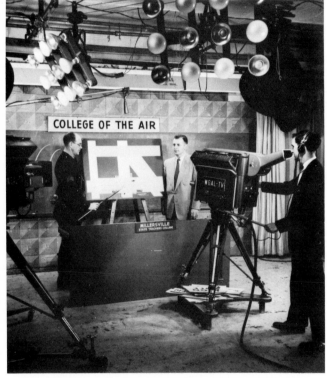

COLLEGE OF THE AIR

WGAL TV studio scene from the early 1950s featuring locally produced College of the Air program.

A successful demonstration of television was first made in the early 1920s, but it was nearly twenty years before the first commercial broadcast was produced in New York in 1941. Since then, the growth of the industry has become legendary; there are over 700 commercial stations and 260 educational stations operating in the country today.

WGAL TV is a pioneer in the industry. It held one of only 108 licenses in the nation when the first telecast began from the studio at 24 South Queen Street in Lancaster on March 18, 1949. The first formal program was produced four days later for a group of RCA television executives, dealers, and radio station personnel during a meeting at the old Stevens House. The show originated in one room of the hotel, and was shown on twenty-five receivers placed in the hotel ballroom. (There may have been more receivers in the hotel than in the rest of the city). In May of the same year, the station's first live telecast was presented to the public; by June, these shows were joined by regular network service.

Important milestones followed in quick succession: 1950 — the daily telecasting schedule lengthened so much that the station was signing on before noon; 1952 — NBC "Today Show" premiered and the station signed on at seven in the morning, and 1952 also marked the move to Channel 8 (from Channel 4 where the station began operations) because of being granted an increase in power; 1954 — in January the station used its special color-transmitting equipment to bring Channel 8 viewers the first colorcast show, "The Tournament of Roses"; 1956 — Christmas Day, WGAL TV broadcast from the new quarters on Lincoln Highway West; 1957 — the station began producing its own local, live color programs; 1958 — first local videotape recording; 1962 — local use of color videotape recording machines.

In 1975 WGAL TV completed a new tower and antenna that stands 1,849 feet above sea level at Hellam, the tallest man-made structure in Central Pennsylvania. A solid-state microwave system sends the television signal from the studio in Lancaster to the transmitter in Hellam at the speed of 186,000 miles per second. The acquisition of the Electronic News Gathering (ENG) videotape camera supplements the station's film cameras and fast-processing equipment.

These are a few of the ways in which WGAL TV continues in the spirit of its pioneering days, by taking advantage of new advances in electronic equipment that enhances TV production capability.

WGAL TV is a primary affiliate of the NBC television network and is the dominant station in the Lancaster-Harrisburg-York-Lebanon area.

Willow Valley Farms

"Anybody that comes to see us really goes out of their way," notes Elmer Thomas, general manager of Willow Valley Farms. That fact does not seem to faze either the local or tourist traffic that consistently go to Willow Valley for meals and/or lodging: "they know what good is."

The complex started as a modest retirement dream of John Thomas, well known as the affable farmer who sold chickens and Thanksgiving turkeys at Central Market. John Thomas's family has been "standing on" market since 1905, long enough to make John dream of something else to offer his boys who were coming along. He envisioned a thirty-room motel that they could help him manage on a small tract of land on the Willow Street Pike. John built that dream in 1966.

Within a year, the Thomases saw the need for a family restaurant to satisfy their guests. In order to offer home-cooked meals at a reasonable price, the one-hundred-seat family restaurant and banquet rooms were opened in 1967. It was an immediate hit.

Numerous expansion projects improving hospitality and food service have followed in swift succession. Today Willow Valley Farms Resort offers 112 rooms, indoor and outdoor pools, sauna, game room, tennis, boating, golf, tours, on-premise bakery and gift shops, as well as dining facilities and banquet rooms for seven hundred people. What a way to retire!

But John Thomas had help: a large family close to each other, close to God, close to the soil. They hired

Willow Valley Farms, a unique motor inn in a country setting. Owned and operated by the Thomas family.

many of their own kind, Pennsylvania Plain People, and trained them to serve the customers willingly and well. Employees now number 300, many of them young people who create a special warm and welcoming atmosphere. Elmer Thomas admits they "work with" the young people they hire. "How else can you keep forty youngsters busy on a Saturday night, off the streets, meeting friends, and making money, too?"

Willow Valley attempts to be a good neighbor to those in the area: Lancastrians think they are, and respond by regularly patronizing the dining and banquet rooms. Consistent in all ways, executive members of Willow Valley Farms Resort are extensively involved in church, community, and business-associated organizations. Willow Valley Farms Resort has been awarded the outstanding four-star rating from Mobil Travel Guide.

The Thomas family opened Willow Woods in 1975, a planned community in the country with 120 garden apartments and townhouses that offer suburban pleasures within the shadow of the city. They look longingly across the highway and speak in terms of retirement village and shopping center.

And, maybe, John Thomas might retire.

Wohlsen Construction Company

"If you want something done well and done cheap, get the Dutchman." The "Dutchman" was Herman F. Wohlsen and the story he told of his past is part of the company's rich lore.

Herman F. Wohlsen came to this country from Germany in 1877 when he was sixteen years old. Lancaster was his destination because his brother already had settled here some years before. Herman's stock-in-trade was an apprenticeship as a carpenter, and little else. His reputation remained to be made. But so many people "got the Dutchman" to do their work that the young carpenter soon branched out from fences and privies to the construction of porches and small homes. By 1890 Wohlsen had formed the corporation that not only bears his name today but is managed by the third generation of his descendants. From that point on, the company's history and the history of the growth and development of Lancaster are closely intermingled.

One of the firm's first big projects was the construction of the stables at the Williamson estate, still in evidence. The Strawberry Street School built in 1895 was their first public building. Many of Lancaster's sturdy row homes were conceived and built by Wohlsen; the first was a twelve-home block stretching from Woodward Street to Dauphin Street.

Both costs and business methods have undergone great changes over the years. When Wohlsen built the Hager Department Store, for instance, a percentage of the cash price for the building was taken out in trade. Hager's issued the builder a credit, their workers came to the management for a chit, and that chit was good for merchandise in the store.

Business methods may have changed, but not the corporate dedication to craftsmanship from beginning to end.

By 1900 the firm had contracts for three famous landmarks: the Brunswick Hotel (now in its third incarnation), the original Woolworth Building, and the YMCA on Orange Street.

Just before the First World War, Wohlsen branched out into industrial building. Today many local churches, schools, college buildings, office buildings, and industrial plants bear the company's stamp.

The company also is prominent in the current restoration effort that abounds in the city and county, and has worked on Rock Ford, the Wright Mansion, the Heritage Center of Lancaster, and the Fulton Bank on Penn Square.

Wohlsen Construction Company: builder of Lancaster landmarks, past, present, and future.

The first edition of the Hotel Brunswick, built by Wohlsen at the turn of the century.

Photo courtesy Lancaster *New Era.*

The original Woolworth building on North Queen Street. Photo courtesy Lancaster *New Era.*

Lancaster County courthouse, North Duke Street.

Woodstream Corporation

◀ *A company on the move: this modern entrance to Woodstream's headquarters building opens on a wide variety of products geared to outdoor recreation and wildlife management.*

Above, *in 1902, John Mast built this rodent-trap plant in Lititz, the site of present-day Woodstream Corporation.*

Typical of Woodstream's ▶ *recreational equipment are these Mark ™ series tackle boxes.*

The story of progress from a lad tinkering in his father's blacksmith shop to the building of an industry whose products are distributed throughout North America and overseas is the story of the Woodstream Corporation in Lititz. It is the world's leading manufacturer of wildlife management products and a major sporting goods manufacturer as well.

Woodstream has been a good neighbor to Lancaster for many years, with a distinguished record of participation in the business, civic, and cultural life of the city. As a matter of fact, one of the company's best-known products, the wood and spring mousetrap, was invented by John M. Mast, a Lancastrian, in 1896. But that is only part of the fascinating story of this company whose products can be found in every town across North America.

The company traces its origins to the Oneida Community, a religious group in upper New York State, that had turned to the manufacture of wildlife traps to supplement a meager income from farming. About 1850 Sewell Newhouse, a convert to the community, erected a trapmaking shop on the Community property. Newhouse had developed his skill at trapmaking in his father's blacksmith shop some years earlier. Looking for something he could use to barter with Indians from the nearby Oneida Reservation, he experimented until he fashioned scrap iron from the blacksmith floor into traps which, though crude and handmade on the forge, worked amazingly well.

As the Community was building its wildlife-trap business in New York, John Mast was working on what he called his "snap-shot" mousetrap business in Lancaster. He soon added rattraps to his line and these proved so successful he moved to Lititz in 1902 and erected a new building. In 1907 the Oneida Community learned that Mast's company was making traps to which they claimed almost a divine right,

216

because of their being pioneers in the trap industry. They secured control of the company, but continued to operate the business in Lititz.

Oneida Community, Ltd. conducted the rodent-trap business as one of its numerous interests until 1924 when three of its executives, including Chester M. Woolworth, who served as Woodstream's chairman of the board until his death in 1977, purchased it and named the new firm the Animal Trap Company of America. In 1925 the company purchased Oneida's wildlife-trap business and moved it from New York State to Lititz. The company acquired Oneida's Canadian plant at Niagara Falls, Ontario, in the same transaction.

One era the company is particularly proud of is that of 1940-44 during which it converted to war production. Mr. Woolworth foresaw the coming need and was prepared. The company provided army cots, coathangers, and parachute springs, then turned to the business of manufacturing over two hundred million bullet cores in addition to fuse plugs, airplane parts, bomb noses, machine-gun parts, and rocket-fuse wrenches under direct and subcontracts from the U.S. War Department and the British Purchasing Commission. The Philadelphia Ordnance Office featured the plant as a model for conversion to war production in several published articles entitled "From Mousetraps to Bullets."

The end of war production marked the beginning of the company's interest in plastics and outdoor recreational equipment. Now, through acquisition and internal expansion, Woodstream, as the company was renamed in 1966, is strongly entrenched in the manufacture of hunting, fishing, camping, canoeing, and boating products, and is still the undisputed leader in wildlife management equipment. There are few sporting goods outlets that do not have at least a few items of Old Pal® fishing equipment ranging from tackle boxes to bait buckets to minnow traps, or Victor® products such as duck decoys or camping seats. In addition to these products, Woodstream plants in Canada also produce fiberglass canoes and snowshoes.

The company's marine products subsidiary at Delhi, Louisiana, acquired in 1971, produces a wide variety of aluminum boats and canoes sold through mass merchandisers as well as Terry® fiberglass bass, deck, and ski boats, sold through independent boat dealers.

In early 1978 Woodstream moved to become an even greater factor in the fishing-equipment industry with the acquisition of the Fenwick Corporation, a California-based manufacturer of tubular fiberglass and graphite fishing rods.

With the continued concern over ecology and the development of toxic-resistant "super" rodents, sales of Woodstream's oldest product line, the well-known Victor mousetraps and rattraps, continue strong. Demand for the company's wildlife traps is also still growing due to worldwide demand for raw furs, the necessity of farmers, ranchers, and stockmen to protect their crops and livestock from predatory animals, and the increasing need for these products in the maintenance of a reasonable balance of wildlife in our environment. The company continues to be concerned with the development of the most humane forms of wildlife trapping and is proud of its record of innovating the trapping systems in use today. Research continues to improve, wherever practical, the methods used in wildlife management.

In light of Woodstream's strong position in the sporting goods industry and the continuing need for wildlife- and rodent-control devices, the outlook for this progressive, innovative company seems better than ever.

Bibliography

Brener, David. *Lancaster's Gates of Heaven, Portals to the Past*. Lancaster: Temple Shaarai Shomayim, 1976.

Ellis, Franklin, and Samuel Evans. *History of Lancaster County, Pennsylvania*. Philadelphia: Everts & Peck, 1883.

Hensel, W. Uhler. *Resources and Industries of Lancaster City*. Lancaster: The Board of Trade, 1887.

Higginbotham, Sanford W. *The Keystone in the Democratic Arch, Pennsylvania Politics, 1800-1816*. Harrisburg: Pennsylvania Historical and Museum Commission, 1952.

Kilburn, Francis. *A Brief History of the City of Lancaster . . . including the Business Cards of the Principal Merchants and Manufacturers*. Lancaster: Pearsol & Geist, 1870.

Klein, Frederic Shriver. *Lancaster County Since 1841*. Lancaster: The Lancaster County National Bank, 1955.

Klein, Philip Shriver. *Pennsylvania Politics, 1817-1832; A Game Without Rules*. Philadelphia: Historical Society of Pennsylvania, 1940.

————. "Early Lancaster County Politics," *Pennsylvania History* III (April 1936): 98-114.

————. *President James Buchanan*. University Park: The Pennsylvania State University Press, 1962.

Lancaster Planning Commission. *Neighborhood Analysis*. Lancaster: City of Lancaster Planning Commission, 1966.

Lancaster Redevelopment Authority. *Annual Report for 1958*. Lancaster: City of Lancaster Redevelopment Authority, 1958.

Lemon, James T. *The Best Poor Man's Country: A Geographical Study of Early Southeastern Pennsylvania*. Baltimore: The Johns Hopkins Press, 1972.

Loose, John Ward Willson. *The Military Market Basket*. Lancaster: Lancaster County Bicentennial Committee, Inc., 1976.

Nolan, John. *Lancaster, Pennsylvania: A Comprehensive City Plan*. Lancaster: The Lancaster Chamber of Commerce and City of Lancaster Planning Commission, 1929.

Reilly, Richard M. *Resources and Industries of Lancaster, Pennsylvania*. Lancaster: Board of Trade, 1909.

Reninger, Marion Wallace. *Famous Women of Lancaster*. Lancaster: Forry and Hacker, 1965.

_____. *Via Mulberry Street and Lime*. Lancaster: Rudisill and Co., 1960.

_____. *Orange Street*. Lancaster: Rudisill and Co., 1958.

Riddle, William. *The Story of Lancaster, Pennsylvania, Old and New*. Lancaster: The New Era Printing Co., 1917.

Sanderson, Alfred. *History of the Union Fire Company No. 1, 1760-1879*. Lancaster: Inquirer Publishing Co., 1879.

Sullivan, William A. *The Industrial Worker in Pennsylvania, 1800-1840*. Harrisburg: Pennsylvania Historical and Museum Commission, 1955.

Twombley, Clifford Gray. *Report on Vice Conditions in the City of Lancaster*. Lancaster: Law and Order Society of Lancaster, 1915.

Welchans, George R. *History of Lodge No. 43, F. & A.M. of Lancaster, 1785-1935*. Lancaster: Lodge No. 43 of Lancaster, 1936.

Wood, Jerome Herman, Jr. *Conestoga Crossroads: The Rise of Lancaster, Pennsylvania, 1730-1789*. Ph.D. dissertation, Brown University, 1969.

Worner, William Frederick. *Old Lancaster Tales and Traditions*. Lancaster: n.p., 1927.

Articles of special interest from the *Journal of the Lancaster County Historical Society*

Barnes, Horace R. "History of the Gas and Electric Industries in Lancaster County." *JLCHS* 52 (1948): 101.

Bowman, John J. "Lancaster's Part in the Watchmaking Industry." *JLCHS* 49 (1945): 29.

Daum, Fred J. "The Cork Industry as Lancaster Knows It." *JLCHS* 54 (1950): 117.

Harbold, Peter Monroe. "Schools and Education in Lancaster Borough." *JLCHS* 46 (1942): 1.

Heiges, George L. "When Lancaster was Capital of Pennsylvania." *JLCHS* 55 (1951): 1; 56 (1952): 45; 57 (1953): 81; 58 (1954): 1.

_____. "Lancaster General Hospital: First Twenty Five Years, 1893-1918." *JLCHS* 62 (1958): 147.

Heisey, Martin Luther. "The Borough Fathers." *JLCHS* 46 (1942): 45.

_____. "How Lancaster Grew and What People Thought of It." *JLCHS* 45 (1941): 87.

_____. "Religious Life in Lancaster Borough." *JLCHS* 45 (1941): 126.

_____. "100th Anniversary of Lancaster's Incorporation as a Borough." *JLCHS* 46 (1942): 83.

_____. "Locomotives Made in Lancaster." *JLCHS* 44 (1940): 1.

_____. "The Famed Markets of Lancaster." *JLCHS* 53 (1949): 1.

Kieffer, Elizabeth Clark. "Social Life in Lancaster Borough." *JLCHS* 45 (1941): 105.

_____. "Libraries in Lancaster." *JLCHS* 48 (1944): 71.

Klein, Frederic Shriver. "Robert Coleman, Millionaire Ironmaster." *JLCHS* 64 (1960): 17.

Loose, John Ward Willson, and Charles O. Lynch. "History of Brewing in Lancaster County, Legal and Otherwise." *JLCHS* 70 (1966): 1.

Teeters, Negley. "Public Executions in Pennsylvania, 1682-1834." *JLCHS* 64 (1960): 85.

Villee, Claude. "A Short History of the Lancaster Fire Department, 1882-1958." *JLCHS* 63 (1959): 137.

Whitely, Paul. "A History of Friends [Quakers] in Lancaster County." *JLCHS* 51 (1947): 1.

Unpublished manuscripts scheduled for publication in the *Journal of the Lancaster County Historical Society*.

Loose, John Ward Willson. "History of the Anthracite Iron Industry of Lancaster County, 1840-1900." [Master's thesis, 1967].

_____. "A Social-Economic-Political Profile of Lancaster City, 1830-1860."

_____. "Building Conestoga Steam Cotton Mill No. 1."

Ressler, Kenneth L. "Banks and Their Role in the Economic Growth of Lancaster County."

Shindler, Richard. "History of the Lancaster Police Department."

Index

225